PLANTS IN ACTION

A SCIENTIFIC BACKGROUND
TO GARDENING

PLANTS

IN ACTION

ALAN HIBBERT AND JUDY BROOKS

BRITISH BROADCASTING CORPORATION

This book is published in conjunction with
the BBC Television series *Plants in Action*,
first transmitted on BBC 2 in Spring 1981

The series is produced by Ron Bloomfield
and Bryn Brooks

The book is edited by Judy Brooks
and Ron Bloomfield

The illustrations are by
Rachel Birket of the Garden Studio (cover)
Joanna Langhorne (plant drawings)
Maggie Raynor (chapter headings)
John Woodcock and Aziz Khan
(botanical diagrams)

Published to accompany a series
of programmes prepared in consultation with the
BBC Continuing Education Advisory Council

First published 1981
Published by the British Broadcasting Corporation
35 Marylebone High Street, London W1M 1AA
ISBN 0 563 16446 8

This book is set in 10/12 pt Monophoto
Century Schoolbook by
Keyspools Limited, Warrington
Colour separations by
Radstock Reproductions Limited
Printed and bound in England by
Butler and Tanner Limited
Frome and London

CONTENTS

For Katharine, Joanne and Andrew,
and for Tamsin

'A poor man will eat better, that has a garden of his own, than a rich man that has none', wrote John London in the Encyclopaedia of Gardening, published in 1822, and that is as true today as it ever was, because little in the garden changes. But in the last hundred years or so gardening has changed. Botanists and horticulturists have made enormous advances, not only in the development of chemical cures, fertilisers and pesticides, but also in understanding how plants work.

That is what this book is about – the way plants grow, behave, flower and seed, and how this knowledge can be used and enjoyed by the gardener.

In this book we have followed the usual botanic convention, in that the names of plant families are printed in Roman type, with an initial capital, and the genus and species are in italics. The name of the genus has an initial capital, the species does not.

CHAPTER ONE

A PLANT'S-EYE VIEW

It's hard, as the gardening chores mount up, to find time to stop and ask, 'What is a garden?' We spend our week-ends cultivating a patch, be it large or pocket-handkerchief, in order to build a community of plants that will provide colour to admire, flowers to pick, a scented arbour in which to rest and dream or, more prosaically, fresh garden vegetables to taste delicious and help with the family budget. In addition, many gardeners cherish a secret wish that the whole thing would look after itself!

Instead, as everyone knows, the plants that you want need care and attention, while the plants that you do not want need to be heavily discouraged – and the sad thing is that it always seems to be the plants that you do not want that keep on coming back. We do not create a natural community of plants in the garden: we build a thoroughly unnatural environment by growing, side by side, a collection of plants that would not normally be seen together. This artificial community needs a lot of maintenance and support. It exists in a state of stress, and if something snaps, the garden will rapidly revert to the natural state.

You can find the natural 'model' for your own part of the country by looking at any nearby piece of uncultivated ground. Here you will find a self-maintaining community of plants and animals, firmly established, well-suited to their home and poised to expand whenever the time is right. This community is a 'seed bank' and is the source of the weeds in any garden, but the plant that is a weed in the garden is just the right one to live in the wild, untended patch, where survival is more important than appearance. A weed is no more than a plant in the wrong place, but, because weeds are built to survive the rigours of the tough world outside, they run riot in the softer environment of the garden. With very few exceptions, none of the cultivated varieties of garden flowers is found on untended ground, even though it may be only a fence away from the garden in which it thrives. And that neatly focuses the problem faced by every gardener.

To bring together a range of flowers and vegetables containing annuals and perennials, shrubs and trees, we have to assemble a collection of plants that would not, in nature, grow either together or in that place. Many of our most familiar garden plants are not even European in origin, let alone native to this country. Generations of plant hunters and botanists have sought new and strange varieties all over the world, and indeed they still do. The smallest and most unsophisticated garden looks like a plant atlas of the world – *Fuchsia* from Mexico, lupins from Central America, spinach from Australasia, tomatoes from South America. The list is very long. Garden plants come from a wide range of environments, and need a lot of care to make up for being expected to grow on the wrong side of the globe.

The plant hunters

Very many of our garden flowers and vegetables are 'foreigners', imported over the centuries. The first were carried by Neolithic man. Others, including onions, vines and fig trees, were brought by the Romans, determined to eat familiar food, even when occupying this strange, cold land at the very edge of their empire.

Since the explorations of the sixteenth century, plant hunters have introduced decorative plants for the garden as well as vegetables for the table. John Tradescant and his son were two of the earliest. They were royal gardeners, under Charles I, and grew the plants they found and brought home in their garden at Lambeth. Within a century, another of the great plant hunters, Joseph Banks, was travelling himself, as well as planning expeditions and dispatching younger botanists to increase the collection of plants in the Royal Botanic Gardens at Kew. An enormous number of plant hunters are responsible for the variety in our gardens, and the names of some are remembered in the names of the plants they discovered and brought home.

SIR WALTER RALEIGH
1552–1618
Potatoes from North Carolina.

JOHN TRADESCANT
the elder
1580–1638
Apricot and Persian lilac from Alicante and Algiers.

Persian lilac

JOHN TRADESCANT
the younger
1608–1662
Virginia creeper, red maple, Michaelmas daisies, lupins, and *Rudbeckia* from Virginia, North America.

Rudbeckia

JOSEPH de TOURNEFORT
1656–1708
Rhododendron ponticum and *Rhododendron luteum* (the common yellow azalea) from the southern shores of the Black Sea.

Rhododendron ponticum

SIR JOSEPH BANKS
1743–1820
Rosa banksiae and *Hydrangea* from China. *Acacia armata* from Australia.

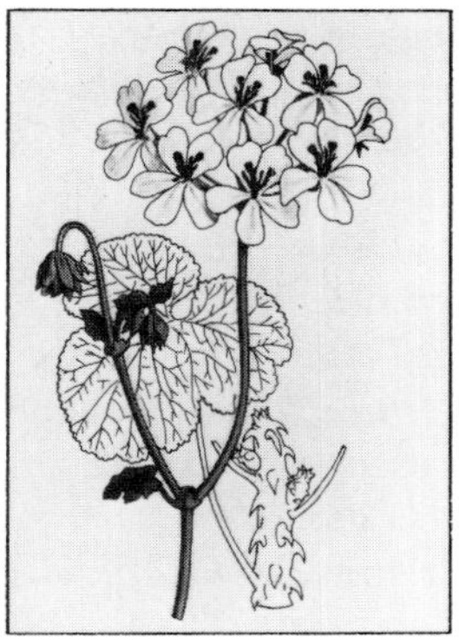

FRANCIS MASSON
1741–1805
Many kinds of *Pelargonium* from South Africa.

Lt WILLIAM CLARK
1770–1838
with **Captain MERIWETHER LEWIS**
1774–1809
Lewisia from western North America.

Captain Lewis & Clark holding a Council with the Indians.

DAVID DOUGLAS
1779–1834
Douglas fir, flowering currant, dogwood, clarkia, California poppy, *Limnanthes douglasii*, *Nemophilia*, *Godetia* and at least seven varieties of pine trees from the west coast of North America.

Clarkia (right)

ROBERT FORTUNE
1812–1880
Winter jasmine, *Weigelia, Mahonias, Chrysanthemum, Forsythia, Saxifraga fortunei* from China and Japan.

CHARLES DARWIN
1809–1882
Berberis darwinii from the Atlantic and Pacific coasts.

CHARLES SARGENT
1841–1927
Flowering cherry, and ornamental crab apple from Japan.

Malus sylvestris.
The wilding or Crab tree.

FRANK KINGDOM WARD
1885–1958
Himalayan poppy, Primulas, lilies and gentians from Assam, Burma, Tibet, and western China

In contrast, the wild community over the fence is made up of plant species that 'fit' together. Their numbers are fairly constant – obviously not identical from year to year, but on average about the same until natural circumstances change drastically or man begins to interfere. Looking, for example, at a piece of woodland, you can see that this community has a spatial structure, with tall growing trees and shrubs standing over an under-storey of annual and perennial herbaceous plants. This community has evolved over thousands of years, mainly in response to the climate, but also modified by the type of soil in the area. It has all happened since the last Ice Age, when the plant life of these islands was either wiped out or drastically changed by the severity of the weather.

As the ice retreated northwards, the climate became milder and birch woodlands developed, followed by a mixture of birch and pine as the weather grew warmer still. By about seven thousand years ago the climate of Britain had become roughly what it is today, and the birch/pine woodland was replaced by mixed oak forest. The kind of wood, containing oak, ash, elm and, in the south, beech, became dominant at that time and remains so to this day. In the north and west of Scotland generally colder conditions prevail, and this, together with the thin, wet, acid soils that predominate there, still favours the growth of birch and pine.

Each woodland plant exists because it is adapted for life at just such a place in just such a community. It is said to occupy a particular ecological 'niche'. In this niche it successfully faces any competition; it thrives and reproduces itself. If it were not so precisely suited to its situation, then, when it died, it would be replaced by another plant, one that was suited to that niche. Some of the habitats occupied by plants in the woodland community are actually created by other plants. Close to the ground there are ferns, mosses and liverworts that could not survive without the shade and increased humidity provided by their taller neighbours. This modification of the climate by one plant that helps the growth of another can be exploited by the gardener in planning his own plant communities. Ferns, bluebells and the Primula family all do best in the shade of a bush or tree, but in the garden it is often the opposite problem that occurs. If you have got a shady corner, you need to search out shade loving plants that can cope with it, things like *Aucuba, Pulmonaria* and periwinkle. A garden that accepts and exploits the natural needs and relationships of its inhabitants grows better and demands less effort from its owner.

Another important feature of any natural community is that it is in a delicate state of balance and it is this balance that ensures its survival. In the natural environment nobody tidies away dead plants or sweeps up the leaves, and a very good thing too, because they contain the nutrients that the next generation of plants will need in order to feed and grow. Fungi and bacteria break down the dead material so that these nutrients can be recycled and released back into the soil where they are available to the new plants that will grow there. Such a community is the outcome of a continual struggle, in which the fit survive and the rest die. It is a stable community, which does not take more from the environment than it can make by its own processes or recycle from its parent soil.

Alan Hibbert, dwarfed by the giant hogweed. This enormous biennial was introduced recently from the Caucasus and has turned the usual rule – that weeds from the wild invade the garden – quite upside down. This cultivated garden plant has escaped and is proving very successful in the world outside, particularly in waste ground near streams, where, once established, it may become dominant. The size of the giant hogweed makes it a dramatic and conspicuous plant. It stands 3.5 metres high, with huge lobed leaves, flowers half a metre across and stems as much as 10 centimetres in diameter. The juice in the stems is an irritant and can cause quite bad blisters. The usual sufferers are children who have been tempted to make toys or blow-pipes of the large hollow stems.

As a cultivated plant, hogweed is really only useful in a large garden, perhaps around a big pond. It grows easily from seed and likes a sunny or partially shaded position in deep, moist soil. The stems should be cut right back to the ground once the plant has finished flowering, before the seeds ripen.

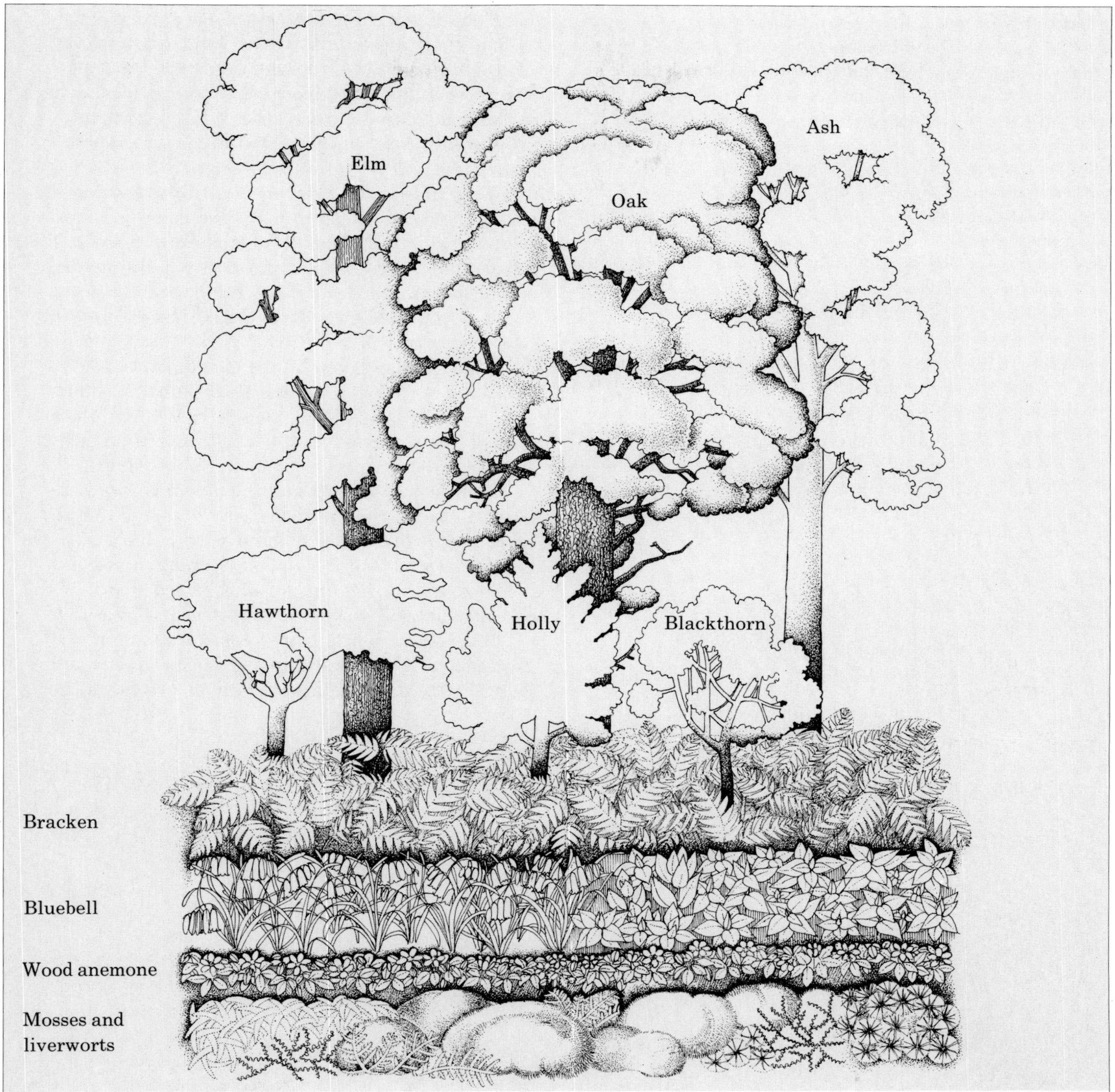

The woodland community

The plants in a stable woodland community grow in three distinct layers. The tallest trees are said to be dominant, and these are the most successful in the competition for light, water and nutrients. They produce considerable shade, and in this shade grows the shrub layer, made up of trees that will never exceed the height of the dominant species but exist quite happily in their shadow. The roots of the trees that grow in these two layers compete for the water and nutrients that are available from the soil. At ground level is a third layer, largely made up of herbaceous plants. There may be several species of grass, along with bluebells, wood anemones, dog's mercury, primroses, wood sage and many others. The combination of plants in this herbaceous layer is the most variable and very dependent on the soil type and the climate. In damp corners, anywhere where the surface of the soil remains moist, there will also be a number of mosses and liverworts.

The major, dominant trees are replaced only as the older ones die and fall down, leaving the space, light, water and nutrients needed by a germinating seedling if it is to grow on and take its place in the higher layers of the woodland community.

Garden flowers: 1 Lily
2 Fuchsia
3 Balloon flower
4 Hosta
5 Nasturtium

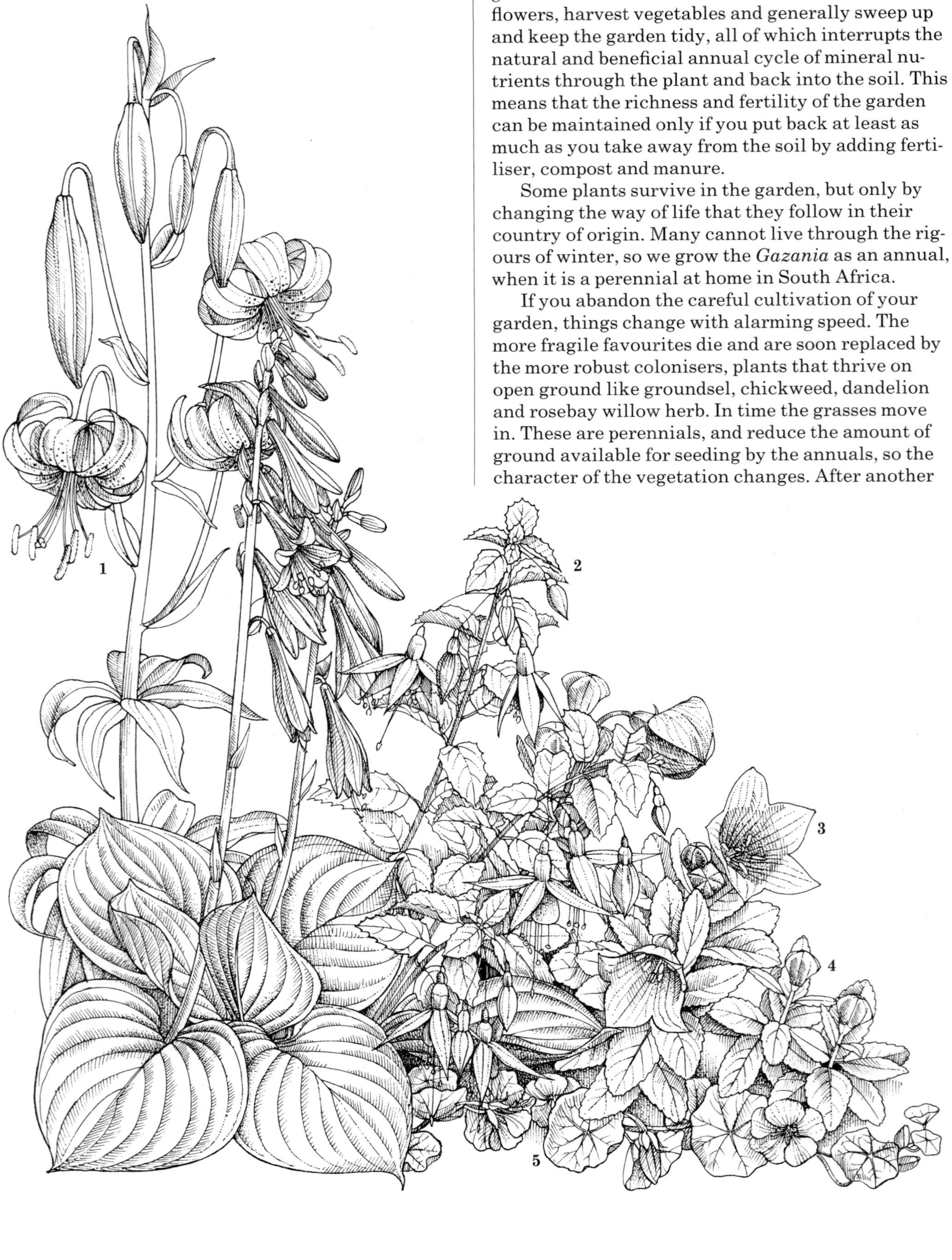

What an amazing contrast in the garden, where most of the plants survive at all only because they have a helping hand from the gardener. We keep down the competition from other plants by weeding, so that the chosen garden species have space to grow and thrive. On the other hand, we also pick flowers, harvest vegetables and generally sweep up and keep the garden tidy, all of which interrupts the natural and beneficial annual cycle of mineral nutrients through the plant and back into the soil. This means that the richness and fertility of the garden can be maintained only if you put back at least as much as you take away from the soil by adding fertiliser, compost and manure.

Some plants survive in the garden, but only by changing the way of life that they follow in their country of origin. Many cannot live through the rigours of winter, so we grow the *Gazania* as an annual, when it is a perennial at home in South Africa.

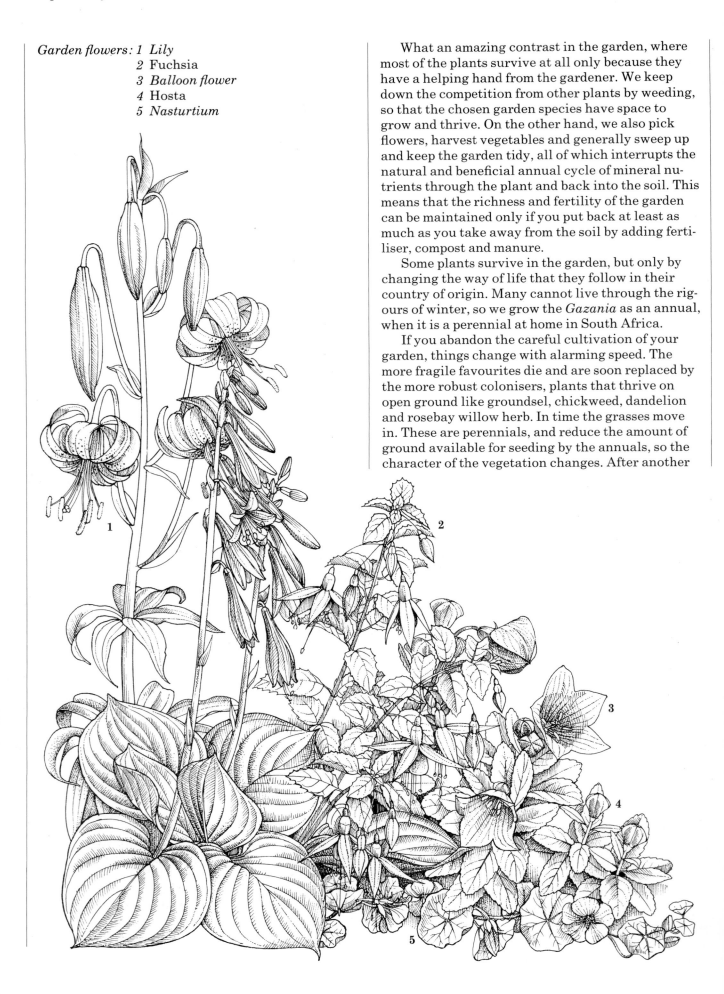

If you abandon the careful cultivation of your garden, things change with alarming speed. The more fragile favourites die and are soon replaced by the more robust colonisers, plants that thrive on open ground like groundsel, chickweed, dandelion and rosebay willow herb. In time the grasses move in. These are perennials, and reduce the amount of ground available for seeding by the annuals, so the character of the vegetation changes. After another year or so there are established shrub and tree seedlings and the beginning of a true woodland community. If man did not exist in this country, and never had, woodland is thought to be the kind of vegetation that would cover our landscape – so that is what will happen in the long run if you neglect the weeding!

Having regard for the ecological principles that decide whether a plant in a natural community lives or dies, we can piece together a scheme for managing the garden. What you do in your garden is to eliminate (in part, at least) the selection pressures that operate in favour of the chickweed and against, say, the lily, so that the garden, in all its unnatural glory, can survive.

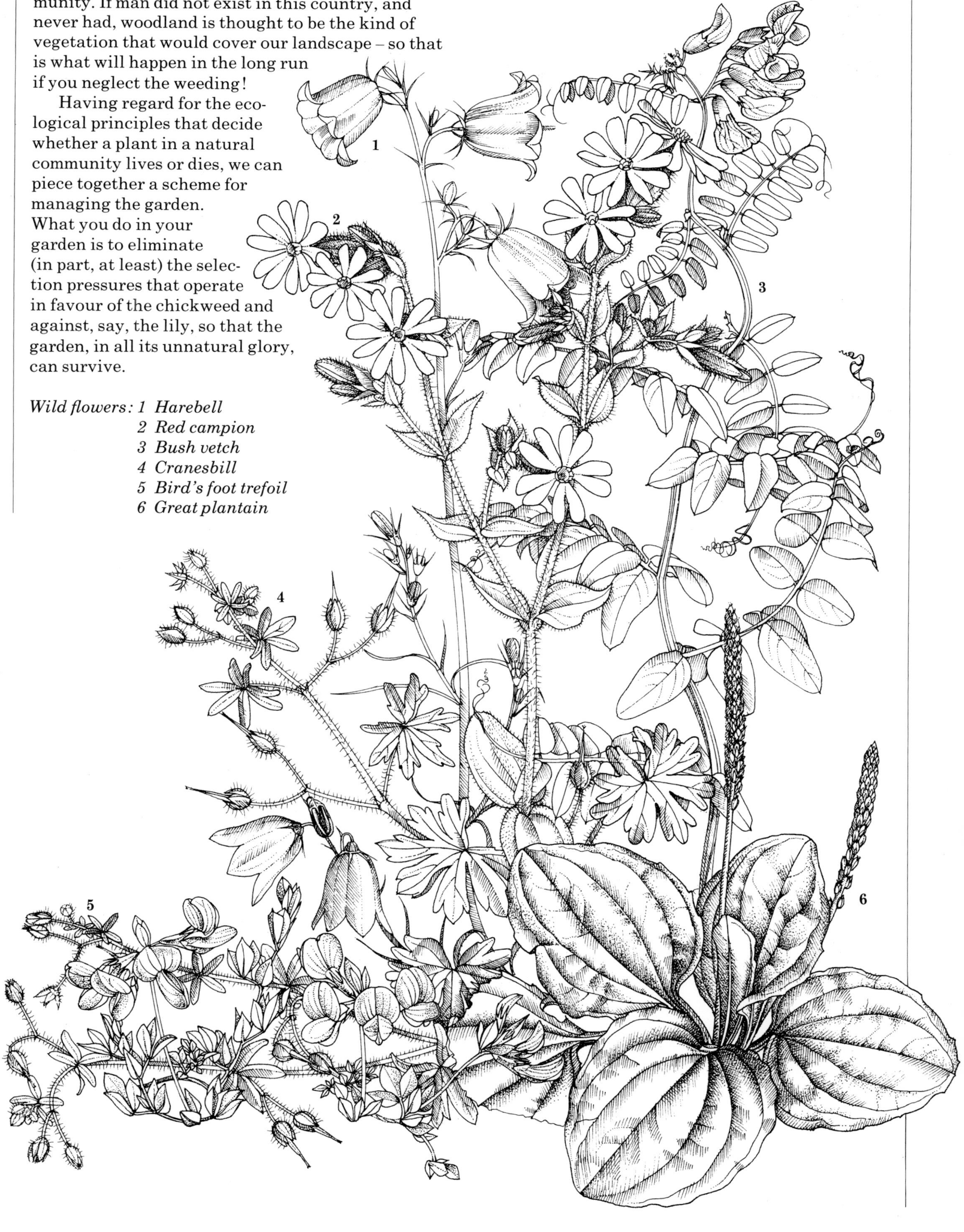

Wild flowers: 1 Harebell
2 Red campion
3 Bush vetch
4 Cranesbill
5 Bird's foot trefoil
6 Great plantain

Take the lawn. The aim and ideal of every gardener who struggles through Sunday afternoon attached to a lawn mower is a neat, smooth, green lawn containing a closely knit community of various species of perennial grass. The precise mixture of grass species that you choose depends largely on the amount of wear that the lawn will get. Some stand the attentions of children and dogs better than others, but whatever types of grass make up the lawn, the real 'baddies' that invade to spoil the dream are broad-leaved weeds (buttercups and daisies, dandelions and clover), mosses and annual grasses like meadow grass.

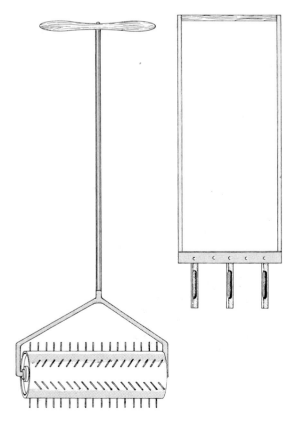

Thinking of the nutrient recycling that supports the woodland community, it is not difficult to see one reason why a lawn can hit trouble. Every time you empty the mower box on to the compost heap (or, worse still, into the dustbin) you throw away the nutrients that the plant has grasped from the soil. The compost made from the clippings may be the saving of the vegetable garden or the herbaceous border, but it is unlikely to find its way back into the lawn. The result is that the soil below the turf slowly and steadily holds less and less nutrient and tends to become slightly acid, which gives the competitive edge to the less demanding weeds and coarse annual grasses. One solution is to replace the nutrients contained in the clippings by applying an inorganic fertiliser. This works, but is quite expensive. An alternative is to leave the clippings on the grass, so that the valuable minerals leach back into the soil. This also works to some extent, but may in the long run do more harm than good, as the clipping eventually form a thick mat which almost suffocates the grasses below.

Another annual chore on some lawns is getting rid of moss, either with a rake and some hard labour or with something out of a bottle. But however conscientiously you attack it, the moss always comes back, because the circumstances in your garden favour the growth of moss more than they favour the survival of fine lawn grass. If you want to keep the moss out, you have either to reconcile yourself to an annual skirmish or you have to change the conditions that tilt the balance in favour of the mosses. In this case the relevant factor is water. On heavy, wet soil mosses grow much better than grass, so the only thing that will produce lasting results is an improvement in the drainage. The thought of taking the turf from an established and otherwise healthy lawn in order to lay drains below it is a frightening one. It is, however, well worth putting drains, or, at the very least, a layer of clinker underneath a new lawn if your garden is on a heavy soil with poor drainage. If your lawn is already laid, you can improve the drainage and aeration by spiking, either with the tines of a fork or with a special tool that can be bought for the purpose. It is also worth remembering that earthworms do their fair share in maintaining drainage by building burrows below the lawn, so if you use a poison to get rid of the worms and their worm casts you are also losing their assistance in the battle against the moss.

So, if your garden is a better environment for moss than it is for lawn grass, then keeping the lawn free from this invader is always going to be difficult. Either you can accept the environment as it is and live with the moss, bearing in mind that it is at least green (which is more than can be said for the bare patches that result from application of a moss killer), or you can spend a fair amount of effort giving the lawn grasses continual help against the competition of the moss, or you can take drastic action and tilt the ecological balance in favour of the grass, once and for all.

A spiked roller (left) breaks up the thick mat that grasses form and aids aeration. The hollow tine fork (right) helps deeper drainage. It removes a core of heavy, compacted and badly drained soil which can then be replaced with sand or a sand and peat mixture. This allows a much better flow of water.

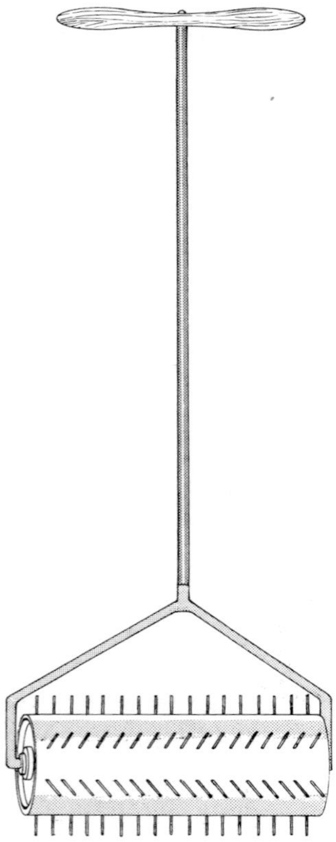

Some common lawn grasses and weeds:
1 Brown top grass
2 Chewings fescue
3 Rough meadow grass
4 Perennial rye grass
5 Yarrow
6 Dandelion
7 Daisy
8 Plantain
9 Creeping buttercup

1
2
3
4
5
6
7
8
9

SOIL AND CLIMATE

Another factor that affects the growth of most plants is the acidity of the soil. Since the inorganic part of the soil is made by the weathering of the bed-rock below it, the composition of this rock greatly affects the character of the soil. Roughly speaking, the rocks in the northern half of the British Isles are igneous in origin and were made many millions of years ago by the action of heat, whereas the rocks in the south were laid down in water, mostly under the sea, and are called sedimentary rocks. Igneous rocks are harder and weather more slowly than sedimentary strata, so, in general, soil in the north is rather more acid and rather poorer in plant nutrients than soil in the south. This difference between north and south limits the distribution of garden plants that are sensitive to the acidity of the soil, and also governs the general character of the wild vegetation. By and large, there are more species of wild flowers on the less acid soils of southern England than there are in the north and in Scotland. Some species demand one type of soil or the other. For example, many of the delicate and beautiful wild orchids need the low acid, or alkaline, soils of the south-east downlands, whereas heathers thrive on the peaty, acid moorlands of the north.

In the garden you must either choose plants that like the acidity of your soil or be prepared to put time and money into tipping the ecological balance in favour of the outsider. The first step is to test the soil, which is easily done using a commercially available kit, called a lime or acidity kit, or sometimes a pH test. It usually involves mixing a soil sample with a chemical reagent and testing this mixture with either a specially treated paper strip or an indicator solution. In either case you get a colour change that can be compared with a standard range of colours supplied with the kit. The manufacturers also give you a long and fascinating list of plants and the acidity level that each likes best, so you can fill your garden with plants that will exactly match your garden soil.

Most plants like a fairly neutral soil and can be catered for quite easily, but the few that demand extremes may be a problem. Lovers of an alkaline soil can be helped by liming, but plants like heather and

The cross-leaved heath (left) grows only on an acid soil while the horseshoe vetch (right) demands an alkaline soil. In the wrong conditions, the plants never thrive and, as the distribution maps show, this means that these plants are hardly ever found in the same area.

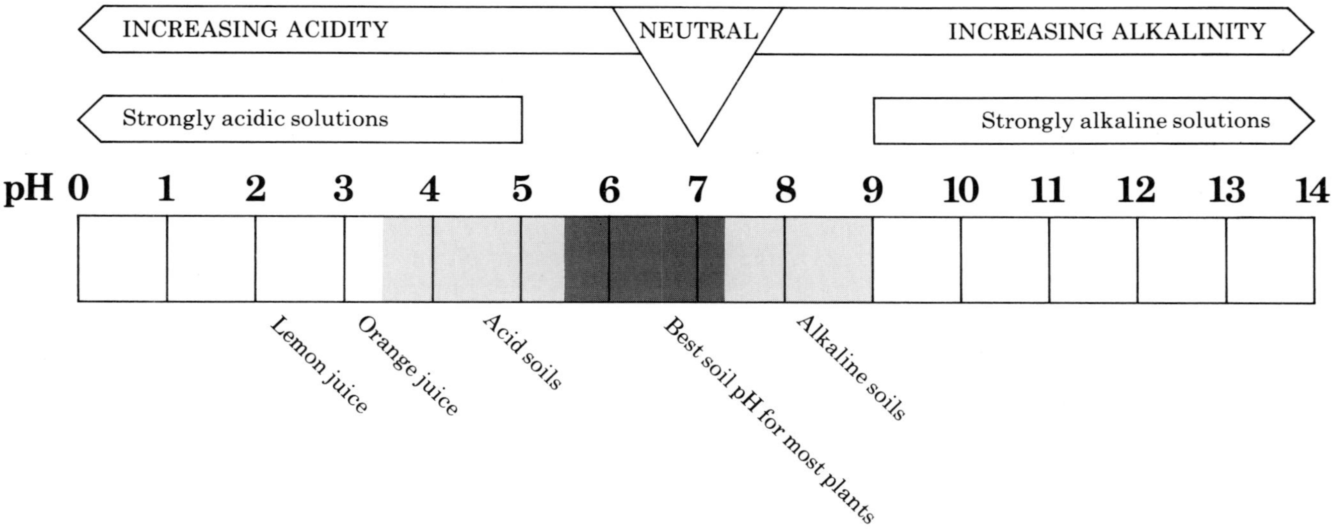

The pH scale

The areas in which the National Vegetable Research Station have found the growing season long enough and tomato crops reliable enough for their growth to be attempted on a commercial scale, out of doors.

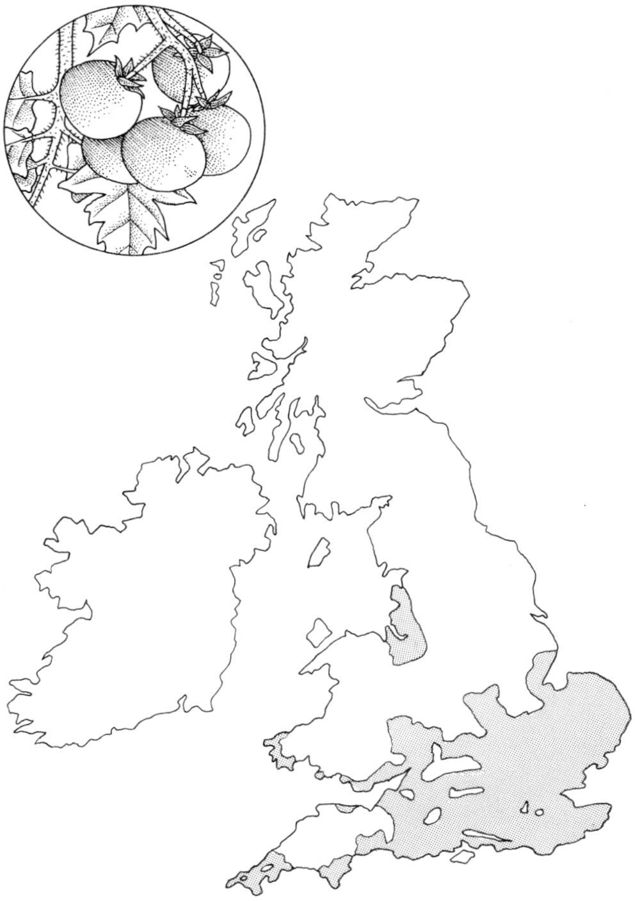

shrubs like *Rhododendron*, *Magnolia* and azalea which all like an acid soil are difficult to grow in an alkaline area like Dorset or the chalklands of Sussex. It is much harder to make a soil more acid than it is to make it more alkaline. There are chemicals that help, but in many cases the best solution is to dig a pit, line it with polythene to isolate it from the soil around, fill it with an acid, peaty soil and plant a real acid lover like the *Rhododendron* in that.

Rainfall gives rise to one of the gardener's great grumbles. Whatever the season, there always seems to be too little or too much. In a drought, the answer lies in a hosepipe and the watering can, but when it rains very heavily and the soil is wet, there is nothing you can do but wait for it to dry. It is equally difficult to manipulate the temperature, which, like the soil type, changes as you travel north. The combination of these factors influences the wild vegetation as well as the garden. In the colder, northern woodland, for example, the dominant species are pine and birch. In the Midlands, oak predominates, whereas in the warmer and drier south-east, with its alkaline and more fertile soil, the most common tree is the beech.

It is not the actual extremes of temperature in the north that do the damage but the length of the growing period – that is, the number of weeks and days in the summer season when temperatures each day are high enough to allow growth, flowering and fruiting. In Britain we are on the temperature limit for a number of popular vegetables. Outdoor tomatoes and sweetcorn can be grown only in the south, and the recent cycle of late spring frosts has so shortened the growing season that runner beans have been a casualty in the north-east. Many of the plants that are taken for granted in England, like the lime tree and even the English oak, are actually on the limit of their distribution and are not found in Scotland.

Planting in the warmest or most sheltered corner of the garden can help the more fragile plants to survive, and cloches and cold frames lengthen the growing season a little. They should be put over the soil, to warm it up, a week or so before planting seeds in early spring. Once the seeds have germinated, a cloche will protect the tender young plants until the outside temperature is high enough for them to cope on their own. Cloches are most useful for seeds and young plants, simply because most plants, with the exception of lettuce, grow too tall and hit the roof of the cloche when they reach full size.

A greenhouse with heaters to mimic the warmth of summer and lighting to copy the length of its days can extend the growing season to 365 days each year. This is, of course, the way that many commercial glasshouses are run, but at a considerable cost in fuel. Hot-house vegetables are always expensive.

House plants, like plants in the greenhouse, suffer no competition from wild neighbours whose seeds fly over the fence and germinate into weeds which then threaten to choke the cultivated inhabitants of the garden, but they do have to cope with the most unnatural environment of them all, the inside of a house. Pretty well everything about the average living room must be unnatural for a plant; no tropical rain for the *Monstera* from the humid forests of Mexico, no beating sun for the cactus from the arid plains of North Africa and no changing seasons to stimulate the annual cycle of the plant's behaviour. It is, of course, possible to create a number of very different environments within the home. The steamy humidity of the bathroom, the baking 'greenhouse' of a sunny window sill in a south-facing room and the draughty gloom of a corner in the hall are all artificial environments, but some of them are very suitable for certain plants. The key to success is to know which 'niche' will suit which plant.

The shortening of the day length and the drawing in of the evening is one of the first signs that autumn has come and winter is not far behind. For the human occupants of the house the long nights indicate warm evenings in front of the fire; outside in the garden, too, the changing length of day and night acts as a signal for changes in the plants' growth and activity. But for the plant on the piano in the corner life gets very confusing. As soon as the natural daylight draws to a close, some interfering human switches on the light, and electric light is quite close enough to daylight to convince the plant that summer is going on for ever.

The plant's confusion can actually prevent it coming into flower, because, in certain plants, flowering is one of the activities that is stimulated

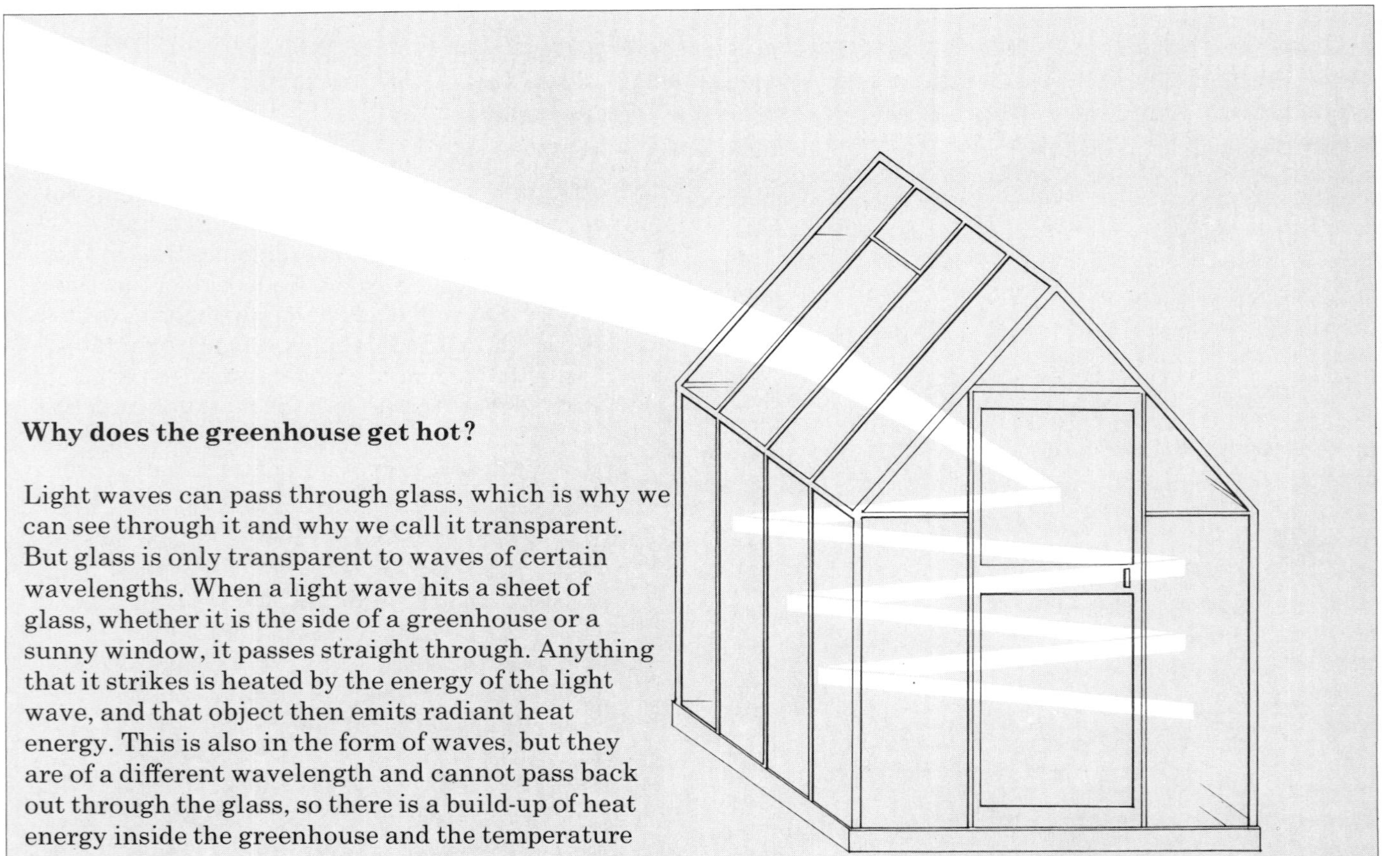

Why does the greenhouse get hot?

Light waves can pass through glass, which is why we can see through it and why we call it transparent. But glass is only transparent to waves of certain wavelengths. When a light wave hits a sheet of glass, whether it is the side of a greenhouse or a sunny window, it passes straight through. Anything that it strikes is heated by the energy of the light wave, and that object then emits radiant heat energy. This is also in the form of waves, but they are of a different wavelength and cannot pass back out through the glass, so there is a build-up of heat energy inside the greenhouse and the temperature goes up.

by the short days and long nights of winter. This is the reason that so many winter-flowering pot plants disappoint the indoor gardener. They are bought in a blaze of colour, but, the following year, the use of electric light extends their day so they cannot 'see' that winter is approaching and they remain stubbornly green.

The influence of day length on the growth, development and reproduction of plants and animals is called 'photoperiodism'. Leaf fall in autumn, the migration of some birds and the reproductive cycles of many animals are all stimulated by seasonal changes in the length of the day and the night. The photoperiodic responses of flowering plants divide them into three groups.

Long-day plants, which require a long day and short night before they will flower. A 'long day' is generally more than ten hours' daylight out of the twenty-four.

Short-day plants, which will begin to flower only when the day is less than a critical length. This 'short day' varies considerably among species.

Day-neutral plants, for example, the tomato, celery and cucumber, which are all indifferent to the length of the day.

Not surprisingly, the response of a plant to day length generally reflects the day length that it would experience when growing in its country of origin. Long-day plants are usually those that grow in the temperate regions and flower in the summer when the days are long. The garden is full of them: spinach, radish and larkspur are all long-day plants. Most of the short-day plants, on the other hand, are found either nearer the equator or are those that flower in winter or early spring in temperate zones.

Several of the popular pot plants need a short day before they will flower. 'Short' is usually less than twelve hours, although plants do vary in their requirements. Pot *Chrysanthemum*, Christmas cactus and poinsettia are all common house plants that will flower only when the days are short, and all of them can be manipulated so that they flower when the market is at its best. Christmas cactus and poinsettia are seen only at Christmas, but the *Chrysanthemum* is now available all the year round. Some of the manipulations practised by the professional horticulturist are beyond the reach of most gardeners, but controlling flowering by regulating day length is relatively easy to do at home.

The important factor, to the plant, is not the total amount of light it receives in the course of twenty-four hours, but the actual length of the day and of the night. A short-day plant needs a 'day' of less than twelve hours, followed by the remainder of the twenty-four in darkness. The mechanism is so sensitive that even a flash of bright light during the 'night' can inhibit flowering, so if you decide to shorten the day length of your house plants by putting them in a cupboard at dusk, choose the cupboard with care. The whole operation could be ruined if you need to open it later in the evening.

Poinsettias, with their brilliant red colour, are spectacular plants when they are first bought. The colour is not, in fact, on the petals but on another part of the plant, called the bracts. In most plants bracts are small green leaves at the base of the flower, but in the poinsettia they are huge and brightly coloured and they surround the tiny, insignificant flowers. The poinsettia is a traditional Christmas purchase, when its red colouring is most

How plants measure night and day

For an animal to be able to react to the length of the day it experiences or to any other exposure to light it must first be able to detect that light in some way. The vertebrate animals whose sex lives are governed by day length have eyes and can see the light. Plants also use the length of the day and the night as a yardstick, but they do not have eyes or any organ that resembles an eye, so how do they cope?

The 'eye' of the plant is a pale blue pigment called phytochrome. It is distributed throughout the tissue of the plant, but in such small quantities that it is quite masked by the plant's green colouring. Phytochrome has been extracted from plants, isolated and chemically identified as a protein which has a pigment molecule attached to it.

Phytochrome exists in two forms, and it signals 'light off' or dusk to the plant by changing from one form to the other, and 'light on' or dawn by changing back. Short-day and long-day plants respond to these signals in opposite ways. At dusk the phytochrome 'eye' signals that darkness has fallen, and a 'biological clock' begins to time the duration of the night.

For short-day plants the night has to exceed a critical length. Once this length of time has elapsed without dawn breaking, a series of reactions takes place, and hormones are released that stimulate the development of flower buds. Even a flash of light during the night can 'reset' the clock and prevent the plant flowering.

In long-day plants the biological clock begins when the phytochrome signals that it is dark, but the flowering mechanism is switched off or inhibited when a critical period of time, or night length, has passed. If daylight breaks before this length of time has elapsed, the change is detected by the phytochrome and flowering is stimulated.

appropriate, but plants are now also grown with bracts of pink or a lovely rich cream.

The problem arises the following Christmas, when the bracts remain obstinately green and the whole plant has grown to twice its original size, making it clumsy in a small room. Colour and size each need separate treatment. The poinsettias on sale in the shops have been chemically dwarfed to make them an attractive and convenient size, but by the following year the effect of this treatment will have worn off, leaving a large and rather lanky plant. If you cut the plant right back in May, it will not be too big by the following Christmas, but it is usually hard to persuade these heavily pruned plants to flower, and when the bracts do change colour they are pale and unspectacular. However, a number of shoots will grow from the cut plant, and when these are about five inches long they can be taken as cuttings, which will flower and be ready to brighten and decorate the house by the following Christmas, providing they get the right conditions of day length.

Poinsettia is a short-day plant, so it needs to be kept away from artificial light as the evenings draw in, but there is a bit more to it than that. Putting a plant away as light fades in the garden reproduces the natural day length of the coming of autumn and winter in the British Isles, but if poinsettia is grown in these conditions of natural day length it flowers in the spring, not at Christmas when it is needed. For a Christmas poinsettia you have to convince the plant that winter is coming a bit early. For a period of eight or nine weeks, starting in September, the poinsettia needs a 'day' of no more than ten hours, so it should be locked away in the cupboard well before night falls outside.

The secret of getting a poinsettia to flower – or, for that matter, getting almost any plant in the house or garden to do its best – lies in imitating the natural conditions in which the plant evolved and in which it would thrive. The garden is an unnatural environment and must always be so, but the more it conforms to or imitates the natural needs of its residents the better those plants will grow.

Many cuttings, including those of the poinsettia, root more easily in the humid atmosphere of a propagator. Even a primitive one like this, made by supporting a clear polythene bag over the young plants, will help.

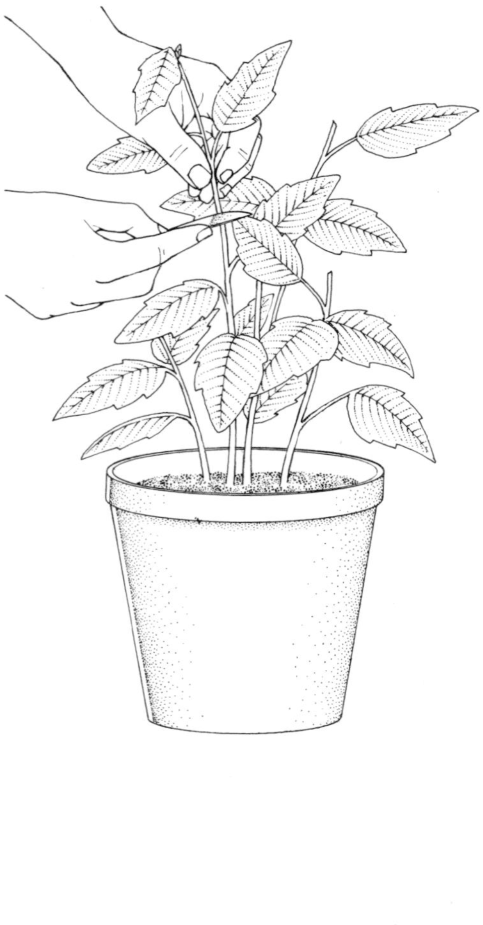

CHAPTER TWO

PLANTS AND THEIR SEX LIVES

As gardeners we have at least two reasons to be grateful that plants have a sex life. The first is that in the sexual reproduction of a plant the inheritable factors carried by the two parents are mixed in the offspring. Without this genetic mixing and changing, both deliberate and fortuitous, we just would not have the countless varieties of garden plants that we grow and take for granted. Without the skill of the plant breeder and the sexual variation that he takes as his raw material, the plants available to the gardener would be more or less the same as the plants by the wayside.

On top of that, the parts of the plant that are important in its sexual cycle are very often the same parts that are important to the gardener. The bright and scented flower holds and advertises the plant's sexual organs but it is also picked and enjoyed by human admirers. The fertilised flower swells to form a fruit that holds the seeds of the next generation, but that same fruit is also harvested and eaten. Without the sex lives of its inhabitants, the garden that we enjoy would hardly exist at all.

The genetic or inheritable information is carried in genes, which are situated on tiny, thread-like structures called chromosomes that lie in the nucleus of every cell. Whatever the organism, the chromosomes always exist in matching pairs, and each species of animal and plant has its own quota of chromosomes, called the chromosome number. Humans, for example, have twenty-three pairs, whereas the apple has seventeen.

Each of the sex cells, or gametes, as they are called, contains just one of each pair of chromosomes. This means that when fertilisation occurs and the male and female gametes fuse, the embryo which results has a complete set of chromosomes, half of which came from each of its parents. As with everything, there are some exceptions, but, generally speaking, that is how variation is introduced in sexual reproduction. Plant gametes are made in the flower. The pollen, which is the male gamete, is made in the swollen part at the tip of each stamen, called the anther. The female gametes are made in the ovary, which generally lies at the centre of the flower. The upper part of the ovary is called the stigma, and is usually sticky or feathery, so that pollen grains will catch on it. This transfer of pollen, or pollination, is the first step towards fertilisation.

Some plants, like the garden pea, are most often 'self-pollinated'. In that case the anther and the stigma ripen at the same time, and pollen just falls out of the anther and on to the receptive stigma of the same flower. When pollen from one flower is transferred to the stigma of a flower on another plant of the same species, 'cross-pollination' occurs, and it is this crossing between different plants of the same species that introduces variation. Because this is an advantage in the evolution of a plant, or of any organism, most plants have some mechanism to encourage cross-pollination. In some plants (like holly and *Skimmia*) the male and female flowers actually grow on different plants, so there is no chance of self-fertilisation. This is why some holly trees persistently refuse to bear red berries for Christmas; however long you wait, the male tree will never carry the female fruit. In other plants (like sweet corn) there are separate male and female flowers on the same plant but in most plants the male and female gametes are produced in the same flower. Whatever the design of the flower, its arrangement is directed towards getting pollen from one plant to another by any means possible.

The dark, string-like objects are the chromosomes, which are only visible when the cell and its nucleus are dividing.

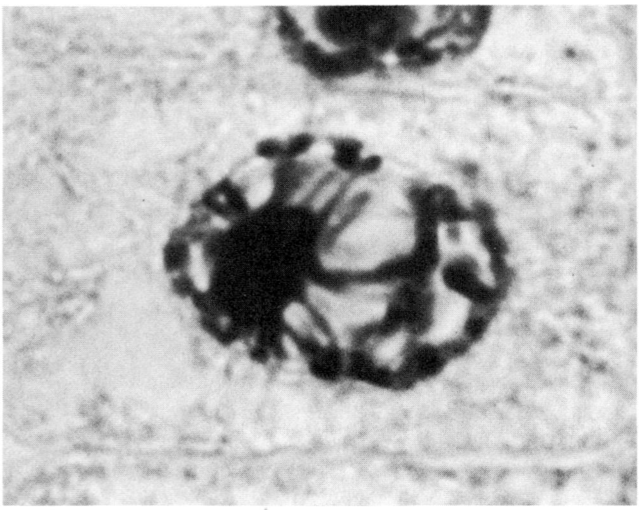

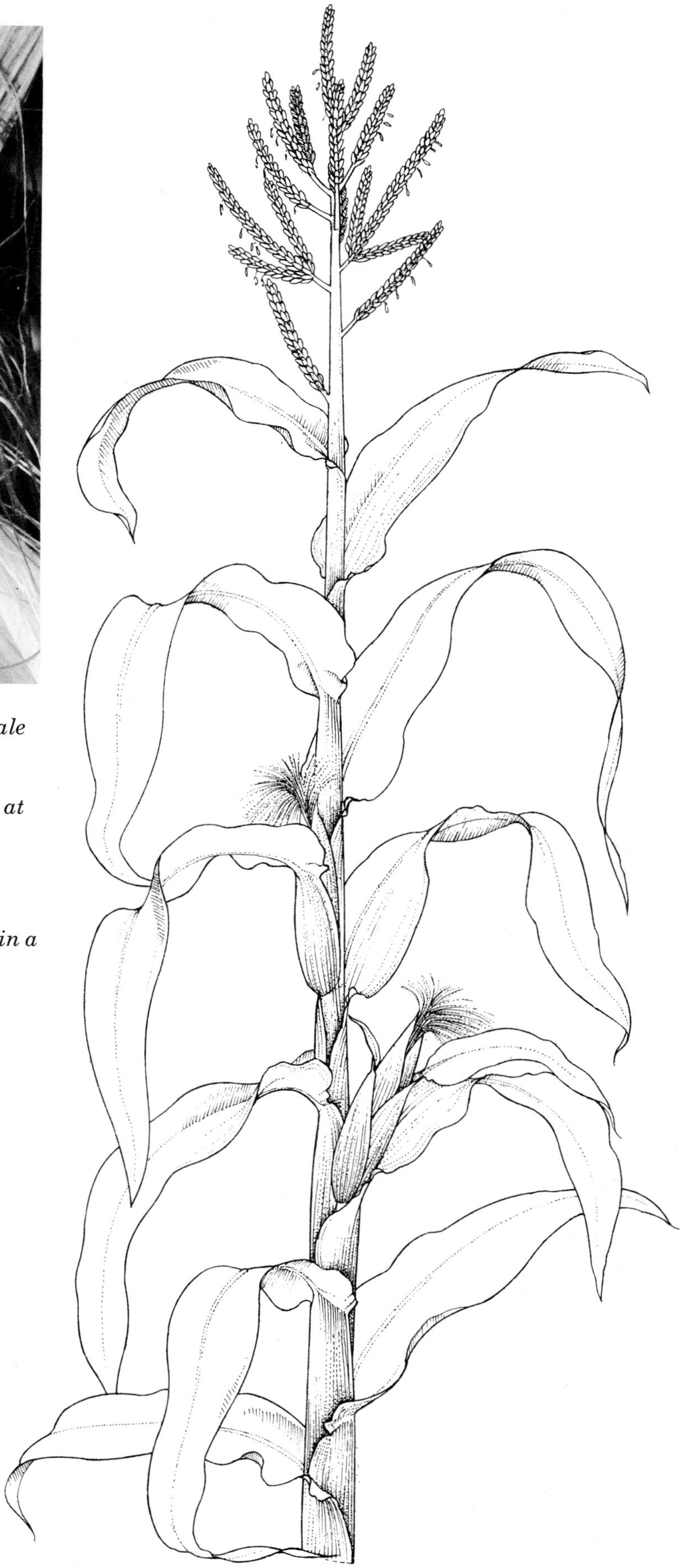

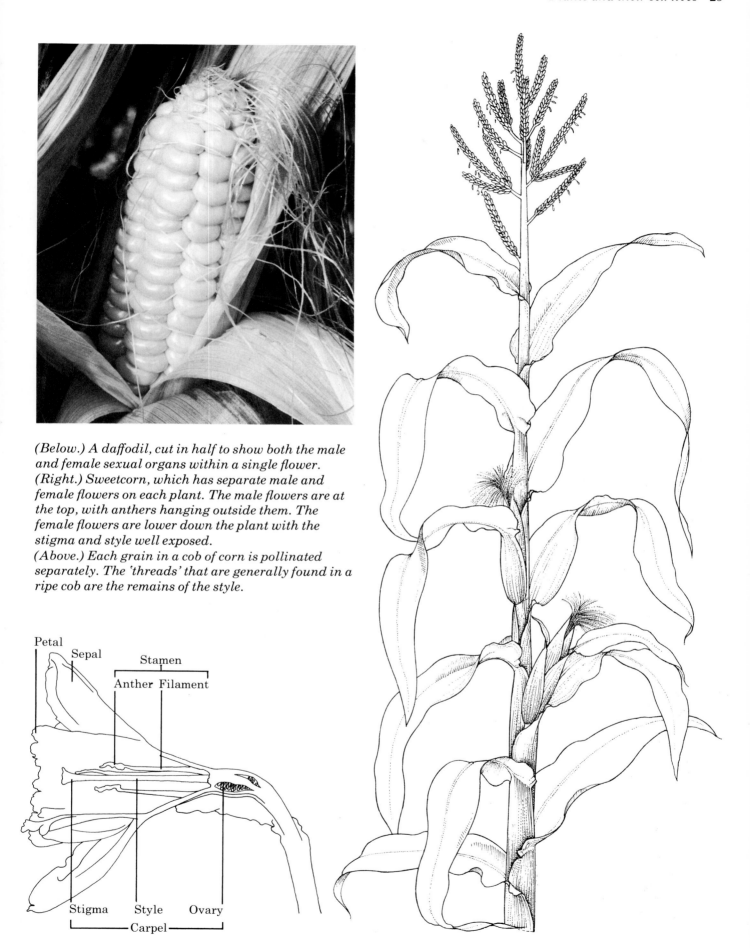

(Below.) A daffodil, cut in half to show both the male and female sexual organs within a single flower.
(Right.) Sweetcorn, which has separate male and female flowers on each plant. The male flowers are at the top, with anthers hanging outside them. The female flowers are lower down the plant with the stigma and style well exposed.
(Above.) Each grain in a cob of corn is pollinated separately. The 'threads' that are generally found in a ripe cob are the remains of the style.

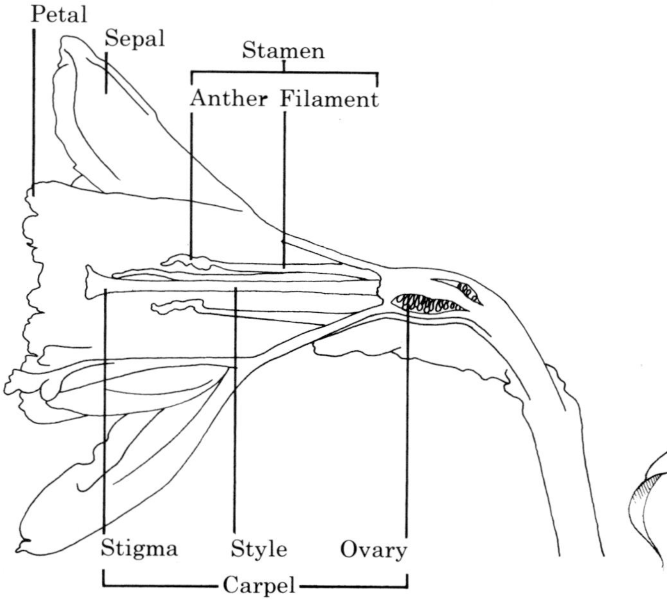

Stereoscan pictures of various pollen grains, showing how their shape and size relates to the plant's means of pollination.
1 Wind pollinated pine ×*1000*
2 Wind pollinated grass ×*4500*
3 Insect pollinated bush mallow × *480*
4 Insect pollinated thistle ×*4500*
5 Insect pollinated scabius × *480*

1

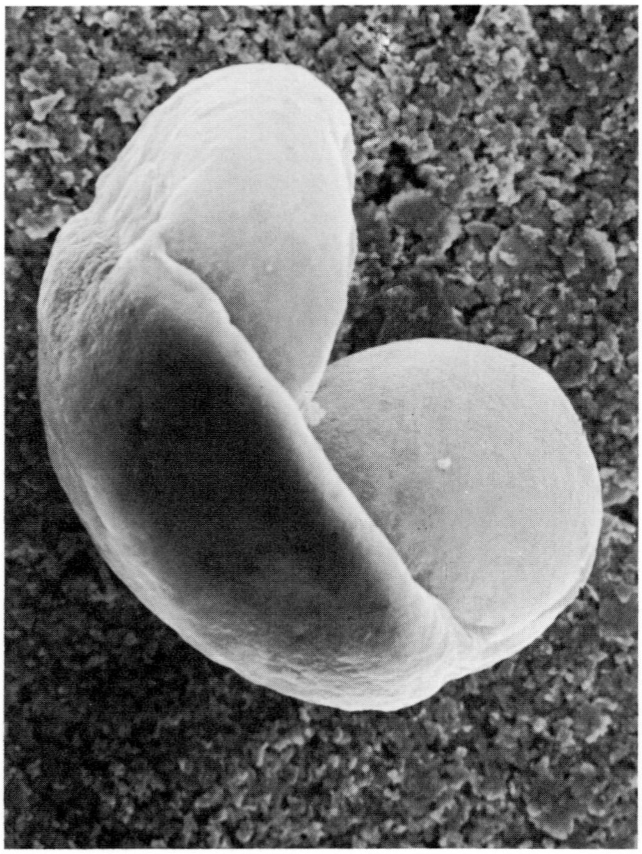

2

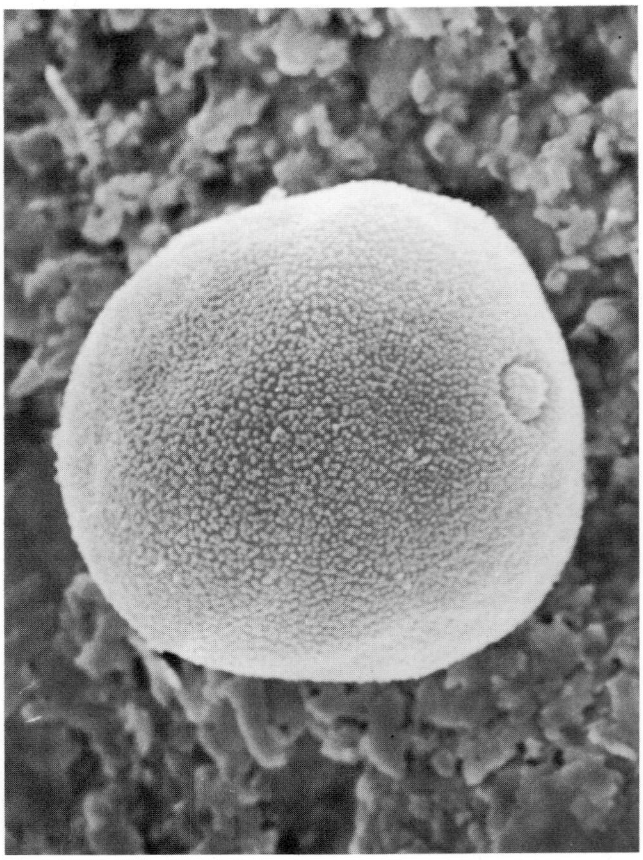

3

4

Some pollen, such as that from grasses and trees, is carried between plants by the wind. The grains of pollen tend to be very small and light, measuring less than 0·05 mm across, and they are easily and invisibly carried on the currents in the air, sometimes for several miles. Anybody who suffers from that curse of the summer, hay-fever, will testify that while the pollen may not be seen, it can certainly make itself felt.

The wind is a chancy thing, and plants that depend on it for pollination do everything they can to help. The flowers of wind pollinated plants are small and inconspicuous, but both the stigma and the stamens hang beyond the petals, outside the flower, so that they are exposed to any passing breeze and can catch every grain of pollen that is blown their way. Inevitably, most of the pollen is wasted in the wind, so each flower produces literally millions of grains, and it is this mass production that is such a trial to the allergic.

Sweet corn is one of the wind-pollinated plants that is grown in the garden. Each of the grains of corn that make up the 'cob' grows from a separate flower, so in order to get full heads of corn, complete pollination is important. The chances of pollination are increased by planting the corn in a block rather than in the usual rows so that each plant has possible donors of pollen on every side.

In this country the other main carriers of pollen are insects, although in the tropics there are bats and humming birds that play their part. The agents of pollination remain, of course, unaware of the important role they play. The transfer of pollen is incidental to their search for food. Plants which rely on insects for pollination are particularly common in the flower garden, where the colour and scent that have evolved to attract insects also recommend the flowers to the gardener. Insect-pollinated flowers have nectaries, usually at the base of the petals, which make nectar, a sugary fluid that insects love to eat. As the insect flies or crawls from one flower to another seeking nectar, it carries with it an accidental load of pollen that can be rubbed off on to the stigma of another flower.

5

Insect-pollinated plants make fewer pollen grains than those that rely on the wind but generally speaking, each grain is larger and covered with spikes and knobs which help it to become attached to the foraging insect. The stigma and stamens, instead of hanging outside the flower exposed to the wind, are set within the flower so that the insect has to push past them in order to get to the nectaries. In this way the plant's structure makes the most of every opportunity to achieve cross-pollination. The whole appearance of the flower – its large size, its bright colour, even the pattern on its petals – all these mark it, to the insect, as a suitable place to look for food. (See colour photos on pages 33, 34.)

Although it does not really matter to the gardener whether the flowers in the flower garden get fertilised or not, it is of vital importance in the vegetable garden. Wide-spectrum insecticides, as the name implies kill everything. They certainly get rid of the pests they are aimed at, but they also threaten the success of your vegetable patch, and that of your neighbours as well. Runner bean plants are insect-pollinated, and if the flowers are not fertilised there will be no runner beans to pick, so it is worth doing something to encourage suitable insects in the garden. *Buddleia* is sometimes called 'the butterfly bush' because of the numbers of these lovely insects that may cluster around its lilac flowers, but bees and many others are equally attracted. They may come to feed on the *Buddleia* but stay to help pollinate the vegetables. A hive at the bottom of the garden, or even a neighbour with bees, is a particular asset because, although the owner of the hive will get the honey, every garden in the area will benefit from the diligence of his worker bees as they stock up for winter.

The honey bee is a particularly useful pollinator, since each bee collects nectar from only one species of flower at a time. You can watch them in the garden. Having collected from one, say, hollyhock, they will search persistently until they spot another hollyhock, completely ignoring the temptations of the rest of the flower bed. This is a great advantage to the plant, since the pollen that can cross-fertilise a flower must come from another flower of the same species. Showering the valuable hollyhock pollen on to the neighbouring lavender is a complete waste for both the plants.

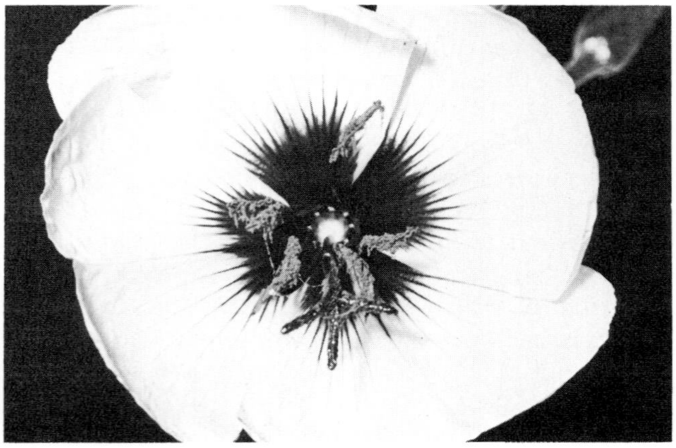

The evening primrose in normal light (above) and ultra-violet (below). A foraging honey bee can see ultra-violet and is guided to the flower's nectaries by its striking markings.

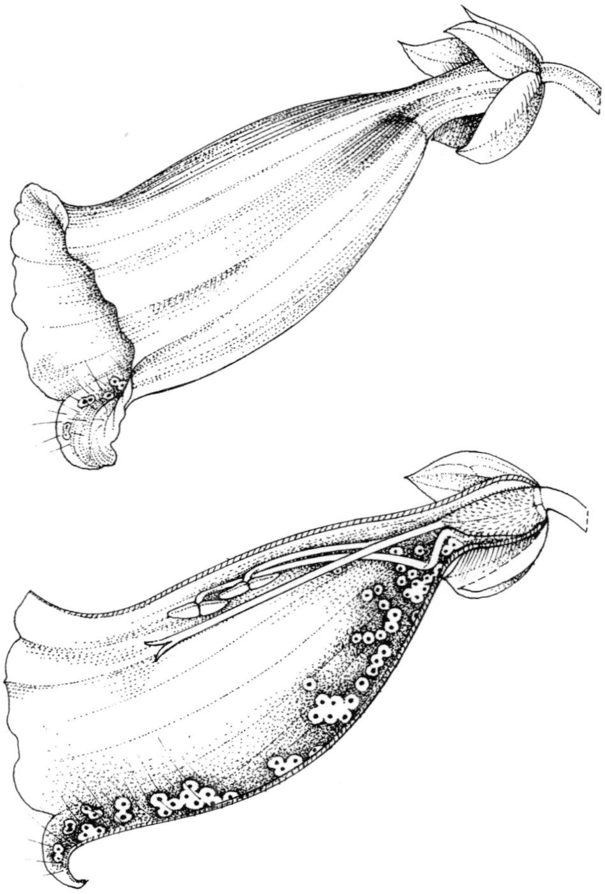

The spots inside the trumpet of each foxglove flower guide foraging insects to the nectary at the base of each flower. They are called honey guides.

Lords-and-ladies: a sexual trap

Lords-and-ladies, or cuckoo-pint, is a strange-looking 'flower', which is often seen in England and Wales during the spring but is less common in Scotland and Ireland. The great green trumpet shape that is seen in the hedgerows is, in fact, an enlarged bract, the lower part of which forms a chamber containing the real flowers. The male and female flowers are separate, but both are carried on the central spadix.

The female flowers are at the bottom of the chamber. Above them is a circle of sterile flowers, shaped like bristles; above those, the male flowers and, at the top, another ring of sterile hairs, this time pointing downwards. On the morning of the day that the bract unfolds, the flowering shoot or inflorescence produces heat and emits a strong smell, reminiscent of rotting meat. This delectable combination is irresistible to small flies and beetles, which believe that it will lead them to a meal. In their search for the

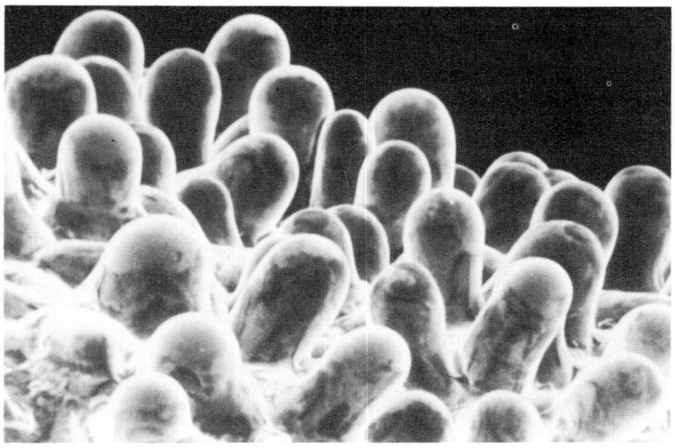

(Above.) Stereoscan picture of the surface of a ripe apple stigma.
(Below.) The same surface with grains of apple pollen fitting on to it.

Some flowers further increase their chances of catching the right kind of pollen by minimising the variety of insects that can get inside the flower. Clearly, only very small insects can get inside very small flowers, but some of the larger flowers restrict the entry of tiny insects by having a trap-door opening that will yield only under the weight of a large and heavy insect, like a bee. The fewer kinds of insect that can get into a flower, the better the chance that its last port of call was another flower of the same kind.

The structure of the pollen grain itself, as well as the stigma upon which it must eventually land, also help prevent the wrong pollen getting to the egg cell. The pollen grains of each species have a unique and often quite complex shape. A pollen expert can easily identify a plant from its pollen by examining it under the microscope; this technique is used a lot in archaeology, to identify plant remains that are discovered when a site is excavated. The receptive surface of the stigma has a matching pattern, so that pollen of the same species fits into it, rather like a key fitting into a lock. Pollen grains that do not fit the lock just fall off, leaving the way clear for others of the right shape and species.

In addition to this matching of shape and form, there is also a kind of chemical matching at the surface of the stigma. The pollen grains of some plants carry molecules of complex proteins and other materials in the ridges and patterns that adorn the surface coat of the grains. These act like chemical 'credentials' that must be identified and accepted at the surface of the stigma before the pollen grain can grow down through the style and towards the egg

source of such an appetising aroma they land on the spadix or on the inside of the bract, both of which are covered with a slippery layer of oily epidermis. The insects, unable to gain a foothold, tumble into the bottom chamber, where they are trapped by the downward-pointing hairs.

The female flowers become receptive as the bract opens so, if the imprisoned insects have already visited another lords-and-ladies and carry its pollen, cross-pollination may take place. During the following night the female flowers cease to be receptive, but the male flowers, further up the spadix, produce pollen and, as the insects crawl about their prison, they pick up a thorough dusting. At this stage the attractive carrion smell ceases, and the downward-pointing hairs wither and fall off so nothing holds the insects in the chamber. They climb out and fly away. If they are again attracted and trapped by the newly-opened bract of another plant, then the load of pollen that they carry will brush off and pollinate the receptive female flowers.

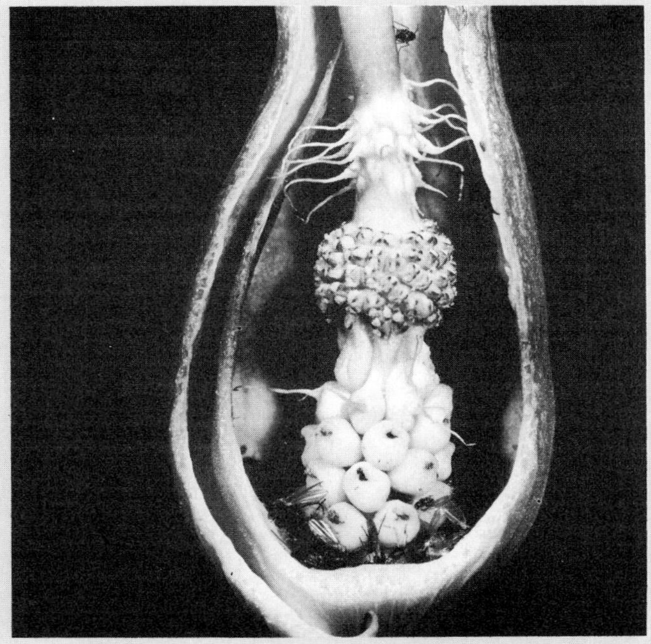

cell. In some species there is yet another check on the identity of the pollen grain and its compatibility with the egg, which takes place within the style. Any growing pollen tubes that fail this chemical test are inhibited in their growth and do not reach the egg cell. It is a complex series of identity checks, a kind of chemical obstacle course going on in every flower in the garden, and ensuring that the pollen grain which finally gets to the egg cell and fertilises it is the right species and is compatible. Once fertilisation has taken place a new embryo plant will then begin to form.

The seedling plant carries inheritable characters from both its parents. It may exactly resemble one or the other, or it may not look very much like either. The new plant may bear flowers of great beauty or fruits with a luscious flavour, or it may be a scrawny little thing that you would not find room for in the biggest garden. The results of most crosses are unpredictable. If you collect seed from cross-pollinated plants, the next generation may or may not exactly resemble its parents.

The first attempt to predict the results of crossing plants which were members of the same species but which had some very different features was performed not by a scientist in the laboratory or by a horticulturist in the greenhouse, but by a monk in his monastery garden. The ways of science have changed a great deal since the nineteenth century when Gregor Mendel made his first experiments in the grounds of the Abbey at Brno, but the rules for breeding plants that he formulated are still in use. He had no idea why the plants behaved as they did; genes and chromosomes were not to be discovered for another half century or so. Mendel based all his work and the 'Mendelian laws', as they came to be called, on his observations as a gardener growing peas in the monastery garden.

Gregor Mendel (1822–1884)

Mendel and the Laws of Inheritance

The pea was an ideal plant for Mendel to choose for his experiments, because, when left to themselves, the flowers self-fertilise before they even open. This meant that he could prevent self-pollination by opening the flower bud himself and cutting out the anthers, and he could then cross-pollinate the flower, using the pollen of his choice, simply by shaking it on to the ripe stigma. On the other hand, if he wanted the flower to self-pollinate, all he had to do was leave it alone.

Peas also show a range of clear characteristics, with no confusing 'half and half' features to muddle the picture. Some pea plants are tall and some are short, but none is medium in height, for example. Some peas are green and some yellow, some have a wrinkled skin, whereas others are smooth and so on, and all these characteristics are inherited. They are also all inherited independently, rather than in pairs or larger groups. A tall pea plant can bear either yellow or green peas, as can a short plant, and a yellow pea can have a smooth or a wrinkled skin.

In Mendel's early experiments he examined just one of these characteristics, height, and this led him to some interesting observations. He crossed tall pea plants with short pea plants, collected the peas (the seeds that resulted from this union) and planted them. When this next generation of plants grew, they were all tall; he did not have a single short plant. He called this the first filial (or F_1) generation and left these tall plants to self-pollinate to produce the F_2 generation. The plants in the F_2 generation were a mixture – some were tall and some were short – so he concluded that 'shortness' was in some way carried as an inheritable factor by the F_1 generation, in spite of the fact that all the plants were tall. Tallness, he decided, was 'dominant' over shortness which was 'recessive'.

Then he counted the tall and short plants in the F_2 plot, and found that there were three tall plants for every one short one and that, however many seasons he repeated the experiment and however many plants he grew, he always got all tall plants in the F_1 generation and tall and short plants in the proportion 3:1 in the F_2 generation. His problem was to explain how a recessive feature, like shortness, could be hidden in one generation but re-emerge in the next in quite predictable numbers.

He assumed that when sex cells are formed the members of pairs of factors separate, so that only one is carried in each gamete. He represented a true breeding tall plant by the pair of letters 'TT' and a true breeding short plant by the letters 'tt'. The individual gametes can then be symbolised by the letters T,T,t and t. The possible offspring from the crossing of a short and a tall plant are represented by the permutations of these four letters, which can be shown in a simple plan.

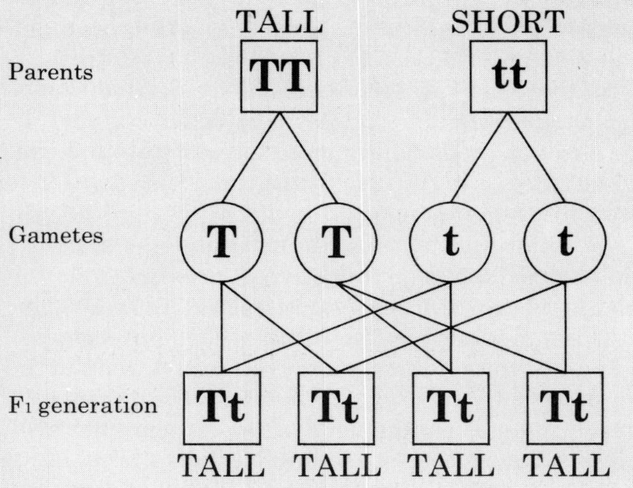

The resulting plants are Tt, Tt, tT and tT, and they all look tall because in every case the plant carries the factor 'T' which is dominant. But in the F_2 generation the shortness emerges.

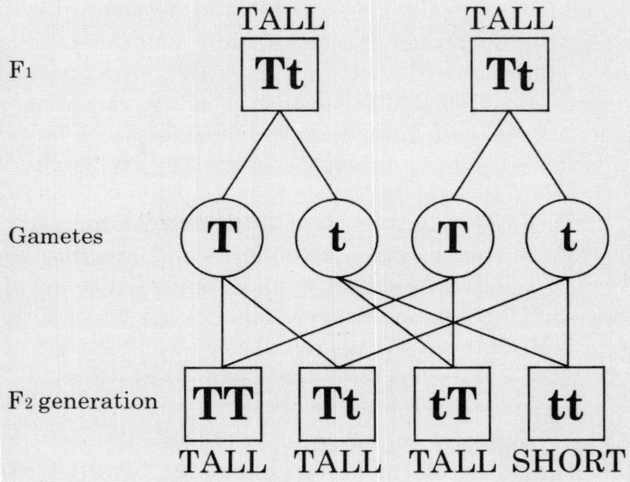

This law of dominance works with perfect simplicity for single characteristics when one is clearly dominant over the other. But there are plants with readily distinguishable characteristics that are controlled by pairs of genes but where one gene is not completely dominant over the other, and this leads to a mixing of the characteristics concerned. For example, a red snapdragon crossed with a white snapdragon produces an F_1 generation entirely made up of plants bearing pink flowers. When this F_1 generation is self-pollinated, it produces an F_2 generation of plants with flowers of red and white and pink – most confusing, but when drawn out in a Mendelian diagram it is still encouragingly simple.

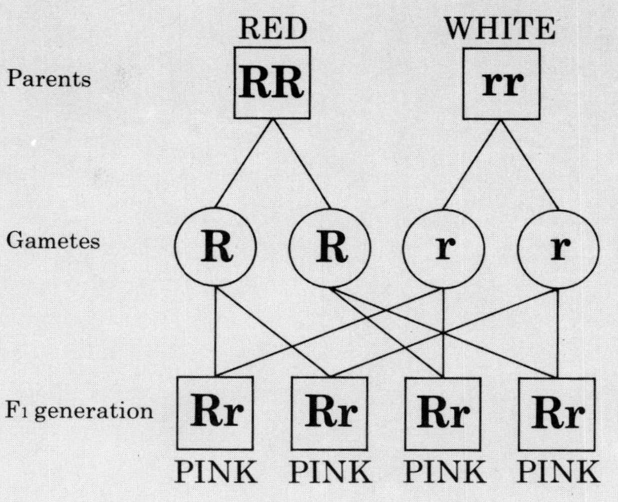

The plants of the F_1 generation all carry an R (red) and an r (white), but because R is incompletely dominant over r the flowers on the plants are all pink.

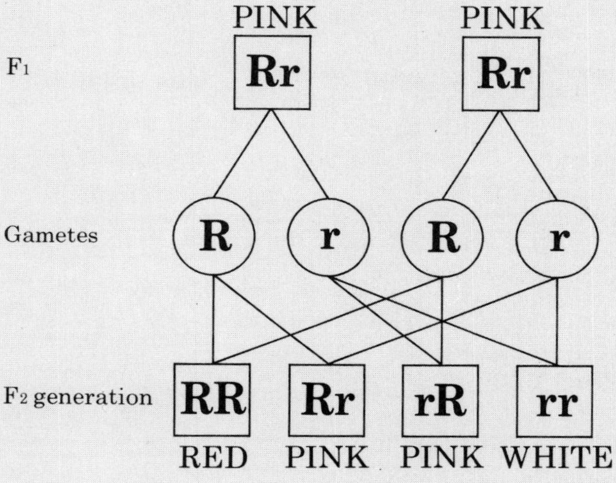

The plants of the F_2 generation are red (RR), white (rr) and pink (Rr and rR) in the proportions 1:1:2.

These examples remain fairly simple because the variations are all either one thing or the other; that is, peas are always either tall or short and snapdragons are either red, white or pink, which is a bit more complicated, but at least they are never dark pink or nearly white. Many inherited characteristics do show a graded series between two extremes, and this is called continuous variation. It occurs when a particular feature is controlled not by one pair of genes but by two pairs or more. It is a matter of extreme good fortune that the plants which Mendel chose display characters with discontinuous variation, since the complexities of continuous variation would almost certainly have defeated even his labour and stopped him formulating any kind of rules or principles.

MODERN PLANT BREEDING

The whole picture of a plant's genetic pedigree is enormously complicated. An apple tree, for example, has seventeen pairs of chromosomes. It has been calculated that for every cross between two apple trees there are 131,000 possible offspring, and even this number could be increased by other, chance gene interactions. The amount of variation that can be introduced in the course of sexual reproduction is absolutely enormous.

It is the application of the science of genetics that has led to the introduction of so many new plants. There have been varieties that increase agricultural productivity, as well as tougher and more reliable vegetables and more colourful flowers in the garden. The number of new hybrids grows every year – the seed catalogues are full of them – but even our prehistoric ancestors practised plant breeding of a kind when they saved seed from the strongest and most fruitful plants to grow next year's crop. In a way, they were doing much the same as nature itself, selecting the strongest and best plants to survive, and, indeed, the production of new hybrids by breeders today is essentially an exercise in accelerated and controlled plant evolution. The evolution is controlled because it is the breeder who selects the plants that will continue; the ones that survive are the ones that will sell rather than the ones that best suit the environment, and it is accelerated because those that do not make the grade very quickly find themselves on the compost heap.

The job of a plant breeder is often to take the desirable characteristics of two plants and combine them in one that has the virtues of both. A process of this kind is going on at the moment at the National Vegetable Research Station in the search for a lettuce that is resistant to the downy mildew fungus, *Bremia*. Downy mildew thrives in damp conditions. Although the first sign of infection is usually a patch of 'down' on the underside of a leaf, the fungus grows inside the tissue of the plant and causes stunted and abnormal growth as well as the down that gives it its name. The down is made up of tiny fungus stalks which poke out of the surface of the leaf and carry the spores that can spread the disease (you can see them with a magnifying glass). It spreads very fast and causes a great deal of damage.

(Left.) Wall lettuce. A common, native perennial and one of the ancestors of salad lettuce.

(Right.) A bumble bee foraging in the flowers of the horseshoe vetch.

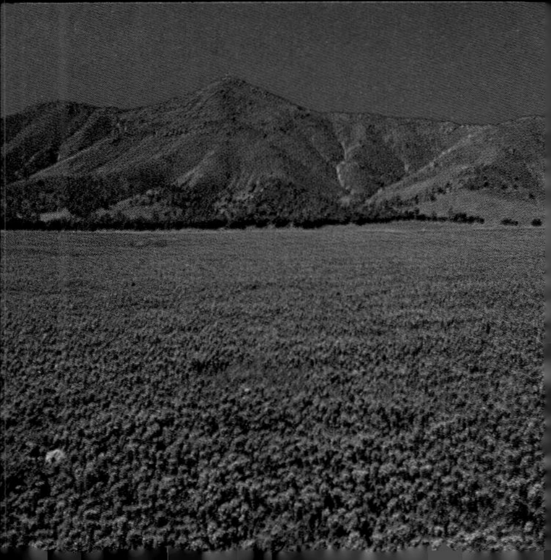

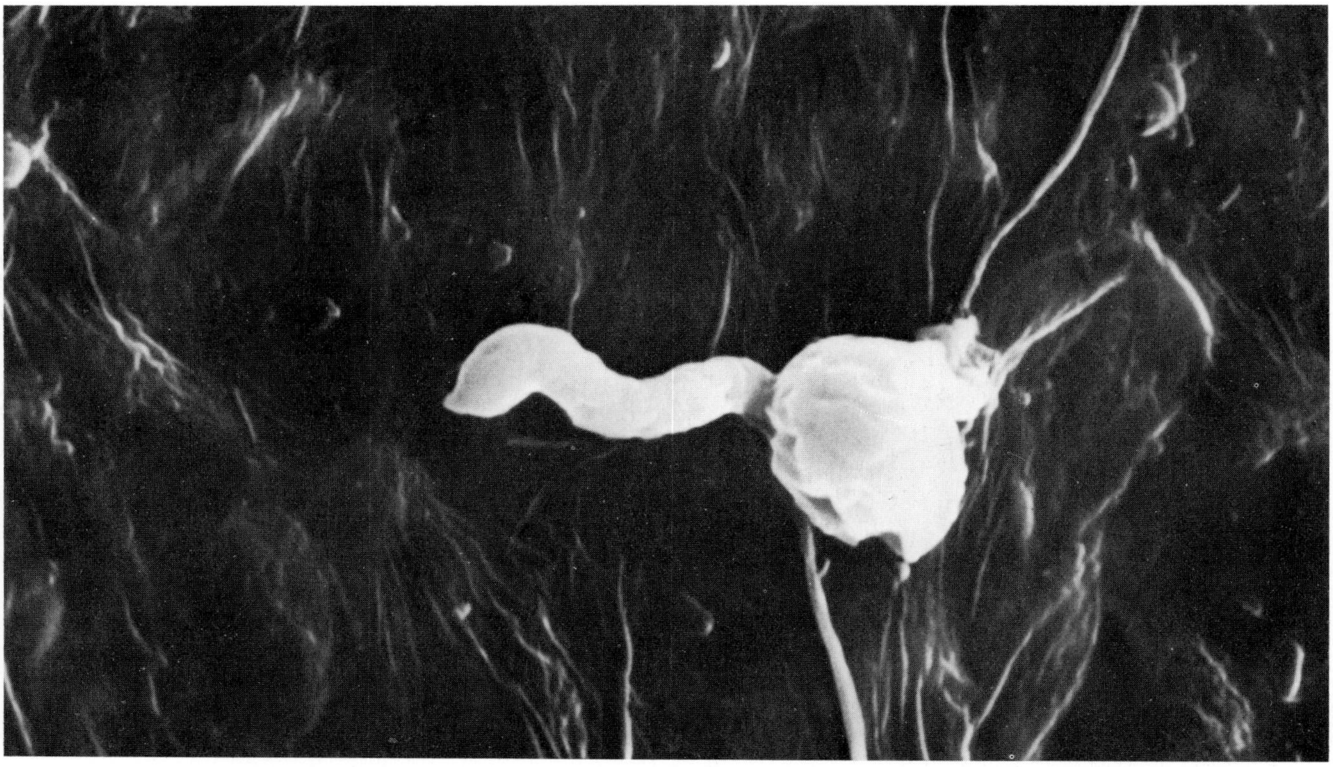

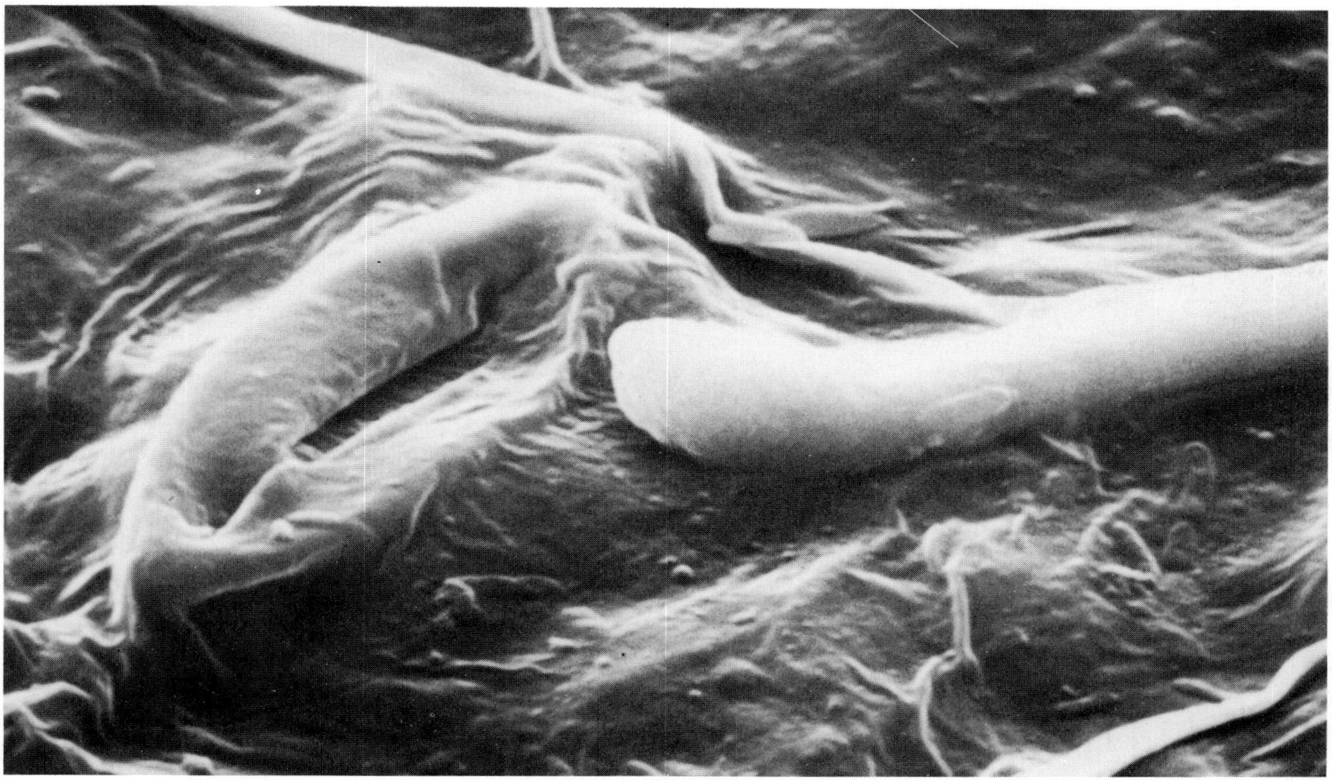

The infective spore of downy mildew beginning to grow (above) and the fungus entering the leaf through a pore or stoma (below).
Opposite page: (top left.) A chrysomelid or flower beetle feeding in a buttercup. A good dusting of pollen has stuck to its body.
(Top right.) A bumble bee foraging in Fuchsia.
(Centre left.) A honey bee feeding on fleabane.
(Centre right.) A honey bee foraging in a crocus.
(Bottom.) The ephemerals of the Arizona desert flower brilliantly whenever conditions are suitable. *(See page 45.)*

(Above.) A bed of wild lettuce used in the breeding programme at the National Vegetable Research Station in Warwickshire.

(Below.) A bed of Avoncrisp lettuce. This variety was bred at the NVRS and is resistant to some strains of the fungus causing downy mildew.

Some of the varieties of wild lettuce have a lot of resistance to mildew, but they are thin and scrawny and taste terrible. It is only the hybrid lettuces that make such lovely summer salads, and these have a much lower resistance to mildew, so the aim is to combine the shape, size and flavour of a modern hybrid with the resistance of its wild but bitter relative. Countless crosses have been performed, and a whole host of different strains of lettuce have been grown in the hope that one will emerge which has just the right combination of taste and resistance.

When the right lettuce is discovered the work is still not over. Before the lettuce seed is put on sale, it will have to be registered on the National List of Vegetable Varieties and before it is placed on this list it will have to pass a number of official tests. They are called DUS (Distinctness, Uniformity and Stability) tests and they protect the consumer by ensuring that the new plants are distinct from other vegetable varieties, uniform in that the plants do not vary much from one another, and stable so that they do not change from one generation to the next. The purpose of these tests is to ensure that when you buy a packet of seeds you can be confident of what will grow from them; however, these tests all take time, particularly when the new variety is a biennial vegetable, like an onion, when each generation takes two years to mature. Between finding the perfect vegetable and getting the seed into the shop there is often a gap of ten years.

Many of the plant-breeding programmes are undertaken to produce new varieties not for the gardener but for the big commercial growers with their vast crops and their dependence on mechanical harvesting. For example, a company like Bird's Eye asks from its breeders peas that are small and sweet and live up to their advertising jingles, but also peas that mature all together on plants that grow at just the right height for the machinery with as few leaves as possible to get in the way of picking and processing. It sounds impossible, but that is more or less what the breeders have produced.

Much of plant breeding is hit or miss. Random pairing of genes results in variation, but most of this variation is of no use to man and of no interest to the plant breeder. Some of it may have a direct application – like height in peas, resistance in lettuce and so on – whereas other variations show a potential which is not wanted at the moment but is kept for experimental breeding in the future. Particularly useful are the variations that reproduce themselves, or breed 'true', and these are often used as a breeding stock from which the plant breeder knows he can get certain characteristics. The more plants like this that a breeder can use as parents, the more easily he will be able to predict the results of the many crosses that he makes in his search for the perfect, disease-resistant plant.

F1 hybrid seeds

Every year there seem to be more seed packets in the shops labelled 'F1 hybrid'. These seeds are obtained by crossing two true breeding but different parents. The results of this cross (the plants you grow from F1 seeds) are predictable but are not like either of their parents.

The parent lines are derived by self-pollinating for about seven generations. This produces plants which are uniform and true breeding, but which often show greatly reduced vigour, hardiness, size and yield. The F1 seeds that you buy are collected after crossing two of these parent lines.

The first thing that is conspicuous about F1 seeds is their cost – they are substantially more expensive. The reason for this is that the parent lines have to be maintained and then hand-crossed each year to produce the seeds. It is no good trying to save money by keeping seeds because the F1 hybrid plants themselves will not breed true – indeed many of the free flowering hybrids are more or less sterile. The extra size and higher yield of the F1 hybrids should compensate for the additional cost.

A pea plant bred for mechanical harvesting, with more tendrils than a conventional plant, but fewer leaves to get in the way of the machinery.

Vegetable gene bank

Many of the older varieties of vegetables and flowers are no longer popular or fashionable, and could easily die out altogether. Some of these are now being conserved at 'gene banks', so that they will be available in the future if breeders need to reintroduce some quality which existed in the older varieties but which has disappeared in more modern ones.

A gene bank for vegetables from all over the world has been started at the National Vegetable Research Station at Wellesbourne in Warwickshire. The scope of the problem, as they see it, is shown by the capacity of their store. They can hold one litre of seed of between eight and ten thousand temperate varieties and between two and three thousand tropical varieties. Storage is in a refrigerator at $-20\,^{\circ}$C ($-4\,^{\circ}$F), and under these conditions the seed should remain viable for between thirty and fifty years, so regeneration of supplies, by growing the plants and collecting the seed, is not needed very often. The aim of the bank at Wellesbourne is to obtain as many varieties as possible and to store them as soon as possible. They will also record all information about the variety and how it grows, but they make no judgements about whether or not it is worth keeping. Any and every vegetable variety that they obtain will be stored, because it is impossible to foretell just which qualities might be important to plant breeders in the future. They are collecting seed from every source they can, including amateur gardeners. The seeds that they particularly want probably will not have an official name but will have been produced for several generations.

The kind of situation that the gene bank will combat is illustrated by recent changes in cauliflower growing. In Italy there are many old types of cauliflower and broccoli, but as the breeders and growers set up in large co-operatives they tend to produce more uniform crops and many of the older varieties may be lost. The value of the older types for breeding is clear. Calabrese, a new vegetable that is popular here and even more so in the United States, was bred from several old Italian varieties of broccoli. If the older types are allowed to disappear, then the scope of plant breeding in the future will be severely restricted.

In this country we have already lost some old Cornish varieties of cauliflower which had a resistance to disease that is not found in the larger, whiter varieties that have replaced them. Unless they are placed in a gene bank, the same is likely to happen to some of the Yorkshire varieties. At the moment, most of the cauliflower seed grown in this country is Dutch in origin, because these varieties have whiter curds which makes them – for the moment at least – commercially more desirable. Some Yorkshire varieties of cauliflower are much hardier, and this is a valuable quality, a genetic resource worth preserving for the future.

In a wider context, the older varieties are often particularly useful when breeding vegetables to be grown in the developing Third World countries. Here at home, though, any minor changes in the climate, the distribution of pests, our eating habits and many other factors could make the breeding possibilities of the gene bank vitally important.

In 1973, EEC legislation established a National List of vegetable varieties in each of the member countries, and made it illegal to sell the seeds of any variety not on that list. The intention was to protect the consumer, both the private gardener and the commercial grower, by ensuring that he got precisely what he expected when he bought seeds. Every variety on the National List has passed the tests for distinctness, uniformity and stability that are undergone by new varieties, so when you buy a packet of seeds you can be perfectly sure that they are what they say they are, grown and packed under proper conditions.

The Martock bean, bred in the twelfth century and grown in this country ever since.

The National Lists of the EEC countries contain some eight thousand varieties of vegetable, and all these can be sold in any of the member nations. That sounds like enough choice for anybody, but the legislation has many opponents. Their concern is that some of the old, traditional varieties, which are often grown in only one region of the country, are not on the list. If these disappear it will be an enormous loss, not just to the plant breeders of the future, but to the gardeners of today, many of whom believe that these old varieties taste better.

Oddly enough, it remains legal to grow, breed and even give away the seed of these vanishing vegetables but it may not be sold. To help the distribution of these varieties without contravening the law, the Henry Doubleday Research Association, in Essex, has founded a seed 'library'. Members 'borrow' seeds, and when they have grown their crop, they collect some of its seed and return it to the library for the use of future borrowers. It is a fairly small-scale operation, but it provides access to the old vegetable varieties for gardeners as well as for plant breeders.

The red and white pea bean, formerly grown in cottage gardens and eaten sliced or dried.

PLANT BREEDING AT HOME

Although the amateur is unlikely to breed a flower or vegetable that will startle the horticultural world (though it has happened), it is interesting to experiment within a species and create something new for your own enjoyment. It is always a slow business, since it takes at least a year for a seed to germinate and the plant to mature and flower, and it will inevitably be entirely unpredictable, for the first few years at least, because most gardeners have no way of telling which characteristics will be passed on. But then the enthusiasts claim that this uncertainty is half the fun!

The *Fuchsia* is a good plant with which to begin. It came originally from Central and South America and from New Zealand, and there are now about a hundred species that are grown in this country. Breeding is long established, and there have been so many successful hybrids that many of the less spectacular species plants have lost their popularity and are rarely seen. The upright varieties can be grown as bushes or standards or against a wall, and the trailing and prostrate forms are ideal for hanging baskets. In the warmer southern counties *Fuchsia* makes a really lovely hedge. It makes a good subject for breeding because the eight stamens are large and easy to manipulate and the stigma and style are both accessible.

The first step is to choose the parents of your new plants; these may be hybrid or species plants. It is not possible to predict the outcome of any cross with certainty, but, generally speaking, blue and purple are dominant in both the inner ring of petals and the outer ring of sepals. In most plants the sepals are small and green and protect the flower bud. Once the bud has opened the sepals are hardly seen, tucked away below the larger and more colourful petals. In the *Fuchsia* both the petals and the sepals are brightly coloured (usually different colours), and this is why the buds begin to show colour even when they are quite tightly closed. Either of your two parent plants can play 'father' or 'mother' or you can perform the cross both ways – but one hint passed on by a *Fuchsia* breeder of forty years' standing is that white or pale flowers often have poor pollen, so they are better as mother than father. Having selected the foundations of the dynasty, you then have to ensure that your parent plants are monogamous; if you want to be sure of the pedigree of any plants you may produce then it is vital that only the father's pollen reaches the stigma of the mother flower.

The technique is this. When the flower is almost ready to open you can 'pop' it by gently squeezing the sepals. In a period of sunny weather a flower bud that looks about to burst open in the evening will generally open in the warmth of the following day, so this is a good time to 'pop' the flower and emasculate it by cutting out the eight stamens. This will be the mother flower, and the removal of the stamens prevents self-pollination. (See photos on page 51.)

You can tell when the stamens of the father flower are ripe, because the pollen will be loose and you can see it. Cut off one of the ripe stamens and use it, like a brush, to dust the pollen on to the stigma of the mother. Some people use a real brush, but it is hard to be sure of cleaning away every last grain of pollen between crosses, so after a while the brush might be carrying the gametes from any number of different plants. It is also important to treat the mother flower very gently, and a stamen is more delicate than the very finest camel-hair brush. If you have judged the right moment to open the female flower, the stigma will be ripe and the pollen will stick to it. If it does not stick, the stigma will probably ripen by the next day, so try again then. Once the stigma of the mother flower is covered with grains of pollen, taken from the father, it is important to prevent pollen from another *Fuchsia* getting near it. Pollen grains grow down the style at different speeds, so a second, accidental, dusting with pollen from another flower could still fertilise the mother egg providing it grew faster than the father pollen. One way of protecting the stigma is to cover both stigma and style with the sort of gelatine capsule that a pharmacist uses for dispensing certain drugs. You can secure it in place with a wisp of cotton wool. If your chemist will not oblige, you can encase the entire mother flower in a tiny bag made of muslin or even polythene.

If the egg has been successfully fertilised, a fruit will swell and grow and be mature by about October. The fruits look like small and rather oval cherries and are not poisonous. Indeed, they have been made into jam, although it was described as rather tasteless. The fruit has four chambers which contain up to three hundred seeds, and these should be planted straight away.

Sow the seeds fairly thickly and keep them at a temperature of about 15 °C (59 °F). The temperature through the winter should never get lower than 13 °C (55 °F), and if you cannot maintain a temperature as high as this it is better to save the seeds and sow them the following January. Results are best if the seeds are sown straight from the ripe, even slightly mouldy, fruit in autumn, but whenever you put them in the germination rate is not brilliant. Some crosses will already have disappointed you by not setting fruit at all, others will now make matters worse by producing hundreds of seeds that refuse to grow. The average rate of germination is about twenty per cent which is not much, but to compensate for its poor germination the *Fuchsia* produces several hundred seeds so some at least should grow.

When the seeds do germinate they appear through the soil after about two to three months, so it is not a pastime for the impatient, but take heart. Some seeds sown in October should produce seedlings that will flower the following year, and then you will know the nature of the new plant that you have created. If you like it you can reproduce it, unchanged, by taking cuttings, and, even if it does not star at Chelsea, it is nonetheless entirely your own.

This is the way that all new hybrids are produced – from roses to radishes. Breeding any of them can be undertaken at home, but *Fuchsia* is a good plant with which to begin. The flowers are relatively easy to manipulate and can be very rewarding too, with the changing shapes and brilliant colours of their sepals and petals.

CHAPTER THREE

SLEEPING BEAUTIES

Variation and vigour are not the only advantages bestowed on the plant by its ability to reproduce sexually. Around the fertilised egg a fruit swells, inside the fruit the egg becomes a seed and a seed is a tough little package that provides the plant with a way of riding out a bad season, missing a whole year or two, or even more if growing conditions are particularly bad.

A seed is made up of two main parts. There is an embryo plant and there is a small store of food that is used to fuel the growth of the embryo as it develops into a seedling. The whole parcel has a wrapping called a 'seed coat' that protects it from damage. The anatomy of a typical seed can most easily be seen on something like a broad bean, simply because it is big enough to get a good look, but you can see the same features in many other seeds. A good example is the peanut; all the vital organs of the seed can be seen perfectly well in a bowl of salted nuts.

The cotyledons look rather like a pair of fat, fleshy leaves, and they contain a food store. Using this, the seed can germinate and grow until it is a plant, big enough to make food for itself. The embryo is tucked safely between the two cotyledons, and if you look closely you can see the beginnings of a shoot and a root. These are the 'bits' that accumulate in the bottom of the peanut bowl when all the tasty cotyledons have been consumed!

Not all seeds are built in this way. Some store food outside the cotyledons, in endosperm tissue, and the cotyledons themselves are much thinner and are used to absorb the food as the seed germinates. Maize, or sweet corn, has endospermic seeds like this. Another interesting difference in the structure of the maize seed is that it has only one cotyledon. This classifies it as a 'monocotyledon', generally called 'monocots' for short, whereas plants like beans which have two cotyledons are called 'dicots'. The monocots include all the plants which look roughly like grasses, with thin leaves showing parallel veins. The larger group of dicots includes all the other flowering plants which, as well as their pair of cotyledons, have a network of veins on their leaves. There are other internal differences too, but the shape and veining of the leaves is a good enough guide when identifying a growing plant as a monocot or dicot.

The broad bean is a dicot. During germination it draws on food that is stored in its two cotyledons.

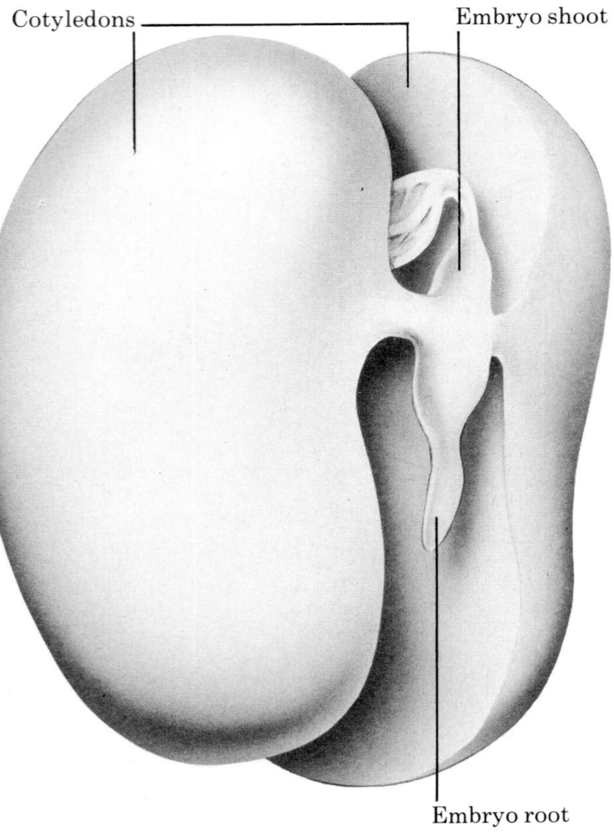

Maize is quite the opposite. Its seeds have only one cotyledon and food is stored in the endosperm.

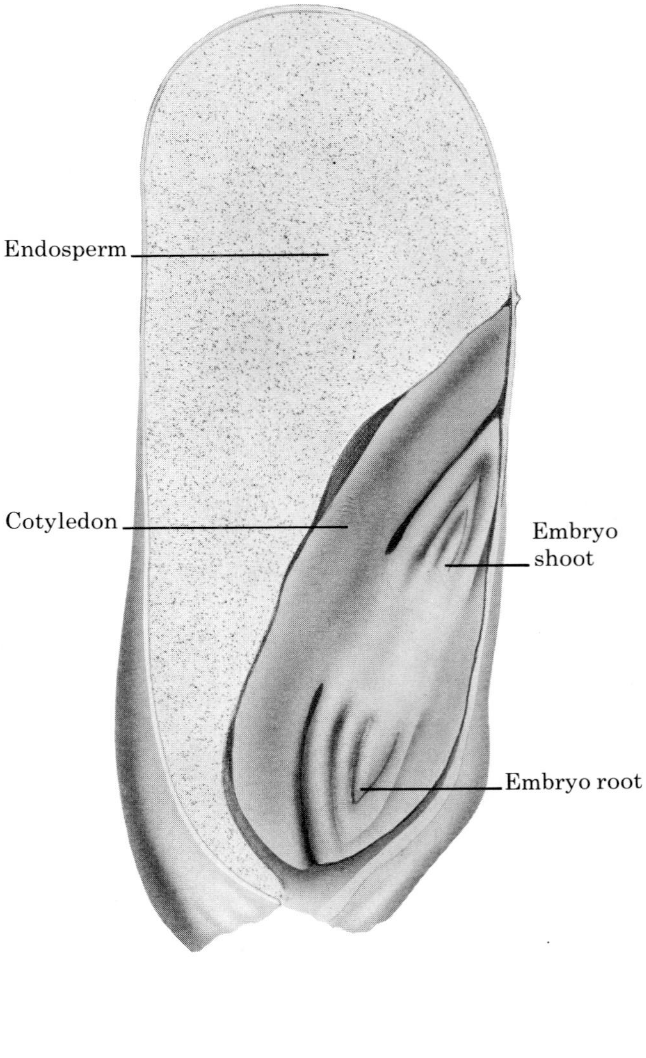

It is the food store in seeds that makes them valuable to man and important in world economics. The food is usually starch but is sometimes protein or oil. The staple cereals, like wheat, maize and rice, all contain a store of starch, and nuts and pulses have their 'high food value' as a result of the protein stored in them. Many seeds are used as a source of natural oil, like olives, sunflower seeds and groundnuts. The food packed away in a seed, whatever its form, was destined to feed the growing embryo, and by farming and harvesting we divert these stores to our own use.

Seeds rattling in a packet show very few signs of life. They contain only a little water and their metabolic or life processes are almost completely shut down. They exist in a kind of coma, a state of suspended animation, but they are very much alive all the same and they do have a definite life span. They remain viable for the duration of this life span and if they have not germinated by then, they die. The length of time that a seed can continue in this comatose state, without either germinating or dying, depends on the circumstances in which it is kept and also varies enormously among species. The seeds of many trees die quite soon after falling from the tree, unless they have germinated – in particular, the seeds of some species of willow, which may remain viable for as little as six weeks. Fortunately, both for the gardener and for the seed salesman, most seeds survive rather longer, at least until the following spring and often for many years.

The idea of longevity in seeds is much abused. Many seeds, stored in suitable conditions, will remain viable for years, but there have been a number of tall tales. At the end of the last century, stories abounded of corn that had been brought home from the tombs of the Pharaohs and that had sprouted when sown. It is now thought more than likely that the corn came from a contemporary harvest and was sold outside the tombs by a local farmer with an eye for a gullible archaeologist. Nevertheless, there are other stories that sound just as improbable but come from rather more reliable sources. During the blitz on London in the last war, the herbarium of the British Museum was bombed, and, in the confusion, some of the plants and seeds that had been stored by drying them and sticking them to sheets of paper got wet. When the staff of

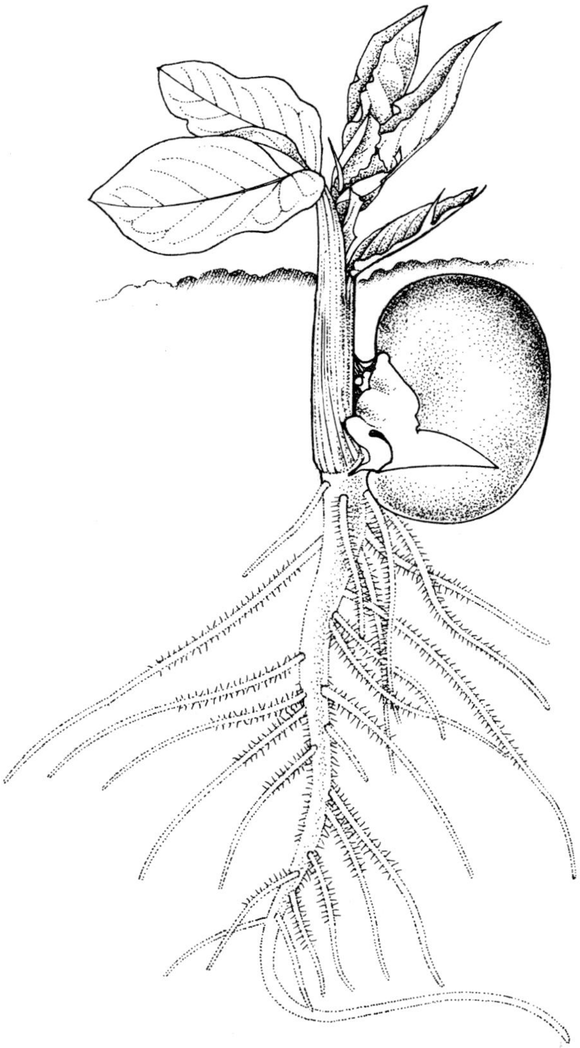

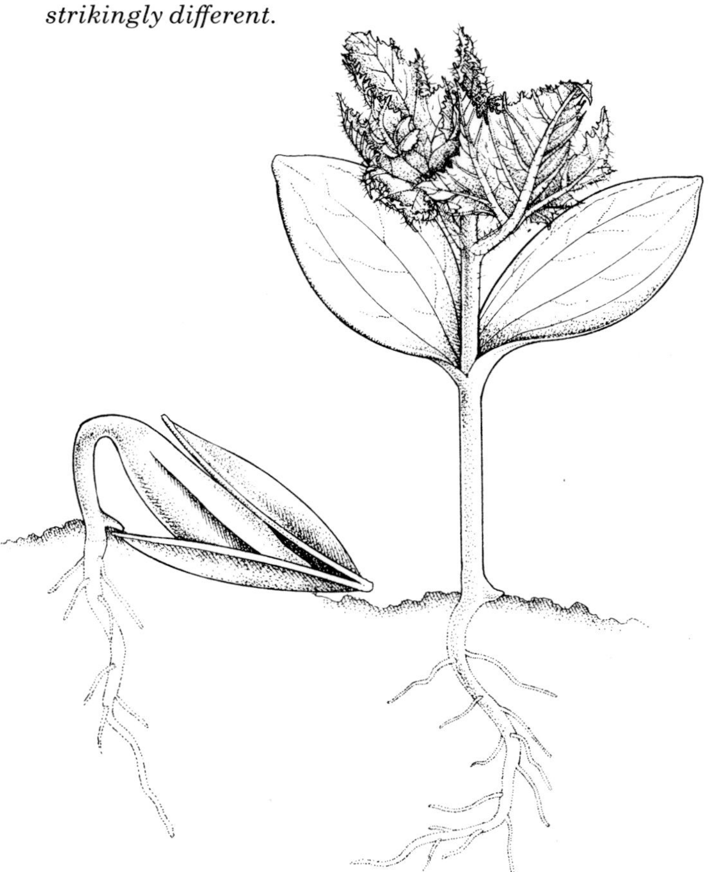

The cotyledons of the broad bean (left) stay under the ground, whereas those of some plants, including the courgette (centre and right), emerge from the soil as the seed germinates. These cotyledons make food, just like ordinary leaves, but their appearance remains strikingly different.

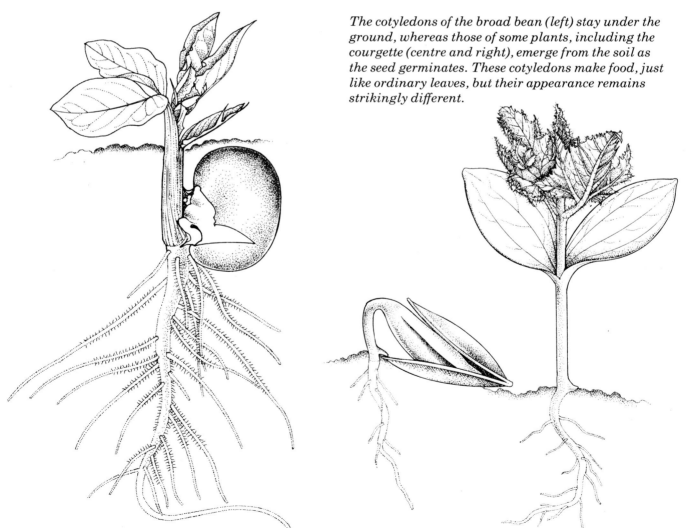

Corn spurrey

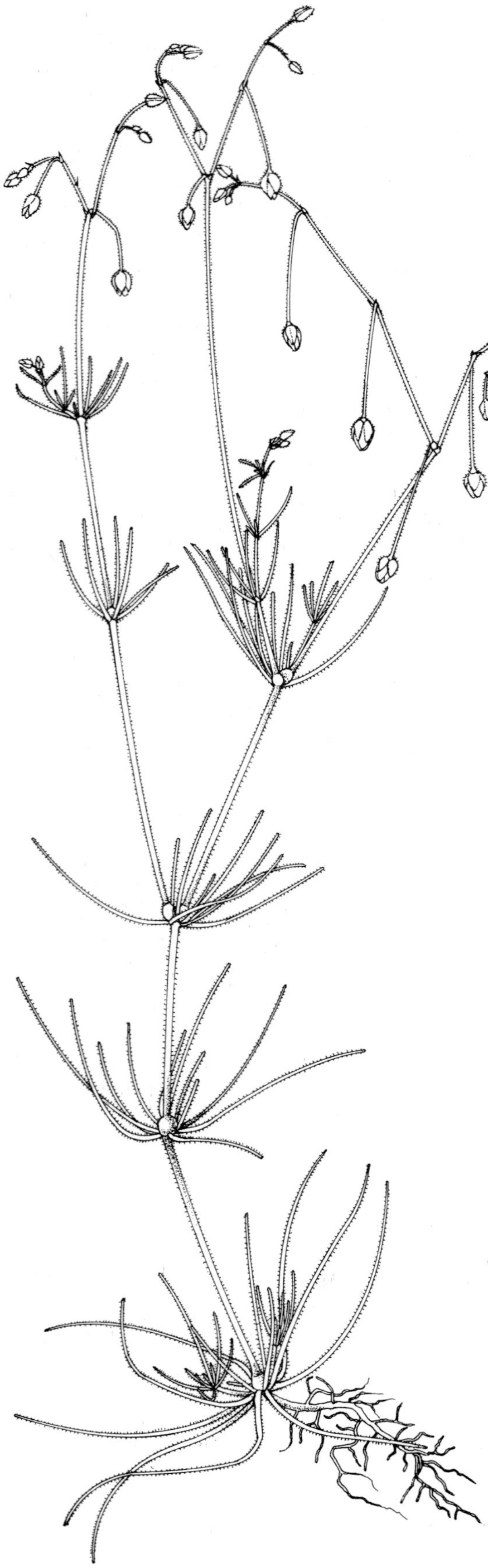

the Museum came to sort out the mess, they found that they had a sprouting garden rather than a museum. Among the oldest of the seeds that germinated was a specimen of the Indian lotus that had been collected 240 years earlier, and there are other reports of even older lotus seeds that have grown. Radio-carbon dating indicated that some found in a dried-out lake bed in Manchuria were a full 800 years old when they germinated. Other species of seed have survived even longer, including some corn spurrey, found buried under a church.

The seeds that we use in the garden have nothing like that staying power, and as time passes the percentage of dead seeds in a packet will increase, so it does not really pay to keep left-over seeds from one year to the next. Some will be fine – tomato, lettuce and runner beans may do well – but the rate of success will amost certainly be less than with 'new' seed. If you do have unused or unfinished packets of seed and they have been kept in fairly cool and dry conditions, try sowing them more thickly than seed bought that season. That way, there should not be too many gaps in the row even if the rate of germination is low.

The Indian lotus

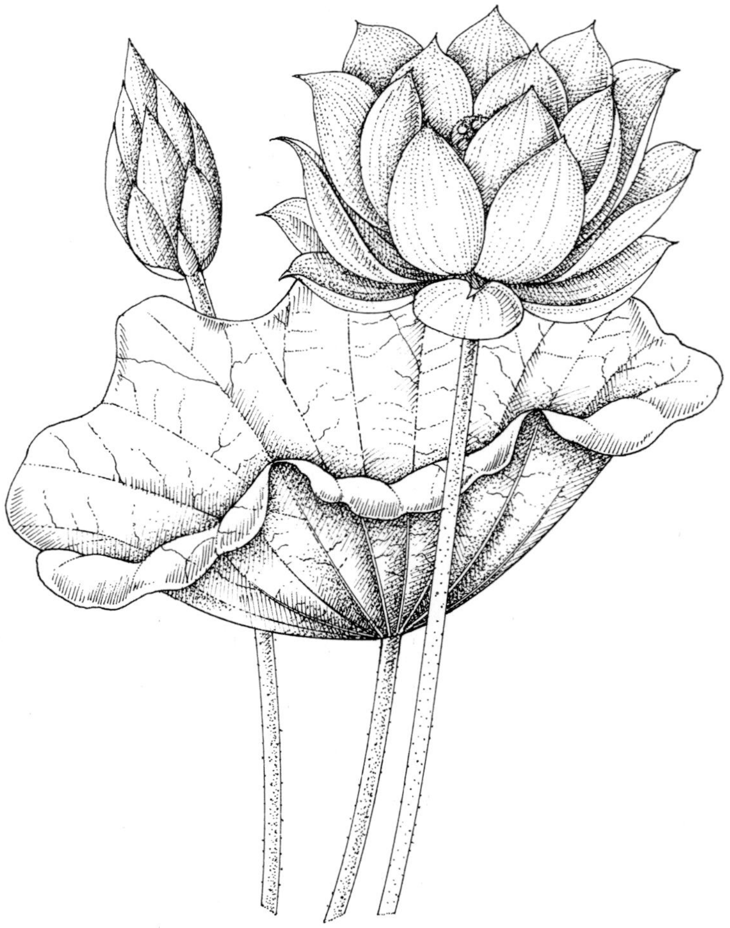

WHY SEEDS GERMINATE

When the time does come for the seeds to germinate, they need some signal to tell them that the world outside their seed coat is friendly and that circumstances are favourable for growth. In many cases this signal is climatic. In dry and desert areas, for example, a very occasional rainstorm saturates the ground and everything seems to spring to life. Flowering plants rapidly grow, reach maturity in a blaze of colour and, having shed their seeds, die. When the rain comes again the conditions that a seed needs for growth will be fulfilled. There will be water, warmth and air, and the desert will blossom once again.

These three conditions are always important for growth. Water is necessary for chemical reactions within the cells as they renew their activity and for transport through the young plant. Anything that needs to be moved from one part of a plant to another is moved as a liquid, in aqueous solution, so without water the plant is paralysed.

Temperature controls the moment at which the chemical reactions within the seed start and the rate at which they continue. As with most chemical reactions, it is generally true that, within limits, the higher the temperature the faster the reaction. But plants vary in their responses, and a wide range of temperatures initiate germination in different plant species. As might be expected, the temperature needed before germination begins reflects the temperature found in the areas where the plant, or its ancestors, grew naturally. So most of the plants that originate in the tropics need to germinate indoors, even though they cope quite well with the infamous British weather once they are mature and well established.

Air is important because, like all organisms, both animals and plants, a germinating seed needs to respire. It needs to take oxygen from the air, and use it to 'burn up' the food stores of the seed to produce the energy that powers its growth into a seedling plant. This is why a badly prepared seed bed can be such a disaster. If seeds are grown in compacted or waterlogged soil, they will fail to germinate because they have suffocated and died.

Plants with seeds that will germinate whenever these three conditions are fulfilled are called 'ephemerals'. They include many desert plants and, in this country, plants that grow around the dry sand dunes along the coast. (See colour photos on page 34.) In the garden, some ephemerals are persistent and irritating weeds. Groundsel grows so fast that it can carpet the vegetable garden several times during one summer, a new plague of it germinating after each rainstorm. Every time a warm day follows a wet one, the groundsel seeds that are lying in the soil will germinate, and up it comes again.

Many seeds, both in the garden and in the wild, germinate as spring begins. As the weather gets warmer all manner of seeds sprout from the moist soil of the garden, cultivated plants and weeds alike. In the autumn very similar conditions may prevail, but in spite of this most seeds stay right where they are, in the ground. They appear to 'know' that it is not spring and it is not time to start growing, even though there may be plenty of the big three – water, warmth and air – all around them.

Storing seeds at home

Although every species of seed has a life span beyond which it cannot survive, the length of time that you can, in practice, keep seed depends on the conditions in which it is stored. It is important to keep seeds in an atmosphere which is cool and dry. If they get too hot then they may dry out altogether and die, whereas if they are too moist they may even germinate, or, if that does not happen, bacteria will get in and destroy the seed.

At the vegetable gene bank at Wellesbourne (see Chapter 2, page 38) seed is kept refrigerated, at a temperature of $-20\,^{\circ}C$ ($-4\,^{\circ}F$), and its lifespan is estimated at thirty to fifty years. However, keeping seed in the fridge at home will not prolong its life because the atmosphere in a domestic refrigerator is too wet.

The best way to keep seed from one year to the next is in an airtight tin or plastic box in a cool shed. If you include a small sachet of silica gel, the kind of thing that comes with a stereo set or can be bought to put in the gap between the panes of double-glazed windows, it will help preserve the seed, because silica has a strong affinity for water and will absorb any water vapour in the box. You can buy silica gel that has been treated with cobalt chloride so that it changes colour as it absorbs water. When it is dry (and therefore absorbing water and helping to preserve the seeds), it is blue. When it has absorbed as much water as it can, and become useless, it turns pink. Its blue colour and its usefulness can both be restored by heating it in an oven. If you do get the coloured silica gel, it is important that the container used for storing the seeds is transparent, so that you can check on the colour change without opening the jar and letting more water vapour in.

Some companies now sell seeds in sealed foil packs and estimate their life at ten to fifteen years, providing the foil is not broken. Once the airtight foil package has been opened, the seeds need the same care as those bought in paper packets.

Fluid sowing

Fluid sowing is a fascinating technique, identical in principle to the 'fluid drilling' used in commercial horticulture. It has a number of practical benefits, but is also a marvellous way of seeing the growth that normally takes place below the seed bed. The seeds are germinated before they are placed in the soil. The tiny seedlings are then suspended in a thin jelly, which is squeezed out along a furrow in the soil. Although this method of sowing was developed for commercial use, it is easy and quite interesting to do at home.

Germination takes place indoors, where the seeds can be given ideal conditions, and this has proved particularly useful for vegetables like celery and parsley, the seeds of which are notoriously difficult to grow. Fluid sowing also makes it easier to spread out fluffy seeds, like those of the *Anemone*, and tiny ones, like lettuce. Carrot sowing, in particular, is improved by fluid sowing, because it lessens the amount of thinning that is needed later on, and it is the pungent scent exuded by the broken stems of thinnings that often attracts the damaging carrot-root fly.

To germinate the seeds you need a shallow box with a lid – something like a plastic sandwich box is ideal. Cover the bottom of it with several absorbent tissues, and put a sheet of 'wet-strong' paper, like a kitchen towel, on top of them. Gently pour water on to the paper, leave it to soak in for a few moments and drain off the excess. This is the 'seed-bed'.

Scatter the seeds evenly over the surface of the paper, making sure that none are touching, and put the lid on the box. The seeds inside have moisture and air, and the box should be kept in a warm place – but not the airing cupboard, which is much too hot. The ideal temperature is around 21 °C (70 °F). Look at the seeds every day to see how many of them have germinated. Small seeds, like lettuce, are ready to be planted out when their roots are half a centimetre long, but larger seeds should be left until their roots are about twice that length. The batch of seeds is ready for planting when the majority of them have achieved this size. Different species germinate and grow at different speeds, but most will be ready for the world outside between one and four days after sowing. Recently germinated seeds like these are very fragile, so it is important to treat them gently and avoid touching them with your fingers. If the seeds germinate before you are ready to plant them, their growth can be halted for a day or so by putting them in the refrigerator but they should not, of course, be put in a freezer.

A jelly that is ideal for distributing the seedlings in the vegetable patch can be bought from specialist suppliers, or you can make a perfectly good substitute using wallpaper paste, providing you make sure that you buy a paste that does not contain a fungicide. Make up the paste and allow it to thicken. About a quarter of a pint of jelly should be used for every thirty-foot row, so you can roughly count the germinated seeds and assess the amount of jelly you need to make up.

Wash the seedlings out of the germinating box into a sieve (1), and gently tip them on to about half the jelly. Then add the other half, and mix it with your fingers until the seeds are evenly distributed. The seeds in this 'frog spawn' should not sink to the bottom. If they do, the paste is too thin, and needs thickening before the seedlings are planted.

Out in the garden, prepare a shallow furrow and squeeze the jelly along it, using a wide-nozzled icing syringe. If tools for icing a cake are not amongst your gardening equipment, then put the jelly into a polythene bag, tie the top tightly and squeeze the seedlings and the jelly through a small hole cut in one corner (2). Cover the seeds with soil in the usual way, and water them if the earth is at all dry. It is very important to prevent the jelly drying out. Once the seedlings have emerged through the soil, they can be treated like any other row of garden plants.

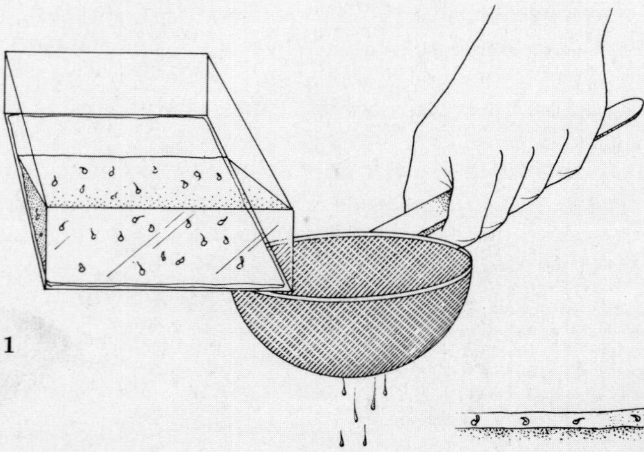

1

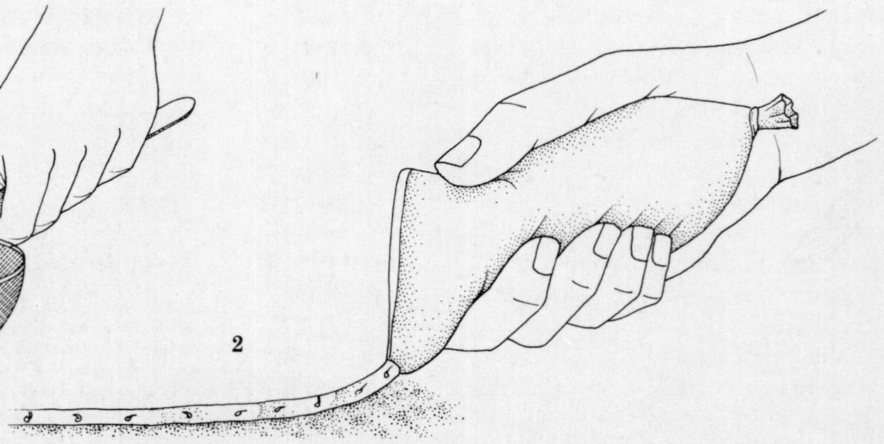

2

DORMANCY

If you collect the seeds of certain plants – like the hollyhock which flowers towards the end of summer – and plant them that autumn, they will not grow. No matter how temperate the autumn weather, they will lie in the soil through the winter and come up the following spring. If you plant the same seeds in the spring they will germinate almost instantly. From the point of view of the plant this discrimination is a very good thing, because if the seeds did germinate in the autumn the tender young plants would be at their most vulnerable just as the winter frosts were at their fiercest. Some plants – like broad beans, which are often sown in autumn – can germinate and grow through almost any weather, but most cannot, and if they did germinate in autumn, just because there was sufficient water, warmth and air, they would all die as winter set in and the species would become extinct. Clearly, then, it is very sensible for the seed to wait until spring before breaking out into the world, but it is an astonishing ability. It means that the seed remains snugly protected within its seed coat, not only until the usual conditions for germination have been fulfilled, but also until it receives some signal or is in some way 'ready' to grow. It has an in-built mechanism that makes it wait before germinating, and this waiting is called 'dormancy'.

An immature embryo within a seed. This seed would be dormant.

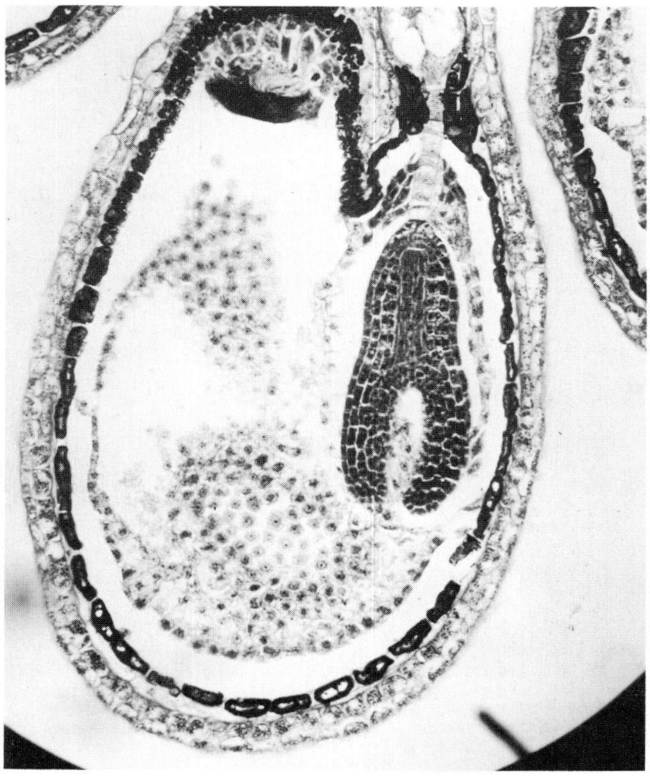

BREAKING DORMANCY

This system evolved for plants growing naturally and, in the wild, it works perfectly. The seeds fall off the plant when the flowers mature and die, and they lie on the ground until natural changes in the seeds and their surroundings have 'broken' dormancy. Then the seeds germinate and the seedlings grow. However, because nature did not design the dormancy mechanism to cope with a world in which men collect seeds, put them in paper packets and sell them to one another, it is sometimes advisable for the gardener to break the seeds' dormancy himself, in order to give his young plants the best possible start in their unnatural life in the garden.

Generally, this is a fairly simple process, but, in some cases, nature refuses to be hurried. In the *Anemone*, for example, the embryo plant is immature when the seeds are shed. It consists of no more than a ball of cells, so that the seeds remain dormant while the embryo grows, rather like a premature baby living in an incubator until it is big and strong enough to face the world alone. There is nothing you can do to get the seeds to germinate before they are ready. You just have to contain your impatience until the spring, by which time the embryo will be mature and the growing conditions will be just right. Delphiniums, lilies and orchids behave in the same way.

A seed from the same plant containing a mature embryo. This seed would grow.

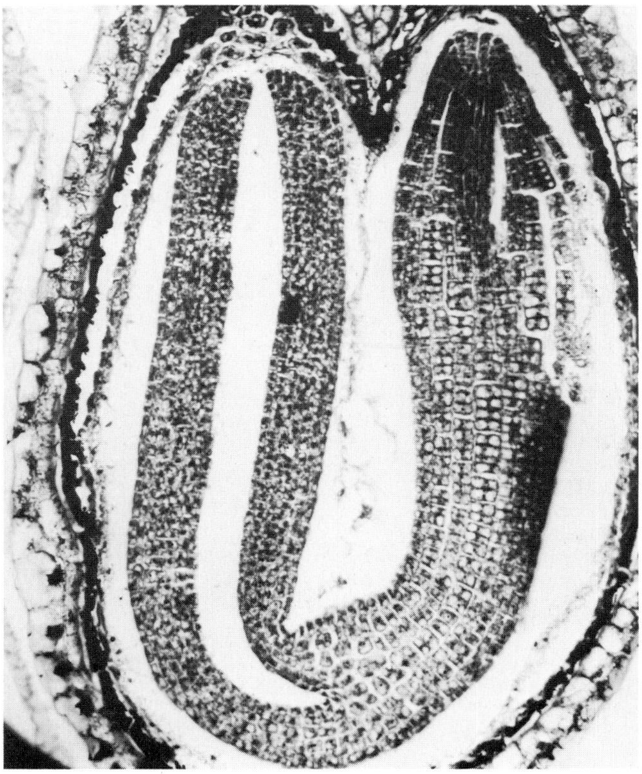

EEC seed regulations

In recent years, packets of vegetable seed have looked slightly different. They have all been labelled to say that the seeds are packed according to the EEC Rules and Standards. These regulations protect the consumer, both gardener and commercial grower, by specifying certain conditions that must be fulfilled by the seed before it is sold. The seeds of plants grown for their flowers are not involved, but for vegetables the law demands that seed must be pure, with as few seeds from other species as possible getting into the packet by mistake. It also requires that the seed be free from certain insect pests and labelled with the date, or at least the year, in which the seed was packed. In addition, the seeds must conform to a standard minimum germination rate, and there is a particular rate laid down for every vegetable you can buy. They are not printed on the seed packets, but here are some of them, taken from the 1970 Common Market Directive that explains the law. They give you some idea of the minimum results you should expect from seed bought this year and carefully sown according to the instructions on the packet.

Aubergines	65%
Beetroot	70%
Broad beans	80%
Cabbages, kale and sprouts	75%
Carrots	65%
Cauliflowers	70%
Celery	70%
Cucumbers	80%
French beans	75%
Leeks	65%
Lettuces	75%
Marrows	75%
Onions	70%
Parsley	65%
Peas	80%
Peppers	65%
Radishes	70%
Runner beans	80%
Spinach	75%
Turnips	80%

Until water gets through its coat the seed will remain dormant, because it needs water to germinate, so some seeds keep dormant through the winter by having a tough, impermeable coat. If the seed were dropped naturally from the plant at the end of the summer, it would spend the winter being scratched by abrasive soil particles, bruised by the action of frost and nibbled by tiny animals in the soil, so that by the spring the tough coat of autumn would be well worn and far from waterproof. Once water can get in and the weather warms up, off it goes. But if the seed has spent the winter in a neat little envelope on the shelf, the gardener will have to give it a helping hand by mimicking the effects of natural weathering. Sweet peas have seeds like this, and that is why they will germinate much faster and better if you nick the seed coat slightly with a sharp knife before planting them.

The cold of winter can itself break dormancy when seeds are shed naturally and lie on the ground until spring. Seeds that are collected before this need some treatment that simulates the winter cold before they will germinate, a process called 'stratification'. Many trees and shrubs have seeds that need stratifying. After purchase they should be put in a

Stereoscan picture of the surface of the seed coat on a freshly harvested sweet pea seed.

box, between layers of sand or a mixture of sand and peat, and either left out in the frost or stored for between two or three months in the refrigerator at a temperature between 0 and 5 °C (32–41 °F). The dog rose and some other wild flower seeds now on the market need the same treatment. It is better to stratify the seeds than to plant them out in autumn and leave them in the cold ground through the winter, because, if they are in the soil, it is inevitable that some of them will perish or be devoured by animals and birds. Wild plants drop so many seeds that they can afford to lose a few without threatening the success of the next generation, but if you have bought a packet of seeds you want as many as possible to grow, so they are safer with the protection of a box of sand.

Some alpine plants, like the lovely blue gentians and Alpine campanulas, also need the conditions that they would experience in their cold mountain home before dormancy can be broken. Each seed contains a small amount of water. When this freezes it expands and bursts the seed coat in just the same way that frozen pipes burst in winter. Once the seed coat has been split like this, the seeds will grow as soon as weather conditions permit.

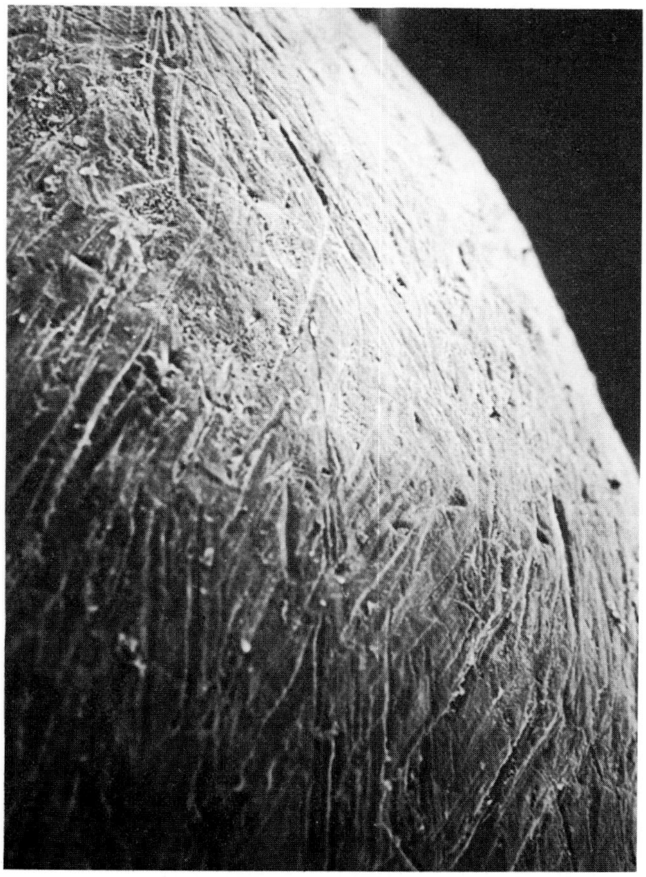

The same seed after a winter's weathering. The coat is rubbed thin and no longer waterproof.

CHEMICAL CHANGES

In addition to all these physical changes it is now known that there are chemical changes going on within the seed itself as it passes through the dormant state. Dormant seeds contain substances that inhibit germination. These do not affect the viability of the seed, but for as long as they are present the seed will remain dormant. If the seed coat is not waterproof or if it has been ruptured, it is likely that the seed's dose of inhibitors will be washed out by rain. As soon as the level of inhibitor in the seed is low enough, and providing the usual essentials of water, warmth and air are present, then the seed bursts into action.

One of the chemical inhibitors that maintains dormancy has been isolated and given the name abscisin. The same substance is found in autumn leaves before they fall and in the dormant winter buds of long-day or summer-flowering plants. If abscisin is applied to seeds, it prevents germination, even in seeds that are not otherwise dormant. On the other hand, there is another chemical, a growth substance called gibberellin, that is commonly found in the parts of a plant that are actively growing, which will induce germination when applied to some dormant seeds.

LIGHT

Light also affects the germination of some seeds, although the species concerned show their response in many different ways. Some cannot germinate without an exposure to light, although in some cases a very short exposure is sufficient; some will germinate only after a period without light, and there are others which will grow in conditions of light or darkness, but at different speeds. The situation is confusing, to say the least, but in most cases where light inhibits germination the effect can be cancelled out by dosing the seeds with gibberellin, so it all seems to be part of the same chemical balance.

The response of a seed to light is mediated by phytochrome, in much the same way that flowering is stimulated in short- and long-day plants (see Chapter 1, page 21). Interestingly, some seeds have a specific light requirement when they are freshly gathered but lose it over a period of time. Sweet alyssum germinates better in light, whereas the Catchfly family is quite the opposite and need a period in the dark, but both will germinate regardless of light conditions after some time in store. Similarly, some Brassica seeds will germinate only after a period of cold, but if they are kept for rather longer in a warm store they will grow anyway. It is as though the species has a preferred signalling system for breaking its dormancy but, if the signal fails for long enough, it will grow anyway. As time passes, the risk of dying of old age without ever having tried to grow becomes greater than the risk of death or damage after germinating at the wrong time. Every organism seems to have some ability to assess the chances of survival and choose the safest bet, and this is one of the gambles taken by flowering plants.

SURVIVAL

For every aspect of a plant's structure and behaviour that is admired for the way in which it promotes its chances of survival, there seems to be another that is just as precise and wonderful. Seeds are no exception. Even when the time of year is right and every dormancy mechanism has been overcome, when the weather is perfect and every condition for promoting germination has been fulfilled, there will still be some seeds that will not come up. They do not die, either. They just sit there in the soil, but when every single growing seedling that did germinate is wiped out by a freak hailstorm, they are still sitting in the soil and the next year – or the year after, perhaps – they will grow. Even though a whole generation of plants perished the species is safe and will not become extinct because of one exceptionally difficult year. It is a marvellous example of 'thinking ahead' and not putting all your eggs in one basket. It also explains the old gardening adage, 'one year's seeding, seven years' weeding'. Indeed, unlike most of the traditional prophecies of gardening, this one turns out to be fairly optimistic. Seeds of several common garden weeds, including plantain, black mustard and the daisy, have survived in soil for twenty years, and those of the dock lasted sixty. It is a dispiriting thought, that the seeds of a weed neglected this year could be giving trouble to your grandchildren!

Despite the complexity of the factors that affect dormancy in seeds, there is a single thread running throughout. The plant needs to ride out the rigours of winter in its dormant state but to be ready to leap into action when the time is right and spring comes. All the mechanisms for maintaining and breaking dormancy are a plant's way of monitoring the weather and checking up on the world outside, to lessen the risk of the seedling poking its head above the ground only to have it bitten off by a sharp frost.

DORMANCY IN TUBERS AND BULBS

The same problems and dangers concern plants that grow from tubers and bulbs rather than from seed, and they solve them in a similar way. The potato tuber, for example, is a modified and swollen stem, and the 'eyes' are dormant buds which are waiting to grow. A newly-formed tuber that is placed in conditions ideal for growth remains stubbornly dormant. To break its dormancy a potato needs either a period in a warm, dry atmosphere or storage in cold, moist conditions. Low temperature alone seems to have no effect, which may give a clue to the best way of storing potatoes to eat, as keeping them dormant sometimes seems more of a problem than getting them started!

Hyacinths need the chills of winter to break their dormancy and signal the coming of spring, the time when they naturally bloom. The bulbs must experience winter, or something like it, before they will flower, so it is no good digging bulbs out of the garden in the autumn, putting them in pots and hoping for a fine display at Christmas. The 'prepared' bulbs that fill the shops in September have spent their summer in a refrigerator, so dormancy has been broken and they are ready to plant. As far as they are concerned, spring is just around the corner.

(Opposite page.) Fuchsia *breeding.*
1 *'Popping' a bud that is ready to open.*
2 *Trimming away the petals and sepals to expose the stamens and the ripe stigma.*
3 *Emasculating the flower by cutting off the stamens but leaving the style and stigma intact. This flower becomes the mother.*
4 *A flower of another variety with ripe stamens covered in pollen. This flower is the father.*
5 *Dusting the stigma of the mother flower with pollen from the stamens of the father.*
6 *A gelatine capsule is used to protect the mother flower from chance fertilisation by unknown and unwanted pollen.*
7 *This cover is held firmly in place by a plug of cotton wool.*
8 *Protected in this way, the fertilised flower is left to develop into a fruit containing seeds.*

For full details see page 39.

1

2
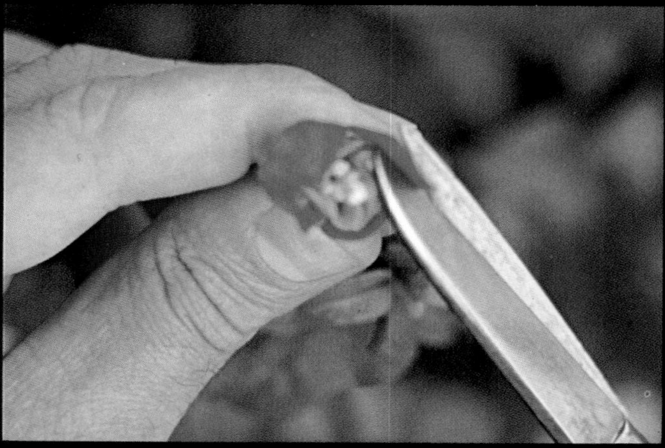

3
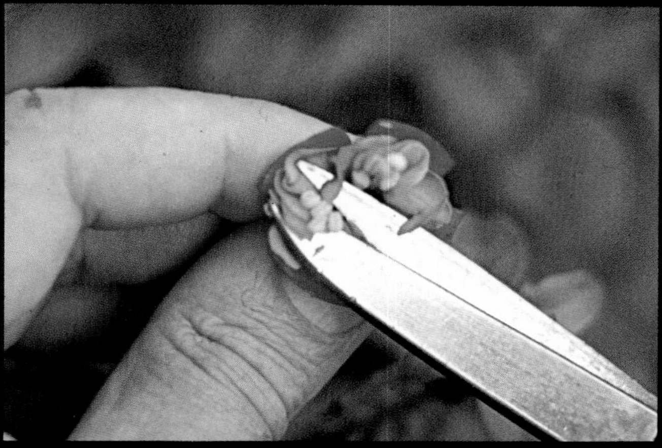

4

5
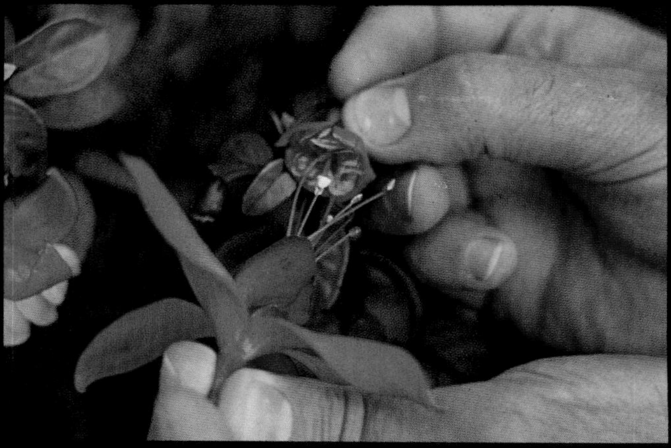

6
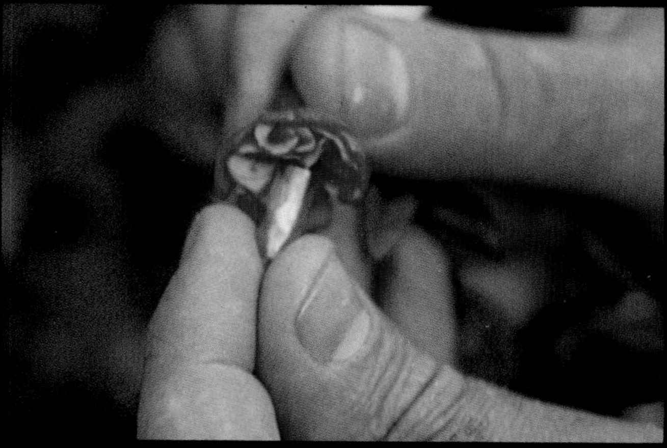

7
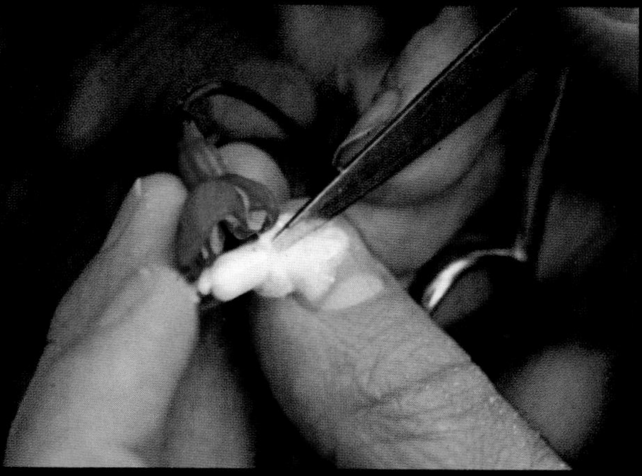

8

(This page.) A hyacinth bulb cut in half. This bulb is ripe and has a flowering stem ready to grow when the bulb is planted.

(Opposite page.) Plants showing the symptoms of a variety of nutrient deficiencies.
(Top left.) Carrot with a boron deficiency. The flesh of the root is separated from the central core.
(Bottom left.) A marrow leaf with the brown, withered edge that is typical of a potassium deficiency.
(Top right.) Yellow and purple leaves on a brussels sprout plant show a nitrogen deficiency.
(Centre right.) Bronze-coloured, lower leaves on a carrot plant with a phosphorus deficiency.
(Bottom right.) A leaf from a potato plant grown with insufficient magnesium. The older leaves turn yellow and show dark patches of dead tissue.
For further details see page 117.

The details of the preparation of hyacinth bulbs, as undertaken by commercial growers, are fairly complex and extremely precise, involving temperature changes of a degree each week and regular checks on the progress of the bulb, performed by cutting one in half to see whether the tiny flower buds are forming correctly inside. If you are planning flowers for Christmas, it is probably easier to spend the extra few pence and buy the prepared bulbs, but if you want to try your hand at treating your own, lifted from the garden, then they should be refrigerated from June to September. If they get wet in the fridge they will slowly but surely rot, so do not let them lie in a puddle at the bottom, but keep them on one of the wire shelves where air can circulate.

Yet another check to the germination of a seed may occur if it falls immediately below the parent plant. Thousands of acorns fall from a large oak tree each year, but they never grow into seedling trees in

(Below.) Sycamore 'wings' and ash 'keys'.
(Bottom left.) Oak trees maintain their distance because seedlings are inhibited by the parent plant.
(Bottom right.) A single fruit from a dandelion plant, with its parachute.

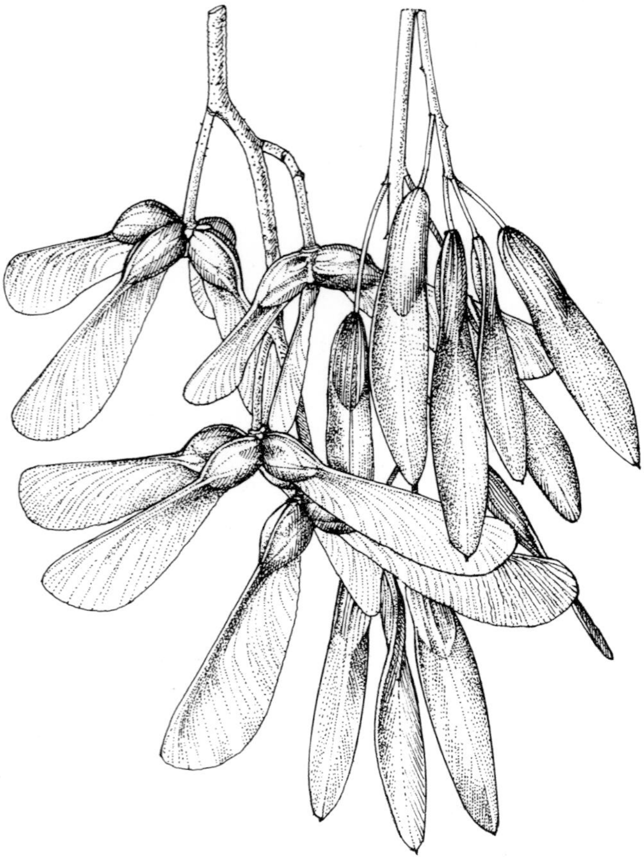

the shadow of the parent oak. In some cases it is the shade of the tree that prevents the growth of its offspring, although in others the parent tree secretes a chemical inhibitor from its roots which prevents the growth of competing young saplings. This is one of many mechanisms that ensure the dispersal of a plant's seeds. If parent and offspring were to grow too close together, they would all suffer in the competition for light, water and soil nutrients. In addition to this, any species is better off, and more secure, if it can extend the area that it occupies, so the dispersal of fruits and seeds is an important part of a plant's life.

SEED DISPERSAL

You can often tell something about the dispersal of a particular fruit and seed by looking at their structure. Almost everything about their shape, size, weight and even taste relates in some way to getting away from the parent plant before trying to germinate. Seeds of the ash and the sycamore are both attached to rigid 'wings', so that caught in a breeze, they whirl away from the tree. Ash 'keys' hang singly whereas sycamore seeds are in pairs, rather like a helicopter blade, but you can see either in action by picking them up and hurling them into the air, where they spin out and away from you. The aero-dynamics of the wing must be very precise because a slightly damaged fruit will not spin at all and just falls to the ground.

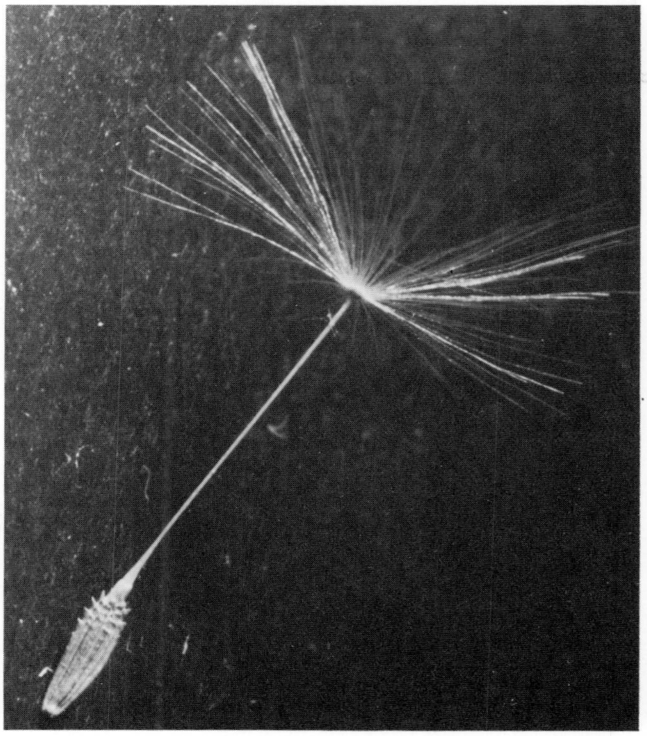

As might be expected, the common and successful weeds, like the dandelion, have a highly efficient method of dispersal. The seeds are very small and light, and each one is attached to a tiny parachute of fine hairs. They are puffed away from the dandelion 'clock' and when ever they land on suitable ground they germinate, which accounts for the speed at which they appear on building sites and waste land. It also explains their persistence in the garden. Even if none of your own dandelions is allowed to mature and set seed, there will be plenty of tiny parachutes floating in on every breeze.

The poppy uses the wind to spread its seed in rather a different way. The seeds grow in a fruit that is built rather like a pepper-pot with a circle of holes around the top. When the seeds are ripe they rattle around inside the 'pot' and fly out of the holes as the poppy head waves in the wind.

Wind-distributed seeds generally have hairs or a 'wing' or something similar to catch the wind, and if you pick up a seed or fruit that looks like that, it is a fairly safe bet that it is the wind that carries it away from the parent plant. Seeds and fruits that are covered in tiny hooks usually depend on sticking to the fur of some passing animal, and being carried away to wherever the animal goes. A typical example is the goosegrass, also known as cleavers and, most appropriately, sticky willie. This is common in hedgerows but is also found, as a weed, in gardens, growing perhaps from seeds that were successfully dispersed and carried away from the parent plant on the clothes of the gardener.

Some animals, like squirrels, collect nuts and store them for the winter, and this storage may serve to plant the seeds, since squirrels are notorious hoarders, burying acorns and so on all over the place and sometimes forgetting exactly where they have done so. These may well shoot up the following year. Fruits that are bright and colourful, fleshy and juicy, are all designed to attract some animal or bird, offering a mouthful of food in exchange for the dispersal of their seeds. If the plant is unlucky, the animal eats the fruit there and then and spits the pip out at the bottom of the tree – one seed wasted. But on other occasions the animal will take the fruit somewhere else before eating it and discarding the seed, or even eat the whole lot, in which case it is anyone's guess where the seed will end up.

Some seeds actually need to pass through the digestive tract of an animal, not just to get away from the parent plant but to break dormancy. The action of the digestive juices may weaken the seed coat, so that, once back on the ground, water gets in and the seed germinates. Or maybe those same digestive juices in some way alter the chemical balance of the seed and stimulate germination. The seeds of a tree called *Calvaria major* need treatment like this before they can grow.

Plants with wind dispersed seeds: willow herb (1), poppy (2), dandelion (3), Welsh poppy (4).

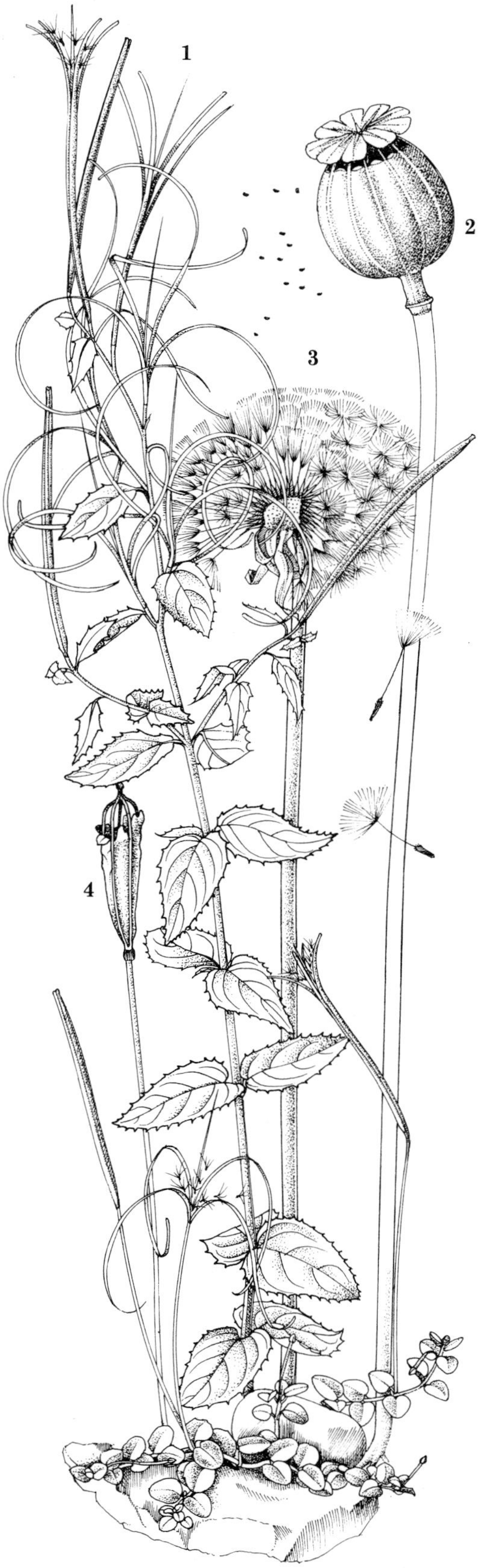

(Left.) The Calvaria *tree.*
(Below left.) The dodo, a flightless bird, hunted to extinction by settlers on Mauritius.
(Below.) The flowers of Calvaria *(1 and 2) with the leaf of the tree (3), its fruit (4) and its seed (5).*

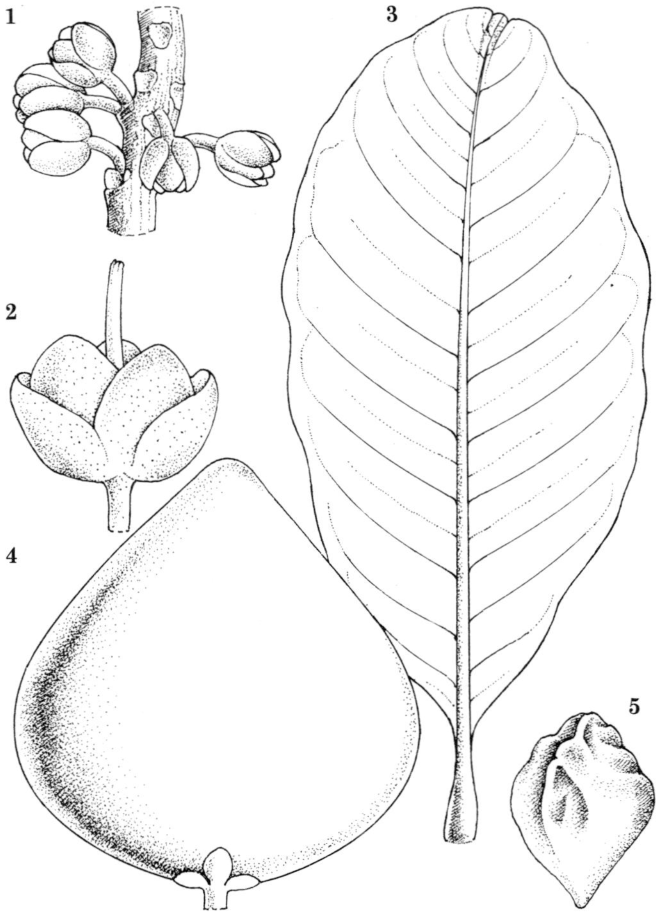

Calvaria grows on the island of Mauritius, where an odd situation arose. There were plenty of mature trees but no saplings. The tree no longer seemed able to grow from seed – in fact, within living memory there had been no seedling *Calvaria* on the island. This was something of a botanical mystery story until somebody noticed that the refusal of the tree to grow from seed dated precisely from the time when the most famous resident of Mauritius, the dodo, became extinct. Perhaps the two were connected. Perhaps the seed of *Calvaria* had to be eaten and excreted by the dodo before it would germinate, in which case the tree would seem to have a rather doubtful future. Fortunately, an understudy was found. The seeds of *Calvaria* were fed to some North American turkeys who gobbled them down with enthusiasm. When the seeds were collected again from around the stockyard and planted they germinated. So there is a happy ending to the tale: there are now turkeys in Mauritius and young *Calvaria* trees are growing again.

Human beings are not exempt from this kind of exploitation by the plant world. The seeds of the tomato are held in a dormant state by chemical inhibitors, but these are not found in the seeds themselves, they are found in the fruit, the flesh of which has to be removed by some means before the seeds can germinate. A visit to a sewage works will amply demonstrate that seeds which have been eaten can germinate quite easily – indeed, seedlings of tomato plants can be used as an indicator of pollution by sewage, particularly when it has been discharged into the sea and washed up on to a beach. So if you notice tomato plants sprouting along the tide line of your favourite holiday beach, be warned. You know how they got there.

CHAPTER FOUR

GROWTH AND BEHAVIOUR

Cress seedlings, growing in light from above (top) and in light from one side (below).

Every germinating seed behaves, in one respect at least, in an entirely predictable and orderly manner: the shoot of the seedling grows up towards the light while the root pushes downwards into the earth. And it is just as well that they do, because they would not be much use to the plant the other way around. This pattern of growth happens with such reliability that it hardly seems worth a mention but, in fact, the way that the plant can right itself, can grow the right way up even when the seed has been planted upside down, indicates just how well organised it is. The plant must be able to find out where 'up' and 'down' are and then alter its pattern of growth to suit the circumstances.

Plants do not have anything remotely like the human nervous system, with its fast-acting nerve fibres and central controlling brain, but they do have a series of 'chemical messengers' that travel through the conducting tissue of the plant, working in a fashion analogous to our own hormone system. It is not, of course, precisely the same. Animal hormones are secreted by glands, and detected by 'target organs' which act in response. Plants have neither of these, but what they do have is a number of hormone-like chemicals that circulate throughout the body of the plant and communicate changing circumstances in a rather similar way. When the contents of a shelf in the garden centre are labelled 'Hormones' these are what they are talking about, but botanists, mindful of their medical colleagues, use the clumsier but more correct term 'growth substances'. Whatever word you choose, it was the discovery of some of these chemicals within the plant and the effects that they have that gave botanists an insight into the way that plants are able to find out about, and respond to, the world outside themselves.

Plants seem to be such solidly static things that it is hard to see, at first, that they respond to anything at all, but respond they must if they are to survive. If you grow a plant in a pot on a window sill, the plant will bend towards the light and if you turn it around it will apparently bend the other way. It is a very necessary thing for the plant to do. It needs light as a source of energy, and so it bends towards the window where the light is strongest. But if you look more carefully you can see that a plant bending is not like a human being bending, first forward and then back. What actually happens is that the plant does not move, it grows towards the light; and only the newly-grown part of the plant responds when it is turned around; the older part does not change at all. This observation is critical, because it demonstrates that newly-developing plant tissue responds the changing circumstances, whereas older tissue has lost this ability to respond.

A house plant on a window sill grows in a bend towards the light. Once it has achieved the angle that will allow maximum illumination, it stops bending and continues growing towards the window.

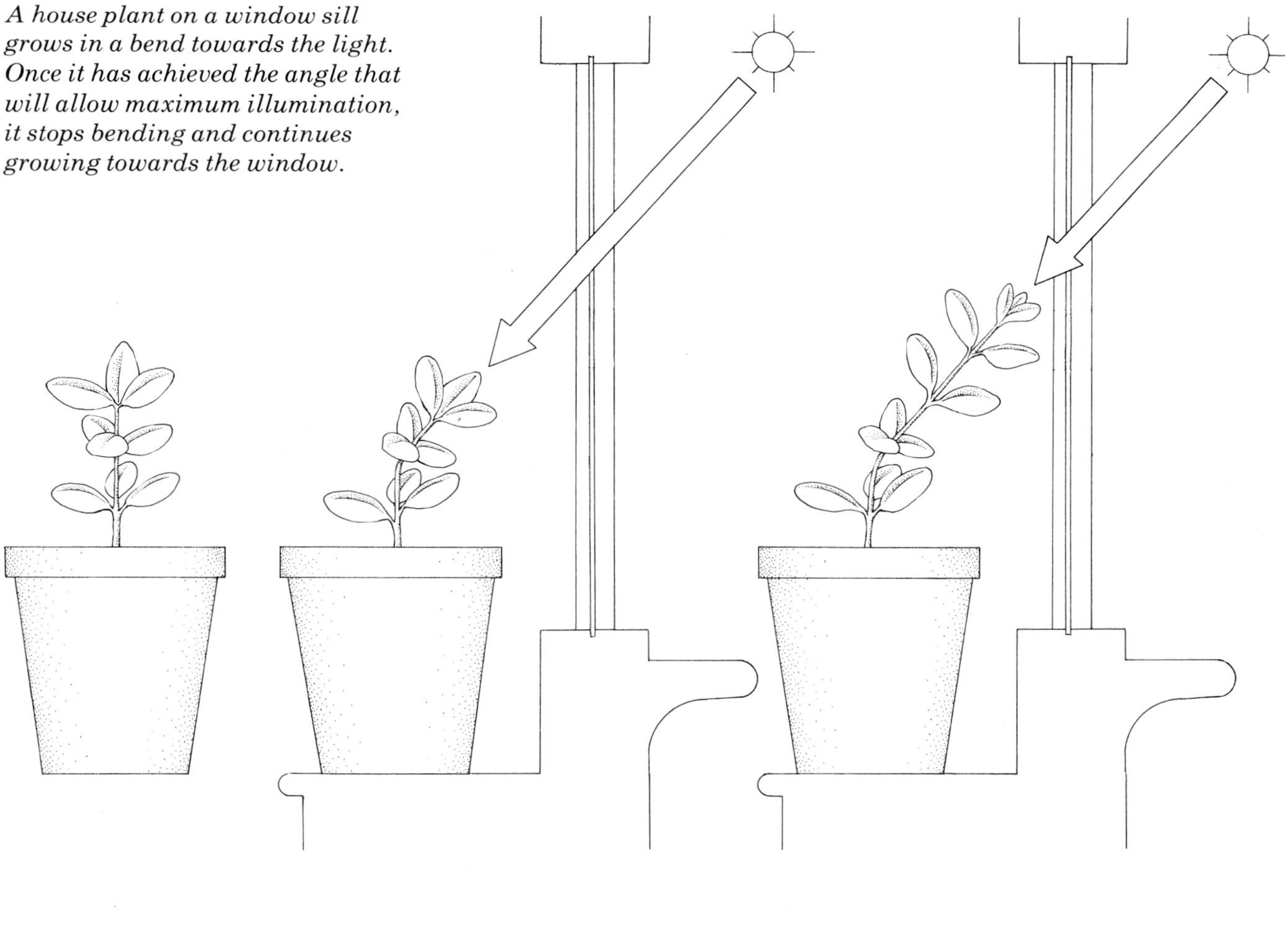

The first person to record this was no less a man than Charles Darwin, whose observations and insights seem to have extended into almost every corner of the living world. He and his son Francis investigated the way in which grass seedlings curve towards the light. They found that if they covered the tip or apex of the shoot with an opaque glass cap, then the shoot did not bend towards the light but continued to grow straight up. Moreover, they showed that while it is the very tip of the shoot that 'perceives' the light, it is an area just behind the tip that does the curving. In 1881 Darwin published a book called 'The Power of Movement in Plants' and in it he suggested that the tip of the shoot detected the light and that some stimulus passed from it down to the growing zone where it had its effect and changed the direction of growth. Fifty years later other botanists, using techniques based on those devised by Darwin, justified his belief. They established the existence of a growth substance which is produced in the tip of the plant and which diffuses down to the growing area, where it acts to determine the growth pattern of the plant. They called it auxin. Since then, many other experiments have confirmed the existence of a whole group of very similar substances and revealed more details about their nature and how they have their effects.

One of the problems for a research botanist working on auxins is that, although the effects of a growth substance can be quite dramatic, the actual amount of it found in the plant is extremely small. Scientists talk casually about one part in a million as the approximate working level of a growth substance, but the difficulties of working with quantities as small as that are enormous. But, however tiny the amounts involved, the effects of auxins are always felt just behind the tip or meristem of the root or shoot. In the meristem the cells of the plant divide and new cells are made, but these cells are minute so they do not add much to the actual size of the plant. The real 'growth' of the plant can be seen just behind the meristem, where the cells elongate and enlarge. You really can see how the plant grows by marking very fine, closely spaced lines on a growing root or shoot and watching how they spread over a day or so.

A seedling growing towards the light (1). A shoot continues to grow straight upwards when the sensitive tip is covered with an opaque cap (2) or cut off (3). If the tip of a shoot that is growing to one side is cut off and left for a few hours on a small square of absorbent jelly (4), then the jelly will take up the auxins produced in the tip. If the jelly alone is then placed on the cut end of a straight growing shoot (5) the auxins will cause bending.

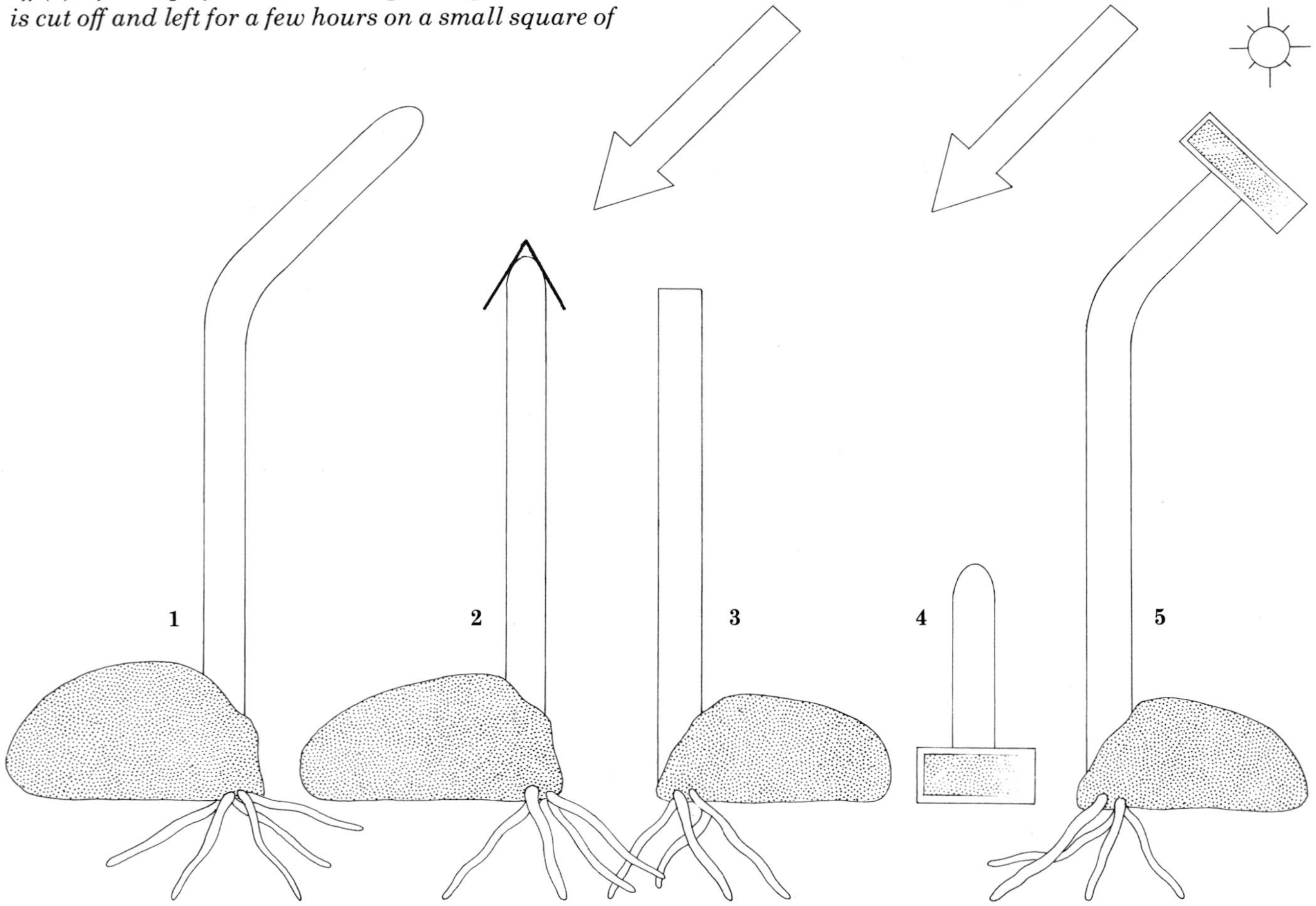

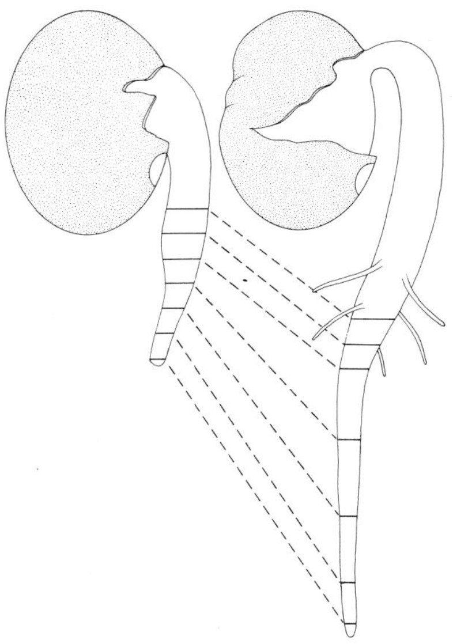

(Above.) The way a plant grows can be seen by drawing equally spaced, fine lines along a length of root or shoot. A couple of days later, the distances between the lines drawn well up the root are hardly changed, while those just behind the growing tip are greatly extended, showing that most growth takes place in this area.
(Below.) The bending of a stem is caused by the differential growth of its cells. Those on the outside grow more quickly than those on the inside of the bend, and this pushes the stem over.

The area that auxin affects most is the area that elongates most, just behind the meristem, and it is here that a plant stem bends in response to light from one side. The concentration of auxin in the stem alters the rate at which the cells enlarge – the more auxin there is present, the more the cells grow. But if there is more auxin on one side of the stem than the other, then the cells on that side will grow more quickly, and this will 'push' the stem over, causing a bend. And that seems to be what happens. When the auxin levels are measured in the stem of a plant that is bending towards the light, there is twice as much auxin on the 'dark' side as there is on the 'light' side. It looks as though light destroys auxin in some way, lowering the level in the side of the stem nearer the light but leaving the other side unchanged. So on the darker side growth proceeds as usual, but on the lighter side growth is inhibited, and the result is the lopsided house-plant sitting on the window sill. Once the stem has bent it will be receiving the same amount of light from both sides. The level of auxin will then be the same on both sides and so will the rate of growth. This means that the plant will continue to grow at the angle it has achieved. Having homed in, as it were, on the light source, the pattern of growth will not change again, unless the distribution of light changes.

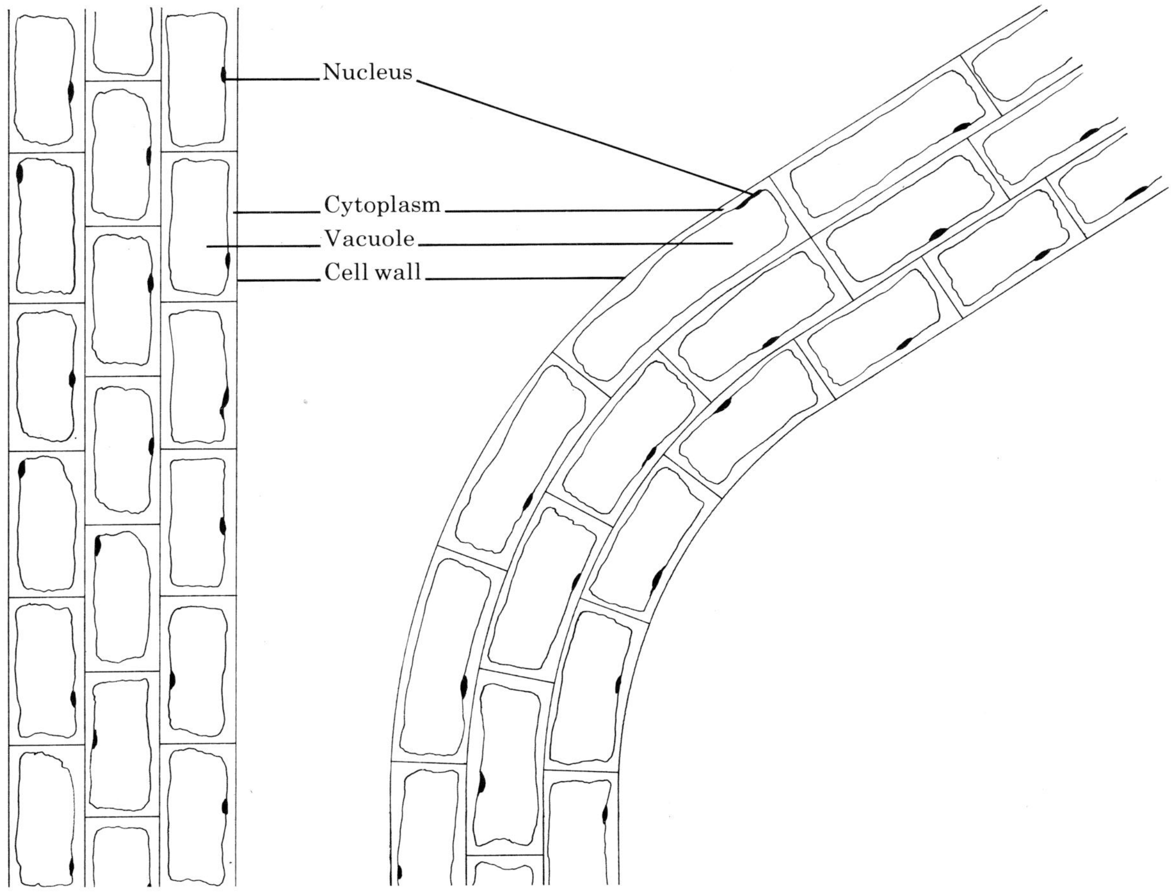

THE EFFECT OF GRAVITY

The growth of a seedling, with its shoot upwards and its root downwards, is in response to gravity. It is easy to see the way that a seed grows in the familiar school experiment of growing a broad bean, or any other large seed, in a glass jar, with the bean held against the wall by a cylinder of blotting paper. Whichever way up the seed is trapped in the jar, the shoot will eventually grow up while the root will grow down, but the seedling may need to perform considerable contortions in order to correct its position. All this growth, all these twists and turns, are fuelled by the limited store of food contained in the seed, so it is inevitable that the resources of seedlings from upside-down seeds are stretched.

Some seed packets carry instructions to plant the seeds flat, on their sides, which ensures that none of the seedlings has to perform a complete somersault in order to get its head above ground. This is particularly important with the seeds of runner beans, which, in this country, are grown about as far north as can be managed. They need every day of their growing season, so a few extra days wasted, struggling to get up out of the soil, really can affect the final crop yield.

1

2

3

The curves in the root and stem are caused by one side growing more than the other and this growth is stimulated by the concentration of auxin, just as it is in the response to light. It is clear that the growth of the seedling is a reaction to the forces of gravity, because seedlings grown in a klinostat, a machine that cancels these forces, do not show the response. They do not grow shoot up, root down in the usual way. What is not clear is how the plant 'detects' gravity and, having received this information, rearranges the auxin within its root and shoot so as to stimulate the appropriate growth.

The roots of some plants contain tiny granules of starch, called statoliths, which fall across the cells and hit the cell walls when the root is tipped to one side or the other. These, it is thought, might provide a mechanism that could sense how the root lay, but statoliths themselves cannot affect the way the root grows. There must be some way in which the movement of the statoliths affects the concentration of auxins in different parts of the root. It may be that their movements in some way alter the permeability of the cell walls so that auxin passes from one cell to another and accumulates on the lower side of the root. Although botanists have demonstrated that changes in the distribution of a naturally occurring substance like auxin can produce a particular mode of growth, they cannot yet explain how the alteration in concentration is brought about by the plant. The stimulation of the moving statoliths cannot in any case be the whole story, because some plants do not even have these granules but still manage to enter the world the right way up.

A change in the auxin concentration in the root seems to have just the opposite effect to a similar change in the shoot. In the shoot, a rise in auxin concentration on one side causes increased growth on that side and a bend in the opposite direction. In the root, on the other hand, a similar rise in concentration actually inhibits growth, and the other side grows faster. So if a growing seedling is turned on to its side, there is an increase in the auxin concentration on the lower side of both root and shoot, but this increase causes the shoot to bend upwards and the root to bend downwards. The two responses combine to produce the best overall reaction for the growing plant.

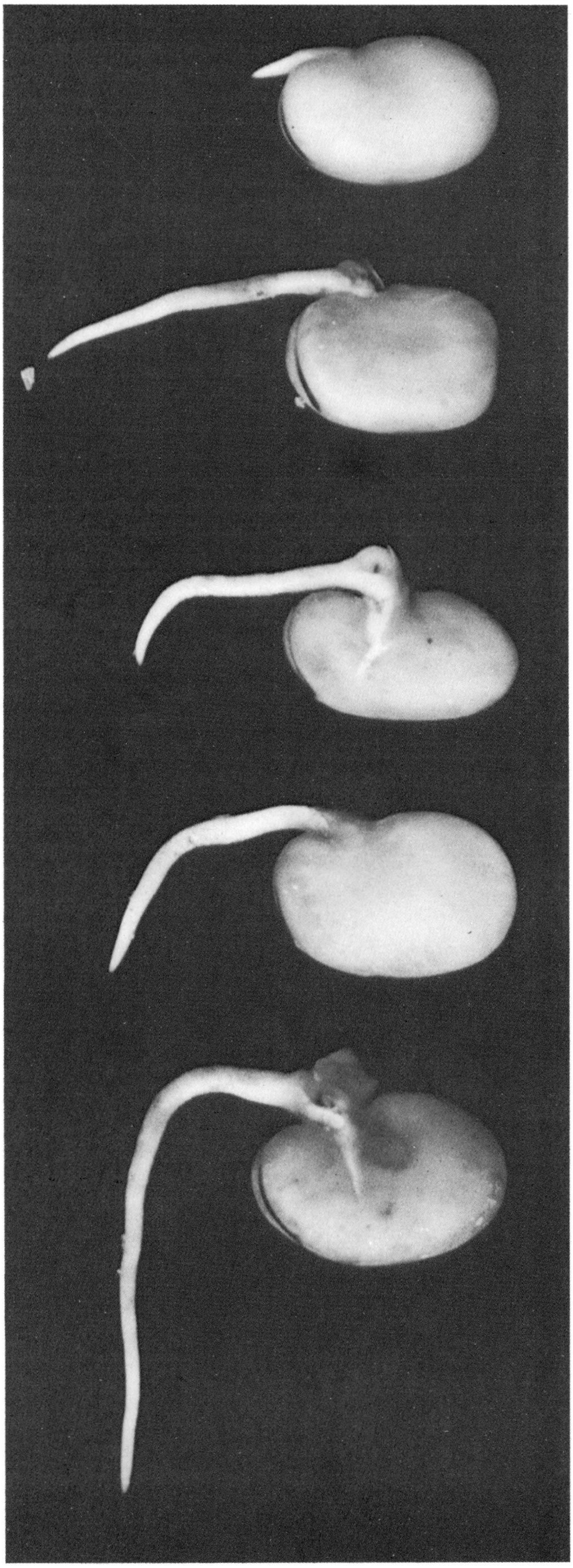

(Opposite page.) Runner bean seeds that have been planted the right way up (1), the wrong way up (2) and, as a compromise, flat on one side (3). (1) and (3) grow unhindered.

(This page.) The effect of gravity on the root growth of a bean. As the root develops, its tip 'detects' the gravitational force and it grows downwards.

Twining plants curl around their supports in the same way that roots and stems bend in light or in gravity, but the stimulus in this case is touch. As a stem touches a support it curls towards and then grows around it. The honeysuckle and the bindweed twine in opposite directions.

Bindweed stems twine in a clockwise direction.

A young beech, distorted by entwining honeysuckle.

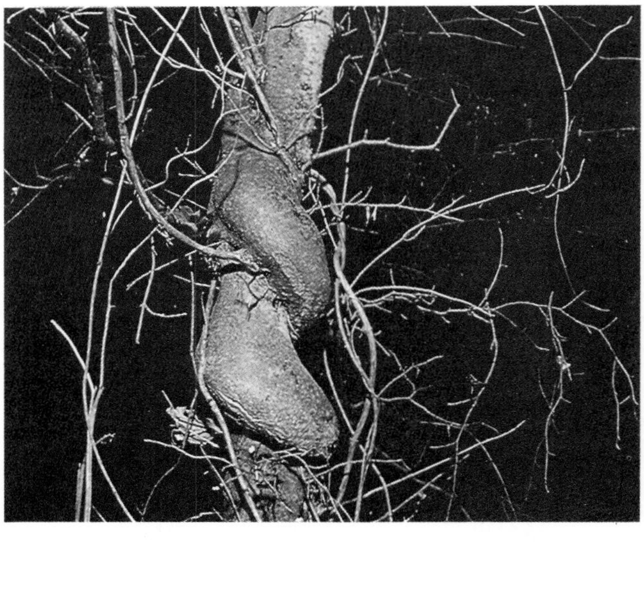

Wild clematis or old-man's-beard. All species of Clematis *are supported by their petioles or leaf stems, rather than their main stems.*

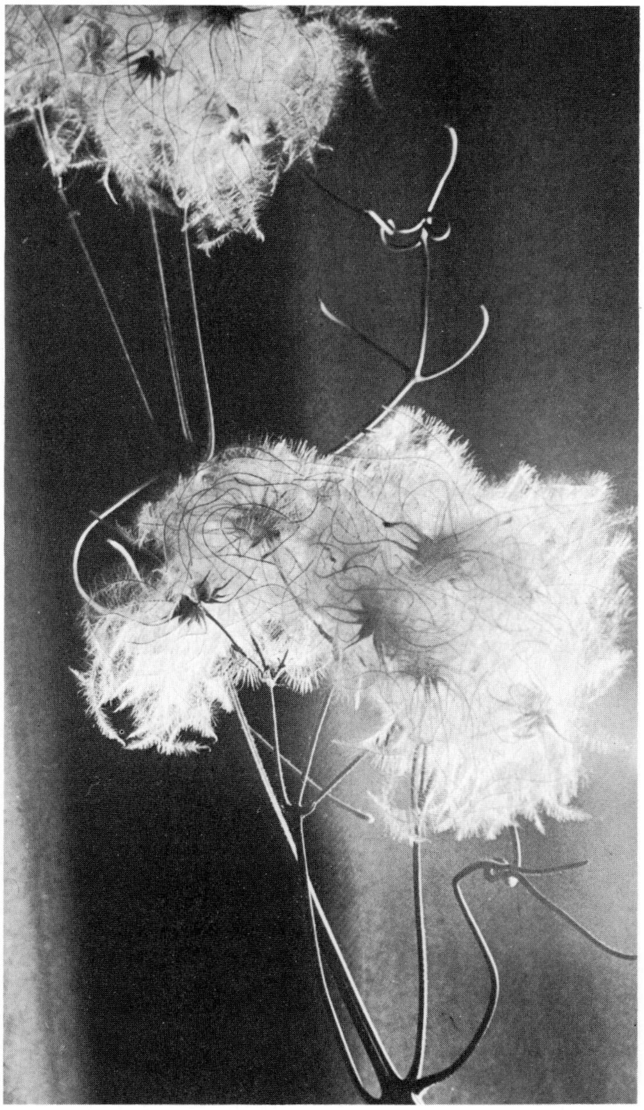

A tendril finds a support in the same way as a twining stem, but can then contract and coil to draw the plant closer to that support.

APICAL DOMINANCE

Another function of auxin in the plant is to determine which of the buds on each stem develops and grows. In many cases the topmost or apical bud is the only one that grows, while the lateral or side buds are all inhibited. The reason is that the apical bud produces auxin which stimulates its own growth but also prevents auxin production by buds lower down the stem. If you pinch out the topmost bud of a *Fuchsia* or *Antirrhinum* it gets bushier, because you have removed the inhibiting effect of the dominant apical bud and allowed the lateral buds to grow.

The same response is the basis of all pruning. Gardeners sometimes call the removal of the apical bud 'stopping', and describe the lateral shoots which then develop as 'breaking'. In spite of the fact that this single plant response is at the heart of all pruning techniques, it still is not really possible to lay down golden rules that will explain just how you should treat every shrub in the garden. Some plants show a stronger apical dominance than others. The dominance of some varies at different times of the year. The lateral buds of different species grow and 'break' in different patterns on the stem, and all these variations affect the way that an individual plant must be pruned. However, it is always important to cut back to a bud which points in the right direction. Once you have removed the apical dominance, the topmost bud still remaining on the stem will usually grow first and grow most, so you can determine the shape of a plant by careful pruning.

We can prune plants successfully because we can observe, understand and then use the plant's responses to its own growth substances. One step further is to synthesise auxin, or something very similar, and then to apply that to the plant in order to control its growth and development. There are now a whole host of 'hormone' products for use by the gardener, farmer and horticulturist. For example, auxin is used to extend the time that potatoes can be stored. The potato is really a stem, considerably modifed to store starch, and like a stem it has lateral buds in the potato's 'eyes'. The growth of these buds is governed by the amount of auxin they receive, just like the growth of lateral buds on a more conventional stem. A freshly-dug potato is dormant, but, after some months of storage, the buds begin to sprout and, for the kitchen at least, the potatoes are wasted. If the stored crop is sprayed with a synthetic auxin, then the growth of the buds is inhibited; potatoes have been kept in this way for as long as three years.

Yet another function of auxin is to stimulate the growth of roots from a cutting. The 'hormone rooting powder' that helps cuttings to 'take' is a synthetic auxin that adds to the natural auxin produced and helps ensure success for the gardener.

Perhaps the most common use of synthetic growth substances in gardening is the application of 2-4-D and other, similar compounds as selective weedkillers. At low concentrations these compounds behave very much like auxins, but, at the high concentration (for an auxin) of 0·1 per cent, they can be killers. Generally, they work better on broad-leaved, dicot plants, and are valuable in the garden as weedkillers on the lawn where they decimate the weeds but do not affect the grass. It is not really quite understood why grasses, grain plants and monocots generally are not affected by 2-4-D when the action on other plants is so dramatic. The growth of most dicots becomes completely disorganised, and the plants appear to burst apart. Slightly lower concentrations cause marked and rather bizarre deformations of the stems and leaves but may not actually kill, and you sometimes find plants like this in the lawn following treatment. Whatever the reason for its effects, 2-4-D has been of great value to farmers all over the world because it will kill weeds in crops like wheat, oats, rice and maize. In this country, the farmer's gain has been the plant lover's loss, of course, with no more poppies, cornflowers and marigolds to decorate the cornfields.

Spraying wheat with weedkiller, on a Sufolk farm.

GIBBERELLINS

Once auxin had been discovered and its importance realised, the hunt was on for other substances that could be used to control and alter plant growth. Many have been found, and doubtless there will be more in the future. One important group, called the gibberellins, was discovered in the first half of this century, almost by accident. In the 1890s some Japanese rice farmers noted the appearance of some extremely tall seedling rice plants in their paddy-fields. They watched them with some care, as particularly large plants are always watched, in the search for a possible source of breeding stock, but the seedlings were a disappointment. They never reached maturity and very rarely flowered, so the disease that caused this unfortunate development was christened 'Bakanae' or 'foolish-seedling' disease. Thirty years later it was found that seedlings like this were all infected with a fungus. When the fungus was transferred from a sick to a healthy plant, the healthy one soon showed the same symptoms of extreme elongation. Eventually the particular substance in the fungus that produced this rather wild growth was isolated. It was given the name gibberellin. Much more recently, gibberellin has been extracted from healthy plant tissue, so it is evident that it is a naturally occurring growth substance which appears in huge concentration in the 'foolish-seedling' fungus. Like the auxins, the gibberellins affect the elongation of cells, especially in the stem. They are made in the apex and young leaves of the plant, again like auxins, and are found in particularly high levels in some fruits and seeds, where they are part of the mechanism that maintains and then breaks dormancy (see Chapter 3).

Many biennials spend their first year as rather squat plants, like lettuce, cabbage and spinach, and then in their second year they make much more gibberellin and shoot upwards, finally forming flowers. Plants treated with gibberellin sometimes show growth which is just like this but rather more so! Some genetically dwarf varieties will grow to the height of the tall varieties when they are treated with gibberellin. Synthetic gibberellin is available but is not likely to be of much use to the gardener, although it is used commercially to control flowering in biennials and some long-day plants and to increase the growth of fruit.

Dr S.H. Wittwer of Michigan State University with some extraordinary cabbages. These giants are in their first year of growth and their rather dramatic bolting was caused by gibberellin treatment. The plants on the left are untreated controls.

CYTOKININS

There is a third group of major growth substances which are very important at the tip of the root and shoot because they stimulate cell division. They are called cytokinins, and these three groups – the auxins, the gibberellins and the cytokinins – together form the basis of control in the growing plant. Cytokinin affects cell division, and the other two act in the region of cell elongation, just behind the growing tip – but how the three interact and how they govern the precise pattern of plant growth has yet to be untangled.

It is known that mixtures of these three plus other, minor growth substances can be used to manipulate the growth of a plant to the advantage of the gardener or farmer. Auxin is produced by fruits as they develop, and this auxin in some way prevents the fruit falling off the plant before it is ripe. If a fruit does not make enough natural auxin, then it will fall early; and for a farmer with acres or even square miles of orchard, these 'windfalls' represent a good deal of money. A dilute solution of auxin sprayed over the orchard will augment the natural auxin in the fruit and save a small fortune each season. More than that, if the 'hormone' spray is a mixture, containing auxin with gibberellin and other ingredients as well, and it is applied when the trees are in blossom, then the cycle of cell division and growth which produces the fruit will begin, even though pollination and fertilisation have not taken place. Left to themselves, unfertilised flowers fall to the ground, but each fertilised flower produ-

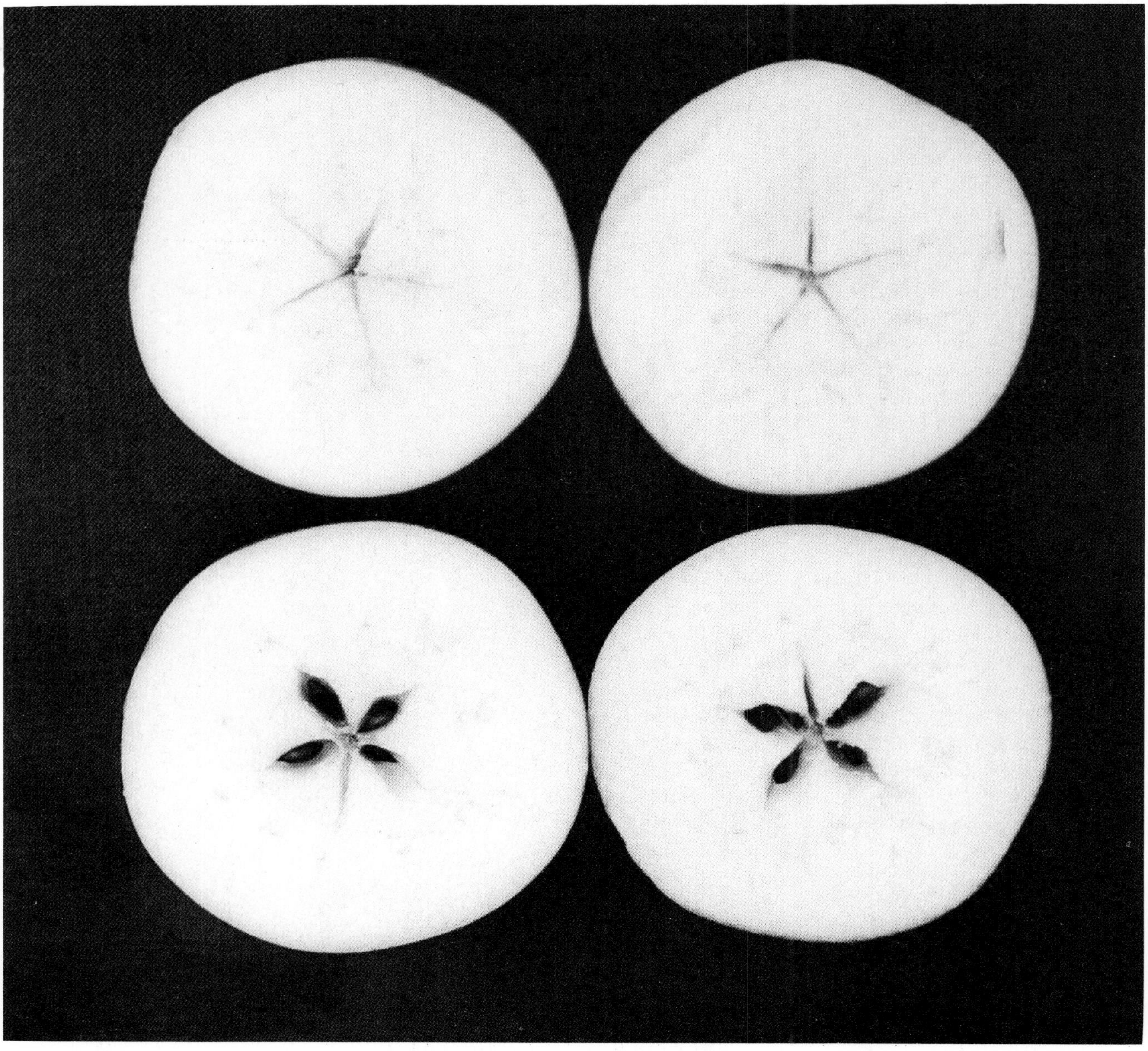

ces a mixture of growth substances that both holds it on the tree and stimulates the swelling of the fruit. An unfertilised flower that is sprayed with a 'hormone cocktail' behaves just like a fertilised flower. The tree is well and truly fooled. It produces a fruit that is perfect in every way but without a pip. The main purpose of hormone sprays like this is not to produce seedless fruits, but to increase crop yield by making sure that every flower on the tree forms a fruit, and not just the ones that have been pollinated by a visiting insect. No hormone recipe yet devised has produced a seed from an unfertilised flower, but the seedless fruits that can be grown are popular and sell well.

Another of these hormone mixtures cuts down the chore of hedge trimming. It inhibits the growth of the main stems and encourages slow growth of the lateral shoots, so you get a bushier hedge with no effort – welcome news, perhaps, for a nation of gardeners with twenty thousand miles of hedge to trim twice each year.

(Opposite page.) Cox apples, formed after treatment with a mixture of auxin, gibberellin and cytokinin (above) and after pollination in the usual way (below). Other seedless fruits can be produced using different hormone recipes – cherries, Victoria plums and Bramley apples with auxin and gibberellin, Conference pears with gibberellin and tomatoes with auxin.

(This page.) The hormone treatment of hedges. Part of this hedge was sprayed about six weeks before the photograph was taken and the difference between the treated and untreated sections is quite clear.

OTHER GROWTH SUBSTANCES

There are a whole host of plant growth substances outside the three main groups, and there are certainly more to find. Our understanding of how the plant organises itself and its growth is far from complete. One of these minor 'hormones', first called 'dormin' but now known as abscisin, is an inhibitory growth substance that prepares the plant for winter. It is involved in leaf fall and in suppressing the growth of buds and branches, as part of the seasonal shut-down that protects the plant and makes it less vulnerable to frost damage.

Another interesting substance is known as 'florigen' because it has something to do with flowering in the plant. Plants are stimulated to flower by a number of conditions, including light and temperature; however once the plant has 'perceived' the right flowering stimulus, there must be something that passes the message 'time to flower' to the apex of the plant where the flower buds will form. Just what 'florigen' is and how it works is not really understood, but there must be some signalling substance circulating around the plant because when a leaf from a plant that has received a flowering stimulus is grafted on to another plant that has not, it will make that plant flower. The leaf must be carrying something that is then transported to the apex of the plant, and that 'something' is called 'florigen'.

It is a hundred years or so since Darwin started the search for the mechanisms that control the growth of plants, but the whole tangle of growth substances, their interactions and effects, is far from unravelled. Undoubtedly this area of research will be important for many years. And it is likely too that as this aspect of a plant's life is explained and understood, the use of precisely acting growth substances will become more and more common and important in the garden.

CHAPTER FIVE

ONE-PARENT FAMILIES

Couch grass. This plant has a variety of regional regional names, including 'twitch' and 'switch'.

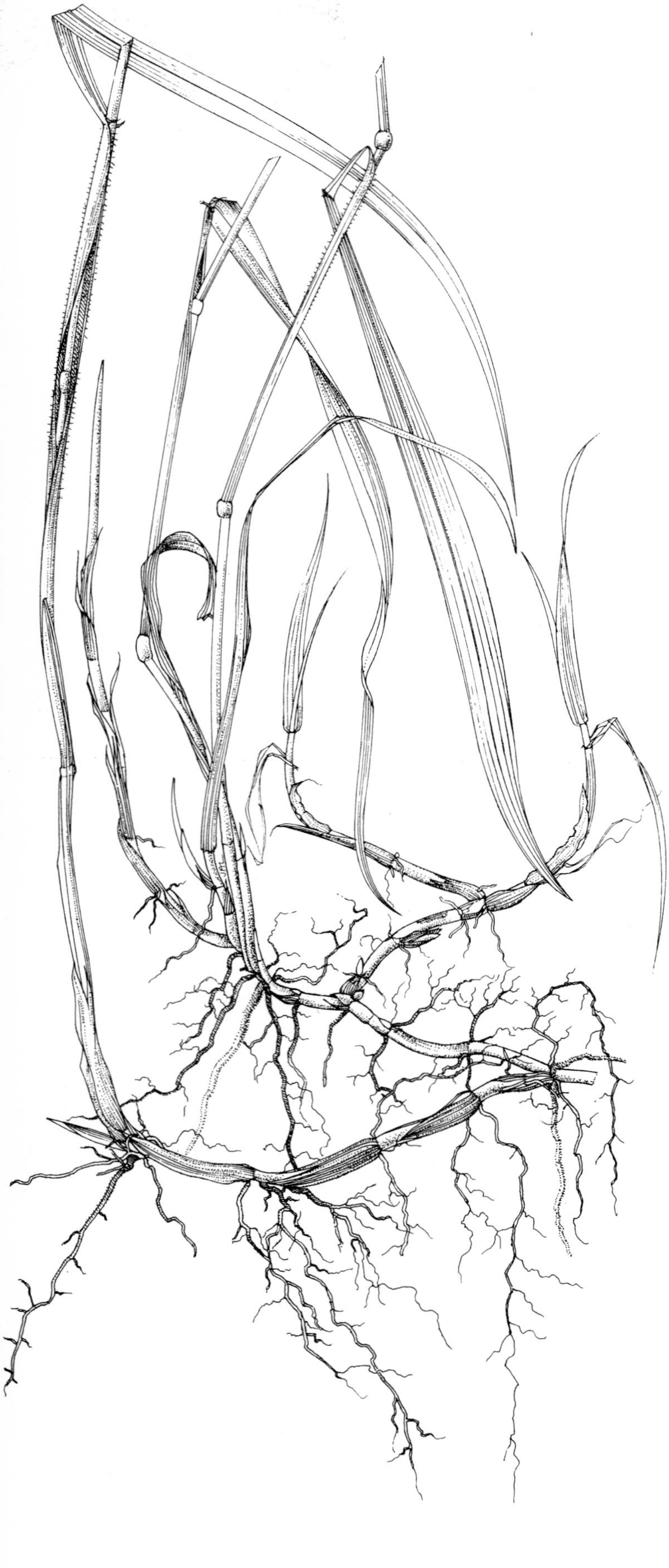

Couch grass is a plague especially dreaded by the gardener because it can spread so fast. More than that, it spreads in a particularly insidious way, underground, so that just as you think you have it beaten another blade pops up somewhere else. The reason for its success (for success it is, however much it hurts to admit it) is that couch produces new plants by the growth of buds on its underground stems or rhizomes. Below the earth is a mass of these rhizomes. One square foot of couch can grow as much as 130 feet of rhizome, bearing up to 1,500 buds. That is 1,500 potential new plants; no wonder the weed spreads at the speed it does! Each new plant remains attached to the parent by the rhizome, until it is established. It gets plenty of nourishment through this 'umbilical cord' until its own root and shoot are big enough to support it, so new plants grow quickly and easily. Mint spreads in the same way, and can take over the whole vegetable garden unless its roots and rhizomes are contained, perhaps by growing it in a buried bucket. The interesting thing about the new plants formed in this way is that they are genetically exactly like their single parent. No variation has been introduced by sexual crossing, so the plants are all truly members of a one-parent family.

This vegetative reproduction, as it is called, is not always a gardener's nightmare. There are many useful or beautiful garden plants that are propagated in this way. The iris has underground rhizomes, swollen and fat rather than long and thin like couch grass, but you can still get a new iris plant by digging the rhizome out of the ground, splitting it and replanting the pieces. Potatoes work in a similar way. Each potato is a swollen stem tuber, modified to store starch for next year's growth. We eat most of them but save some to plant, and can be certain of getting just the same variety of potato again next year. They must be the same. There has been no sexual crossing to introduce any kind of change into their genetic make-up.

(Above right.) An iris with a fat, swollen rhizome and finer, fibrous roots.

(Below right.) To propagate an iris by splitting the rhizome, make a clean cut to separate a single branch (1 and 2). Cut back the leaves (3) to reduce water loss and lessen wind resistance, so that the young plant cannot be uprooted in a gale. Plant the cut rhizome so that about half its diameter is covered with soil (4). Iris rhizomes are best split every three years, after flowering or in September.

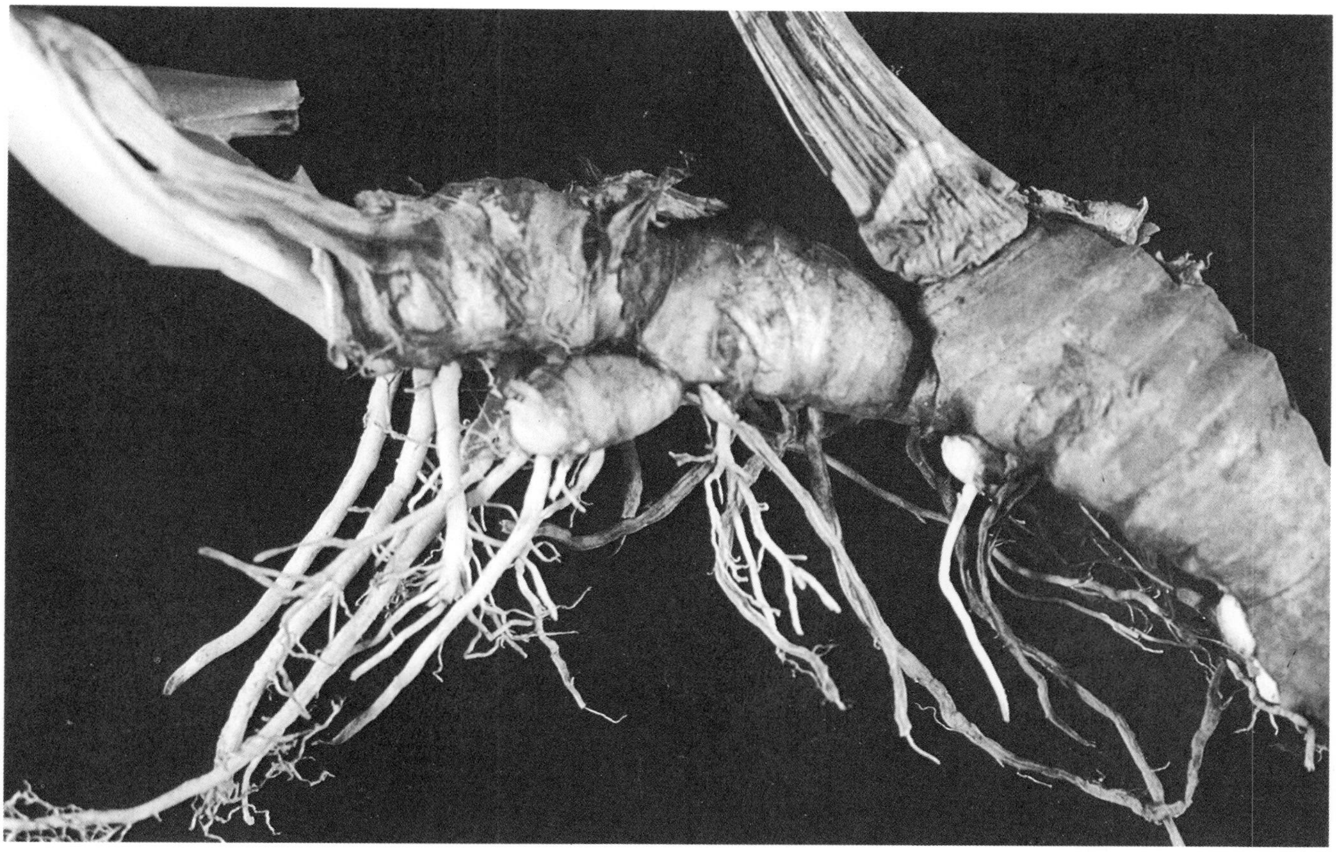

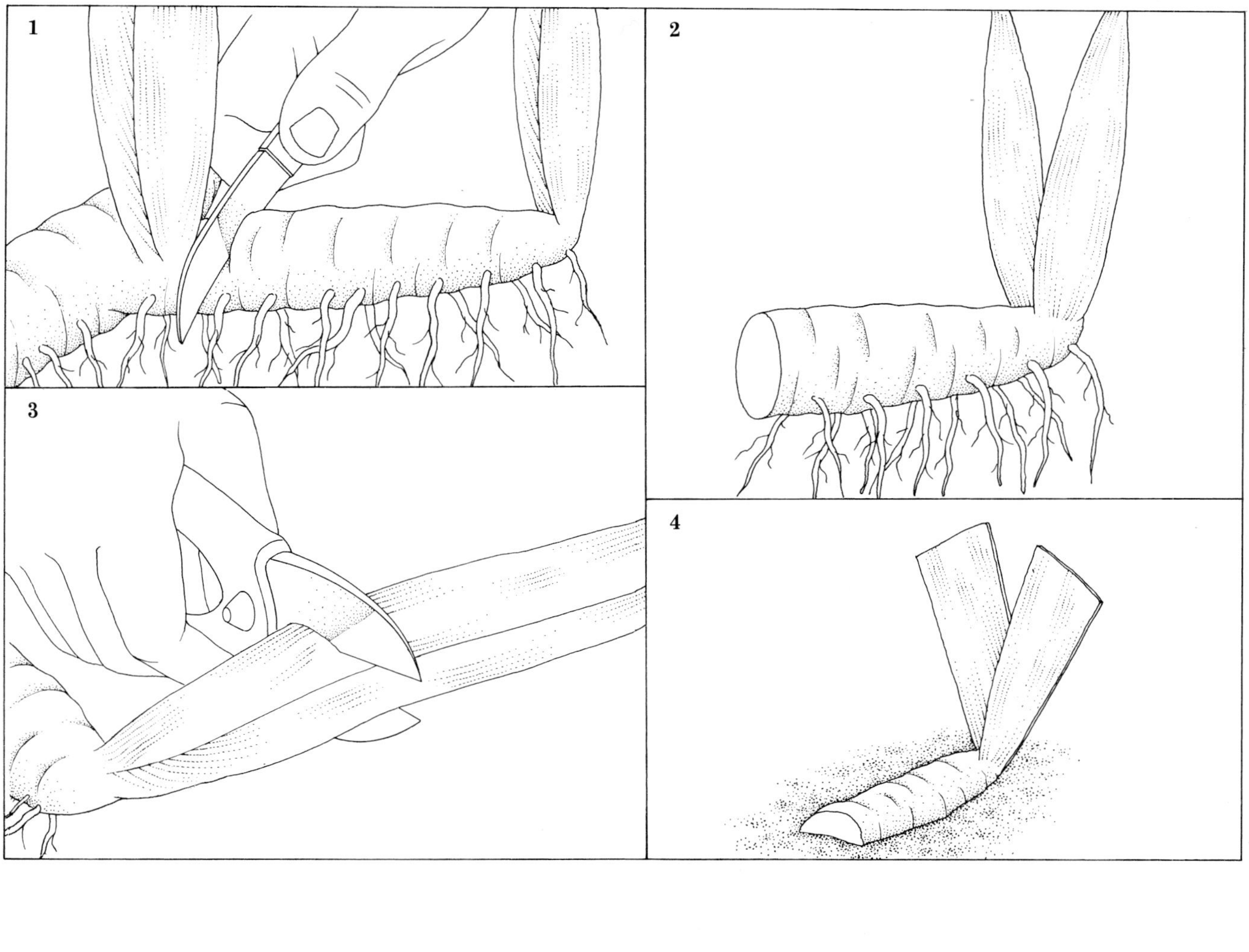
1
2
3
4

The developing food stores beneath a potato plant.

(Below.) A twig of dogwood, with the bark peeled off to show the root initials.

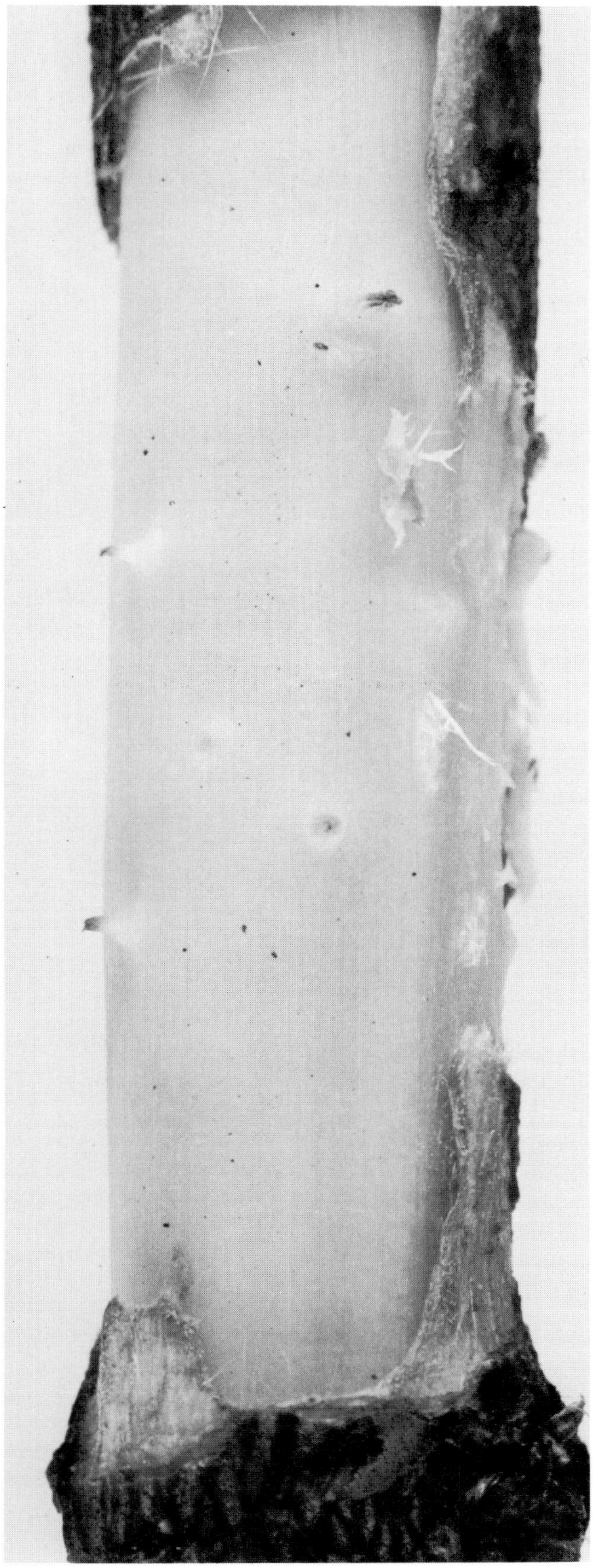

There are countless other techniques for propagating plants by exploiting their ability to reproduce vegetatively. For commercial growers these methods are important, for every type of plant, from house plants to fruit trees; and at home they mean that once you have a specimen that, you particularly like or admire, you can get another just the same at little or no cost.

The most usual way to propagate a plant vegetatively – for the gardener, at least – is by taking a cutting from either the stem, a leaf or the root. Some plants, like *Impatiens* (Busy Lizzie) and some species of *Pelargonium*, get so leggy and ugly as the plants mature that it is easier to maintain strong plants with full foliage and good flowers by continually taking cuttings and discarding the parent plant.

STEM CUTTINGS

The taking of cuttings in the garden or greenhouse (or of house plants in the kitchen) is such a common, frequently used technique that it is easy to forget what a wonderful business it is. When you make a cut across a stem, the two surfaces separated must be, in all respects, very similar. After all, until a few seconds ago, when you made the cut, they were joined and performing their function as part of the stem. However one of them, the cutting, will go on to grow roots, whereas the other, the stock, will grow another shoot. How can such similar pieces of plant grow in such totally different ways?

The answer lies in the fact that there are, throughout the plant, cells which have never become specialised to perform any particular function. They are called 'undifferentiated cells'. They remain alive, with a nucleus and cytoplasm, and they retain the ability to divide and produce more cells that can then take on any function needed.

The first thing that happens when a stem cutting takes root is that a group of these undifferentiated cells become active and divide to form a 'root initial', the very tiny beginning of a root. As the root initials grow into recognisable roots, they force their way out of the stem, rupturing the other stem tissue as they emerge. The ease with which a stem cutting from a particular species takes root depends, in part, on the ease with which the plant is able to form these root initials. Some plants which root very easily, like jasmine and poplar, actually have pre-formed root initials in the stem, lying dormant but ready to spring into action if the stem is damaged. Until this happens the latent root initials remain dormant, and can be seen as small bumps by peeling some of the bark off a twig. In some apple and quince varieties the pre-formed roots cause swellings called 'burr-knots' as the trees get older.

LEAF CUTTINGS

The ability of a plant to grow from a leaf cutting also depends on the renewed division of undifferentiated cells, but in this case they must produce both a root and a shoot. African violet plants can grow in this way from mature cells at the base of the petiole or leaf stem, and the *Begonia* can produce new growth from cells around the midrib. The *Camellia* and the pot plant *Crassula*, also called the jade plant, can be propagated from leaf cuttings, but the cuttings must include a piece of the stem and an intact axillary bud. The plants are able to direct the undifferentiated cells in their leaves only into root making, so without the bud there will be plenty of roots growing from the base of the petiole but the new plant will not have a stem or shoot. The axillary bud completes the plant by providing the shoot.

(Above.) Young African violet plants growing from leaf cuttings.
(Below.) Several cuttings can be taken from each leaf of Sansavieria *or mother-in-law's tongue, but they must be planted the right way up. To mark the difference between the top and bottom of each cutting, some gardeners cut one at right angles and the other at a slight angle.*

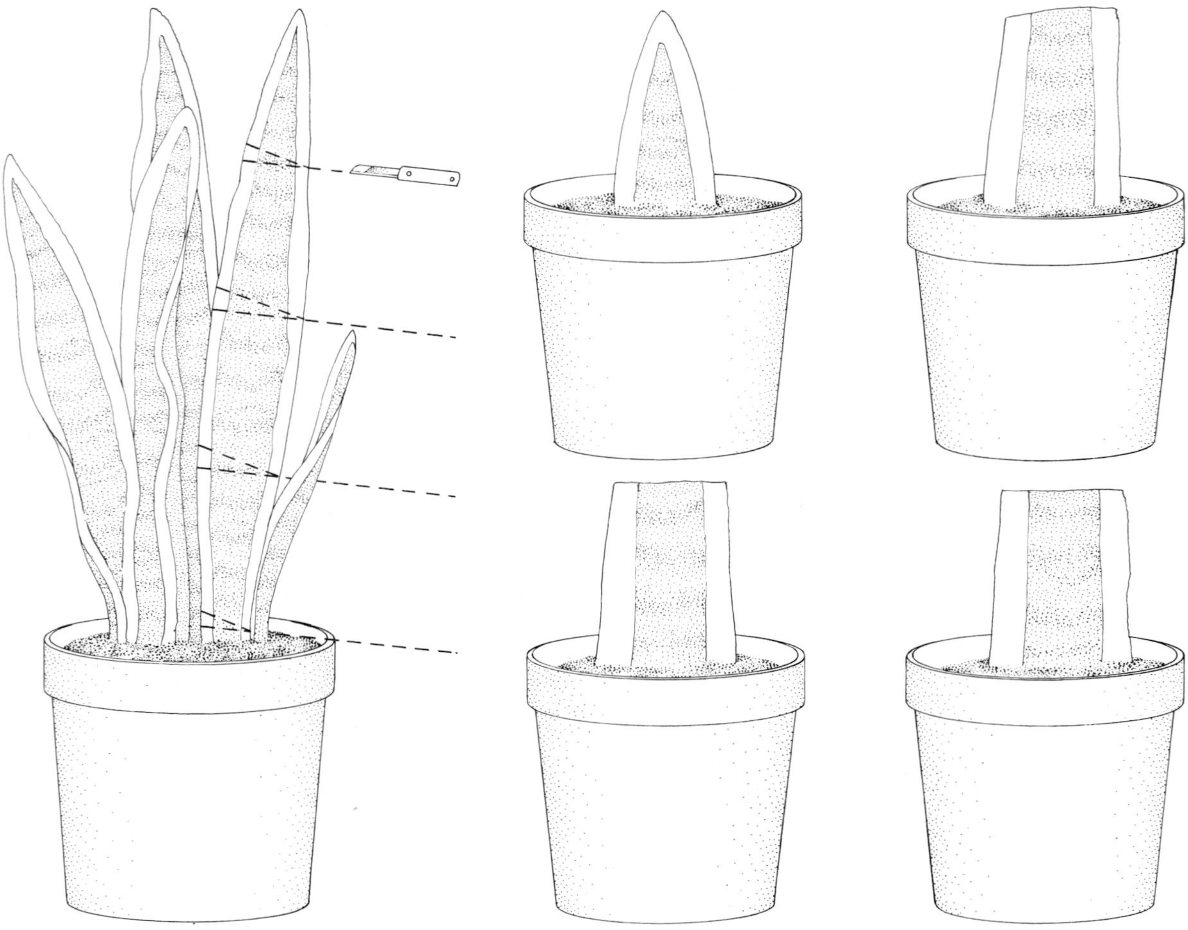

The transformation of undifferentiated cells into shoots or roots is stimulated by a change in the level of growth substances around the cut surface. When the plant is growing normally, auxin is made in the growing tip, in the leaf blade and in the buds of side shoots, and it is passed back down the plant through a system of tubes called phloem. When a cutting is taken, the phloem is severed along with everything else, and this prevents the auxin from continuing on its journey down the plant. But the cutting carries on producing the growth substance, so an accumulation of it builds up just above the cut surface of the stem; it is this change in concentration that stimulates root growth.

Auxin flows from the shoot to the root regardless of gravity, so it is important to get stem cuttings in the right way up. For most plants that sounds a singularly useless piece of advice, because nobody is likely to make the mistake of burying a geranium or *Fuchsia* cutting with its head in the soil, but some plants, like the *Yucca*, have bare wooden stems that can be chopped into short lengths with no very clear features to distinguish the top from the bottom. If they go in upside down, they will produce a root and shoot upside down as well. The same care needs to be taken with leaf cuttings from the unkindly named 'mother-in-law's tongue'.

The more leaves and buds a stem cutting bears, the greater its chance of rooting successfully. This is partly because there is carbohydrate food in the leaves that the young plant can use for energy and growth, but mostly because the leaves and buds make auxin. The more leaves there are the more auxin is made, and it all passes down the plant and adds to the accumulation at the base of the cutting.

Auxin is not the only growth substance involved in rooting a cutting. There are traces of several others, and it is the presence or absence of these co-factors that may account for the fact that it is harder to get some species to root than others. In every case, however, it seems to be auxin that is the most important.

A single Yucca *log can be sawn up to produce many young plants, but again, each piece must be planted the right way up, or the leaves will grow from the bottom (right), leaving an unsightly stump. Market stalls sometimes sell these upside down* Yucca *plants very cheaply, like 'seconds'.*

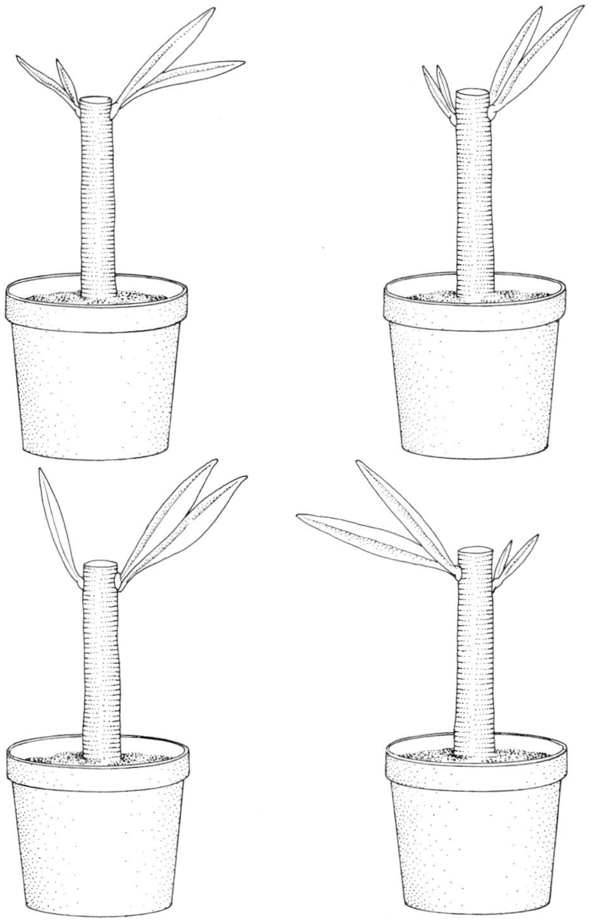

GREEN FINGERS?

Green-fingered gardeners may seem to be able to snap off a bit of a shoot and stick it into the earth with no apparent thought or care and then sit back to watch as a new plant flourishes, but those of us less favoured can do with all the help available. The 'rooting powder' or 'hormone rooting powder' that is sold in garden shops is made from synthetic auxin, and can be used to give a bit of a boost to the plant's natural supply. The freshly cut stem should be dipped into the powder and tapped lightly to shake off the excess before the cutting goes into the soil. This excess powder should not be shaken back into the pot, as it will carry with it all manner of dirt and bacteria from the cut stem and this may make the whole tub of powder degenerate very quickly. If you want to do a large number of cuttings at one time it is worth transferring a little of the hormone powder to something like a saucer or an egg cup and dipping all the cuttings into that to avoid contaminating the rest of it.

The synthesis of auxin was quite a milestone, for both the botanist and the gardener. It certainly made taking cuttings much easier and more reliable, but before that there was a host of ingenious techniques that a gardener could use to help his cuttings on their way. A germinating grain of barley pushed into a split at the base of the cutting was said to increase its chance of rooting. That sounds like the horticultural equivalent of an old wives' tale, but we now know that sprouting grain is a powerful producer of all kinds of growth substances, including auxin, so it is quite possible that some of the hormone 'leaked' from the grain and on to the base of the cutting to stimulate root growth. Another thing that we now know about auxin is that it is found in human urine, excretion and sweat. Could it really be that the coveted green fingers amount to no more than a pair of sweaty palms? Whatever the colour of your fingers, there are a few golden rules that might help when taking cuttings.

The best cuttings come from young plants. Apart from the relative ease with which some species will root (regardless of the age of the stock plant), cuttings from young plants root more easily. This is especially true of conifers. The reasons are complex, but probably relate to the decrease in the production of the co-factors, the growth substances that work alongside auxin to encourage root growth and also to an increase in some growth inhibitors.

Cuttings need a large concentration of carbohydrate in their leaves so that they can feed while getting established. This carbohydrate is made by the plant by a process called photosynthesis (see Chapter 9). For photosynthesis to proceed as well as possible the plant needs good light and ample water, so there is no sign of wilting. The part of the plant that you choose to take for the cutting should be a good, bright dark green. The accumulation of carbohydrate can be helped by lessening feeding a few weeks before taking the cutting. The effect of stopping fertilising the plant is to reduce growth, so that all the carbohydrate that is made by the photosynthesising plant is stored and is ready to fuel the growth of the cutting.

Many gardening books refer to the desirability of taking a 'heel' or a small slice of the older wood along with the cutting. This is likely to be of greatest benefit when there are pre-formed root initials in the mature tissue but probably does not help in the rooting of softwood cuttings.

The time of year that is best for taking cuttings varies immensely. For softwood cuttings of deciduous trees the spring is best, just as the leaves have

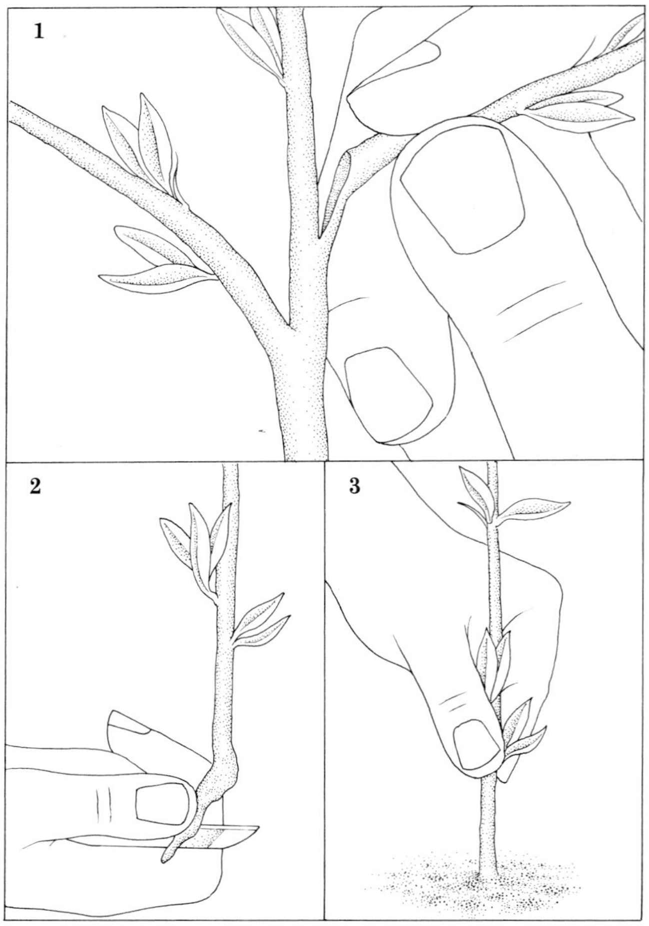

Heel cuttings. Pull a side shoot from the main stem along with a strip of bark or heel (1). Trim the heel (2) and plant in the usual way (3).

unfurled and expanded, because the supply of both hormones and carbohydrates is likely to be high. On the other hand, the cold of winter stimulates rooting in conifers, so you will get the best results between late autumn and the end of winter.

In almost all species it is essential to give the cuttings good conditions of temperature, moisture and light. Adequate temperature for most plants is around 20 °C (68 °F) during the day and about 15 °C (59 °F) at night, so it is easier, in this country, to cope with cuttings during the summer, apart from the exceptions, like conifers, which need the cold.

A moist environment lessens the rate at which the new plant loses water from its leaves. This is important because, although the presence of the leaves and the auxin they produce stimulates rooting, the loss of water from the leaves through transpiration could cause the cutting to dry out and die long before root formation has taken place. A propagating box is like a fish tank with a transparent lid; it maintains an enclosed and fairly moist atmosphere while letting in as much light as possible. If you are putting just a few cuttings in a pot you can get the effect of a propagator by enclosing the pot in a clear polythene bag, supported on sticks or a wire frame to hold it off the cuttings themselves.

Light is of major importance for cuttings, as for all plant growth, because it is light that powers the process by which a plant makes carbohydrate, and it is carbohydrate that fuels the growth of the plant. On the other hand, the part of the stem on which roots are expected to form should be kept in darkness. If you are rooting cuttings in soil or compost, then this will obviously be the case, but it is worth bearing in mind when rooting cuttings in water.

Although this ability of the plant to sprout roots from a cut surface is a great convenience for the gardener, it is not immediately obvious that it is an advantage to the plant, particularly when you remember that all the parts of the plant, the root initials, the hormone balances and so on, must have evolved millions of years before man even walked the earth, let along brandished a pair of secateurs. In fact, the rooting response of the plant is designed to cope with trampling and other accidental damage in the natural environment, rather than with the tidy cuts of the gardener. In taking cuttings, we exploit the natural ability of the plant to our own advantage.

A home-made propagator. If the polythene bag touches the leaves of the cuttings, they are continually wetted and will soon rot.

LAYERING

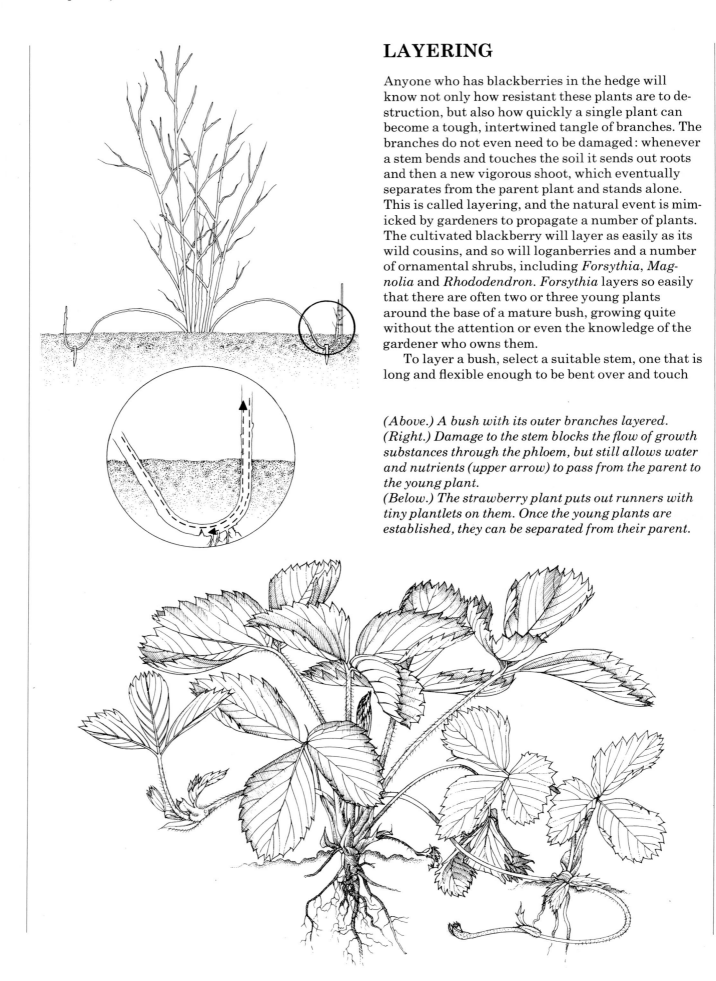

Anyone who has blackberries in the hedge will know not only how resistant these plants are to destruction, but also how quickly a single plant can become a tough, intertwined tangle of branches. The branches do not even need to be damaged: whenever a stem bends and touches the soil it sends out roots and then a new vigorous shoot, which eventually separates from the parent plant and stands alone. This is called layering, and the natural event is mimicked by gardeners to propagate a number of plants. The cultivated blackberry will layer as easily as its wild cousins, and so will loganberries and a number of ornamental shrubs, including *Forsythia*, *Magnolia* and *Rhododendron*. *Forsythia* layers so easily that there are often two or three young plants around the base of a mature bush, growing quite without the attention or even the knowledge of the gardener who owns them.

To layer a bush, select a suitable stem, one that is long and flexible enough to be bent over and touch

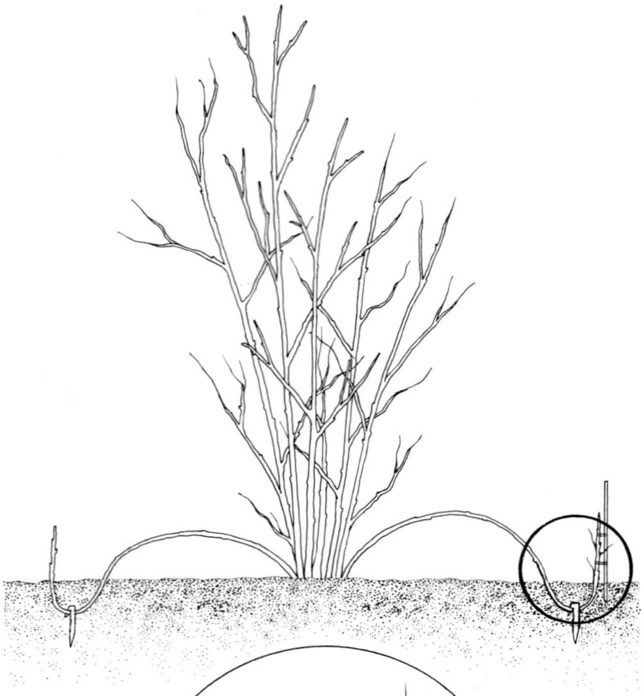

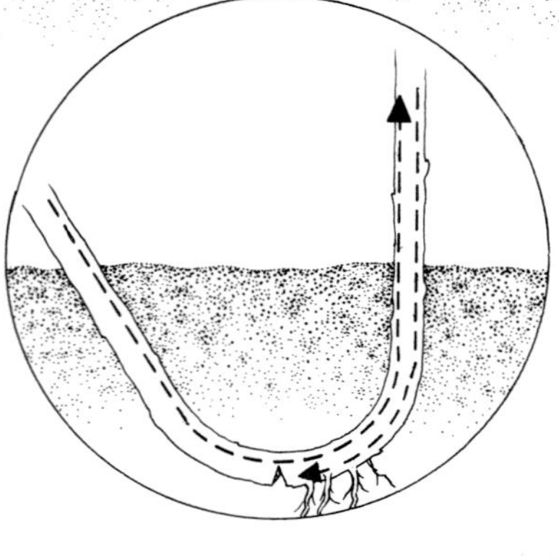

(Above.) A bush with its outer branches layered.
(Right.) Damage to the stem blocks the flow of growth substances through the phloem, but still allows water and nutrients (upper arrow) to pass from the parent to the young plant.
(Below.) The strawberry plant puts out runners with tiny plantlets on them. Once the young plants are established, they can be separated from their parent.

the ground. Then either make a shallow cut part way through the stem, or bend and twist the branch until it fractures but does not break. Strip the leaves from the damaged area, peg it to the earth and bury it under about an inch of soil. The damage to the stem stimulates rooting, just as it does when you take a cutting by blocking the downward flow of auxin and causing it to accumulate just above the broken section. The stem of layered plant, however, is not completely severed, so the new plant retains some contact with the parent – it keeps a lifeline that provides it with water and soil nutrients.

Commercial growers, particularly of house plants, rely more and more on vegetative techniques of propagation. The advantage for them is that they can guarantee the exact similarity of all the baby plants they grow, and this has become increasingly important as sales of house plants have risen in recent years. Not only are we buying more plants, we are buying more of them from chain stores and supermarkets, rather than from florists and garden centres. The buyers from the big stores want all the plants they get to be identical, so that they can have a consistent policy for pricing. A single price for all the plants also cuts down damage caused by customers handling the plants to look for a price tag. However, if a *Monstera* with three leaves and one bud is to be sold at the same price in every branch of a national chain store, then the buyer for the stores must at least be sure that every *Monstera* on the shelves has three leaves and one bud. And that is the sort of order that the big growers have to meet – five thousand rubber plants with three big leaves and one small one, ten thousand African violets all with the same number of leaves and the same number of identically coloured flowers. Their glasshouse benches are covered with identical plants for as far as the eye can see, and the only way of producing plants as reliably as this is by propagating them by one vegetative technique or another and then rearing them under identical conditions. The appearance and size of a plant is always determined by the interaction of these two elements – its genetic make-up and the circumstances in which it grows.

Air layering

This is a very old and well-established technique of vegetative propagation, sometimes called Chinese layering because it originated in China, where it is reported to have been in use as much as four thousand years ago.

A plant can be layered 'in the air' for just the same reasons that it can be layered on the ground – the phloem is damaged in order to block the flow of hormones that stimulate root growth, and the xylem tissue remains whole and supplies the shoot with water and nutrients. The difference, of course, is that air layering can be performed on plants with branches that could never be bent to touch the soil. It is practised on a number of common garden shrubs, but the plant that many people propagate in this way is the familiar rubber plant.

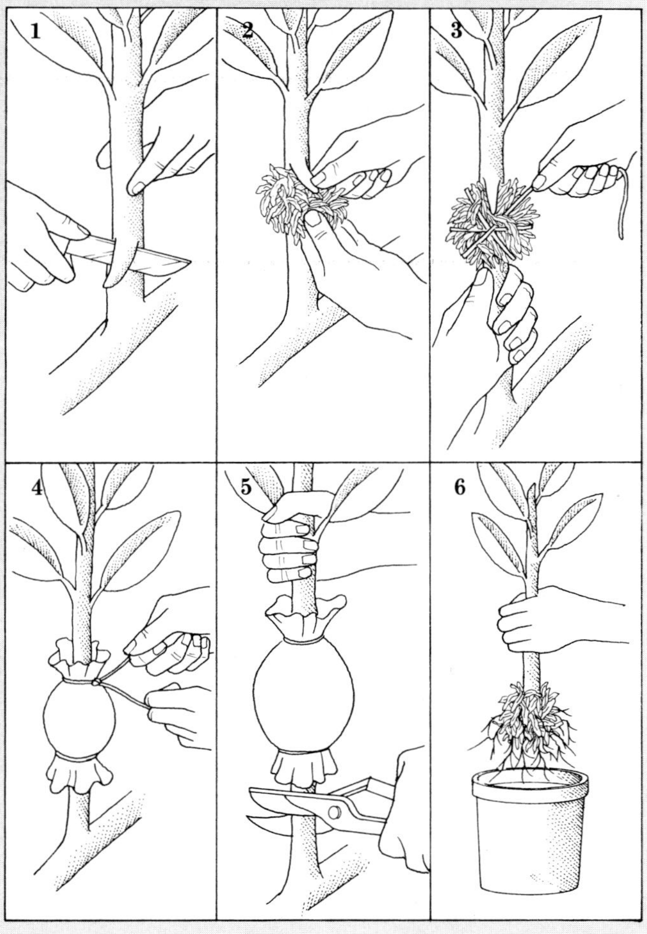

1 Make an angled cut half way through the stem.
3 Wrap a handful of moist Sphagnum *moss around the damaged area. Tie it down firmly.*
4 Cover the moss with black polythene. Make the ends as watertight as possible with string or sticky tape. Leave for a year.
5 At the end of the dormant season, normally winter, cut back any new growth above the layer. Then detach the layered stem from the parent.
6 Gently loosen the roots and pot.

TISSUE CULTURE

The more individuals that a house plant grower can get from one parent the better. Leaf cuttings are more productive than stem cuttings but one of the new propagation techniques, called tissue culture, is the most productive of all. This process starts with a few cells, a speck too small to be seen by the naked eye – and ends up with a fully grown and perfect plant. There are many millions of cells in every plant that can be used to begin the culture, so the number of plants that can be raised from one individual is almost unlimited.

Tissue culture depends on the ability of undifferentiated plant cells to divide and make a tiny mass called a callus, and then, given the right mixture of hormones and growth substances, to grow a root and shoot and to develop into a full size plant. It is really no more than a very sophisticated exploitation of the plant's ability to respond to and survive damage.

The methods by which the process is carried out are the subject of a great deal of commercial competition and accordingly shrouded in secrecy, but basically what happens is that a number of undifferentiated cells are cut from the chosen parent plant. The operation is carried out in sterile conditions, and the cells are placed in a dish on an artificial growing medium which looks rather like jelly and contains all the nutrients the cells need as well as the hormones that direct their growth. It looks like a miracle, but out of this gelatinous puddle emerge tiny plants, with roots and shoots, which can then be transferred from their sterile glass homes into conventional pots and earth, and grown on until they reach a size suitable for sale. You may already own one of these test-tube babies without even knowing it, but the sterile conditions and complex mixtures of hormones that are necessary for their growth make it hard to imagine producing your own. They are more at home in the laboratory than in the potting shed.

A tissue culture from a tobacco plant, showing the effects of changing hormone levels on its growth and development. The bottle on the left contains callus, which will only differentiate to form a root and shoot when it is exposed to the correct mixture of growth substances. One mixture of cytokinin and auxin induces the formation of a root alone (centre), while another mixture, with a greater quantity of auxin, stimulates the growth of a shoot without a root (right).

GRAFTING

Grafting, in contrast, has been part of the gardener's box of tricks for generations. It is the art of joining two plants together in such a way that they continue to grow as one – but as one which has the best characteristics of both. The upper part is called the 'scion' and the lower part is called the 'root-stock', 'under-stock' or just the 'stock'. It seems odd to describe grafting as a method of propagation when you begin with two plants and end up with only one, but in fact it has been used to produce hundreds of thousands of plants, all genetically identical and all directly descended from one individual that was right in every way.

One of these ideal individuals, now the 'father' of a gigantic family, was sown as a seed in 1805, the year of the Battle of Trafalgar. In that year a girl called Mary Ann Brailsford ate an apple from her next-door neighbour's garden and planted one of the pips.

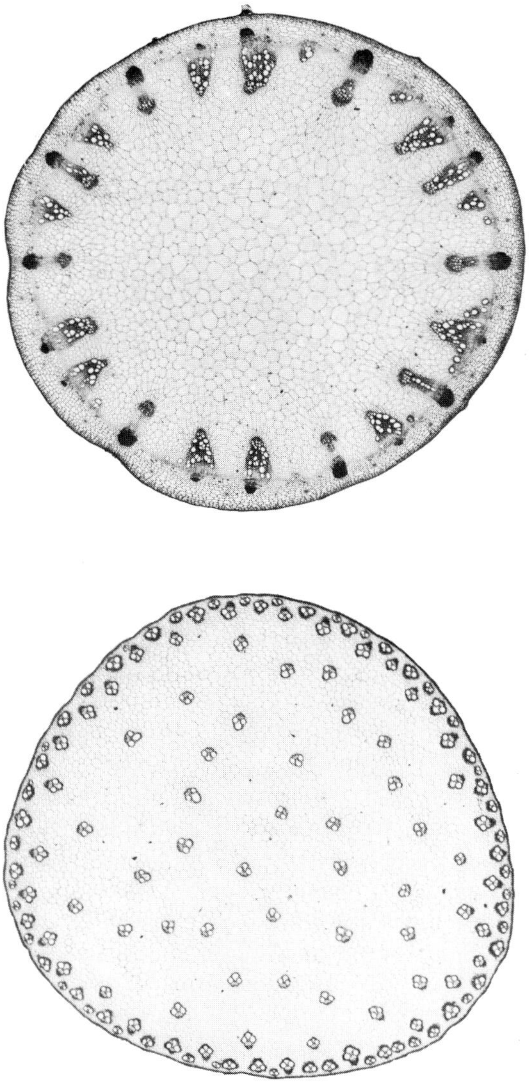

The pip germinated, and she planted the seedling in the garden of the cottage where she lived with her mother in Southwell, Nottinghamshire. Eventually it became a tree and bore fruit, and as the years went by it became well known in the area. Its fruit was good, especially for cooking, so other identical trees were grown by taking scions from it and grafting them on to root-stock plants. By the time there were enough of the trees for them to need a name, the cottage and its garden had changed hands, so the apples took the name of their new owner – Mr Bramley. Every Bramley tree and every Bramley apple is descended from that first tree, grown from a pip planted by a child.

The original Bramley is still in Mary's garden, rather gnarled and elderly but carefully tended and still producing a fine crop of handsome apples. It is quite a thrill to see this patriach but, perhaps, no more than the thrill of getting an apple from the greengrocer, holding it in your hand and knowing that it is one of the direct descendants of the apple that Mary held as Nelson braced himself to face the French.

Grafting is probably used more by the commercial grower than by the gardener, but, although it requires a bit more effort than taking a cutting, it is not really very difficult. The scion and the root-stock are cut so that they fit closely together. They are then bound tightly so that the two cut surfaces are pressed together, and the whole graft is sealed with wax, which stops either part losing water and also prevents infection. Any branches that grow up from the root-stock should be cut back so that they cannot swamp the scion before it gets established.

A graft 'takes' when a successful vascular connection is made between scion and stock – in other words, when all the plumbing is connected up properly the new 'mongrel' will grow. All the complicated cutting and fixing is to give the plant the best chance of making this connection.

The part of the stem that is most important in grafting is called the 'cambium'. This is a layer of cells which lies between the two types of tube that make up the plant's plumbing system, the xylem and the phloem. The cells are meristematic – that is, they can divide to make new cells. When they divide on one side they make xylem, and when they divide on the other side they make phloem. In the stem of a woody plant the cambium is cylindrical, with xylem tissue in the middle and phloem around the outside. Grafting is much harder when plants have some other arrangements of the vascular system, as in monocots, for example.

A section through the stem of a dicot plant (above) and a monocot (below). The asymmetric arrangement of the vascular bundles in the latter makes successful grafting virtually impossible.

An orchard of dwarf apple trees.

The careful cutting and binding of a graft is to make sure that the cambium layers of the scion and the stock are pressed closely together. If they are not touching, the graft will not take. When they are touching, cells at the cut surface of both stems will divide and together make a mass of undifferentiated cells called 'callus', which locks the two parts together. Where the new callus cells are in line with the cambium of both scion and stock, they will differentiate and become cambium cells. These can then divide and produce the xylem and phloem tissue that will join the scion and stock into one plant. Once this has been achieved, water can pass from the stock to the scion, and sugar, growth substances and so on can travel through the phloem and back down the plant into the root. A new plant is born.

The two parts of the new plant still retain most of their own characteristics – indeed, this is often the reason that grafting is useful. A rose with beautiful, scented blooms but puny roots can be grafted on to a rose with insignificant flowers and tough, virile roots to produce a bush with strong roots and prize-winning flowers. Buds growing from the stock will differ from the main plant, (see page 101).

Some root-stocks have the capacity to dwarf whatever is grafted on to them. Scientists at the East Malling Research Station have bred a new apple root-stock, called Malling 27 (or M27), that produces tiny apple trees, only four or five feet high, that crop heavily in the second year after planting. They have grown many of the popular British varieties of apple grafted on to this root-stock, and found that M27 gives a higher yield, in relation to tree size, then any other root-stock. The main advantage for the gardener is the small size of the trees; a ten-year-old Bramley grafted on to M27 is about three feet wide. This means they need only be planted about three feet apart, so in even a small garden you could grow a whole range of different cooking and eating apples.

Whip and tongue graft

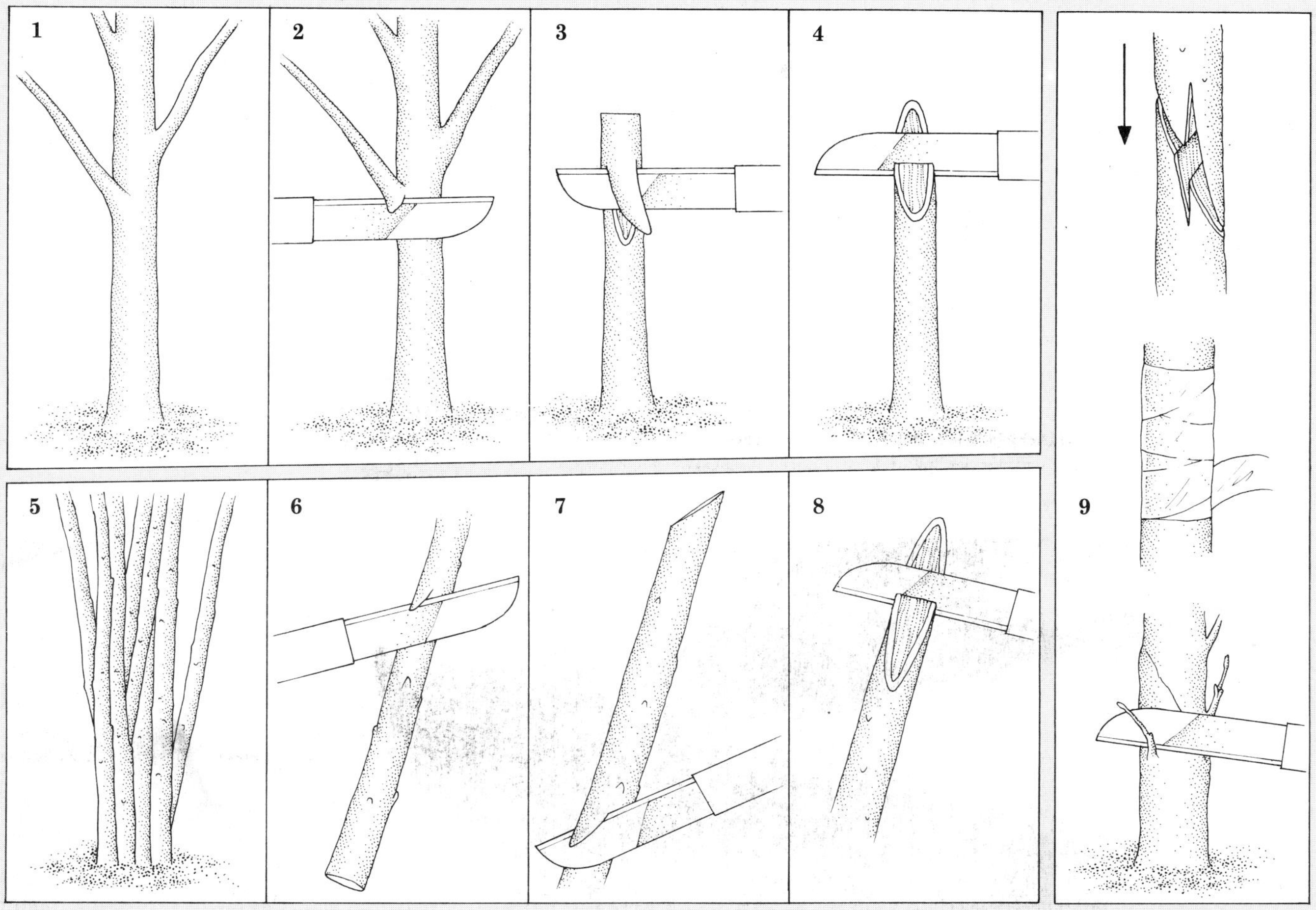

Preparation of the stock.
1 Select a young, healthy plant as the rootstock.
2 When the sap rises in early spring, trim back all the side branches, leaving a single shoot.
3 A few weeks later, cut back the rootstock to the level required (ground level for ornamentals, nine or ten inches higher for fruit trees). Then make an angled cut at the top of the stem.
4 About a third of the way down this cut, make a second, shallow cut, half an inch into the stock.
Preparation of the scion.
5 In the middle of winter, cut a number of scions from a suitable plant. Heel a bundle of them, six inches deep in the soil.
6 In spring, lift and trim each scion to within four buds of the base.
7 Make an angled cut at the base.
8 Make a second cut to match the rootstock.
Making the graft.
9 Fit the scion and rootstock together and bind with grafting tape. Continue to remove any buds that grow from the stock.

Whatever the method of grafting that you choose, there are five golden rules to be followed:
1 The scion and the stock must be compatible, which generally means that they must be closely related.
2 The cambium of the scion and the stock must be in contact and held tightly together.
3 The scion and the stock must be in the right condition for the method of grafting you are using, which normally means that the scion should have dormant buds, but the condition of the stock depends on the method used.
4 All the cut surfaces of both scion and stock must be covered with grafting tape or wax to prevent them drying out.
5 The new plant needs to be watched carefully as growth begins – the scion may need staking, and any shoots from the stock should be cut back.

Apical-wedge graft

The apical-wedge technique is probably the simplest of all the ways of grafting because the 'carpentry' involved in cutting and fitting the scion and stock is quite easy.

It is used for a variety of shrubs and a great many trees, including the *Cotoneaster*, flowering cherry, rowan and crab-apple. It can also be used to graft tomato plants – in particular, to combine a variety which has tasty fruit and a high yield with a disease-resistant root-stock. In this case the scion is inserted into a cut made in the newly emerged shoot of the root-stock, right down between the cotyledons.

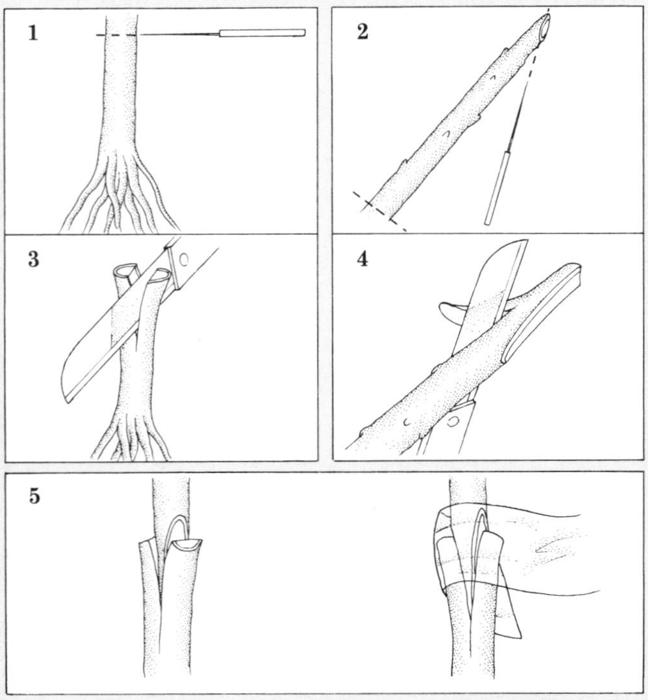

Preparation of the stock.
1 In late winter, choose a rootstock plant, dig it up, gently wash the roots and make a horizontal cut across the top.
2 Make a vertical cut, one and a half inches into the stock.
Preparation of the scion.
Select scions and heel into the ground, as for whip and tongue grafting.
3 In spring, lift the scions and trim the top, leaving four healthy buds.
4 Make two sloping cuts, one each side of base of the scion.
Making the graft.
5 Fit the scion and stock together and bind with grafting tape. A number of grafted plants can be heeled in together, and potted on when the graft has taken.

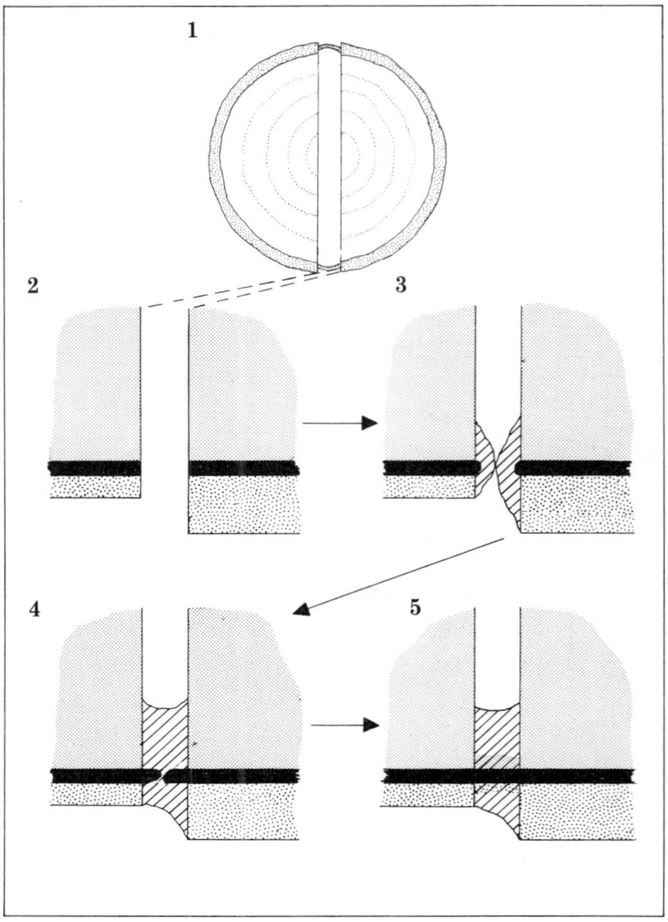

For a graft to be successful, a series of quite complex growth patterns must take place in the tissues of the scion and the stock, as shown in the diagrams above.

A section through an apical wedge graft (1). For the graft to take, the cambium of both parts must be approximately in line and must touch, or very nearly so (2). If these conditions are fulfilled, callus tissue will grow from both scion and stock (3), and will begin to unite the two parts. This callus is undifferentiated tissue, but where it is in line with the two cambial tissues, differentiation takes place and a bridge of cambial cells is formed (4).

Once this cambium has formed (5), it functions and divides as in a normal stem. To the inside of the stem, it forms new xylem cells to transport water and nutrients up the plant and into the scion. To the outside of the stem, it forms new phloem cells. As the scion begins to function, this tissue carries the food that it makes back down to power further root growth.

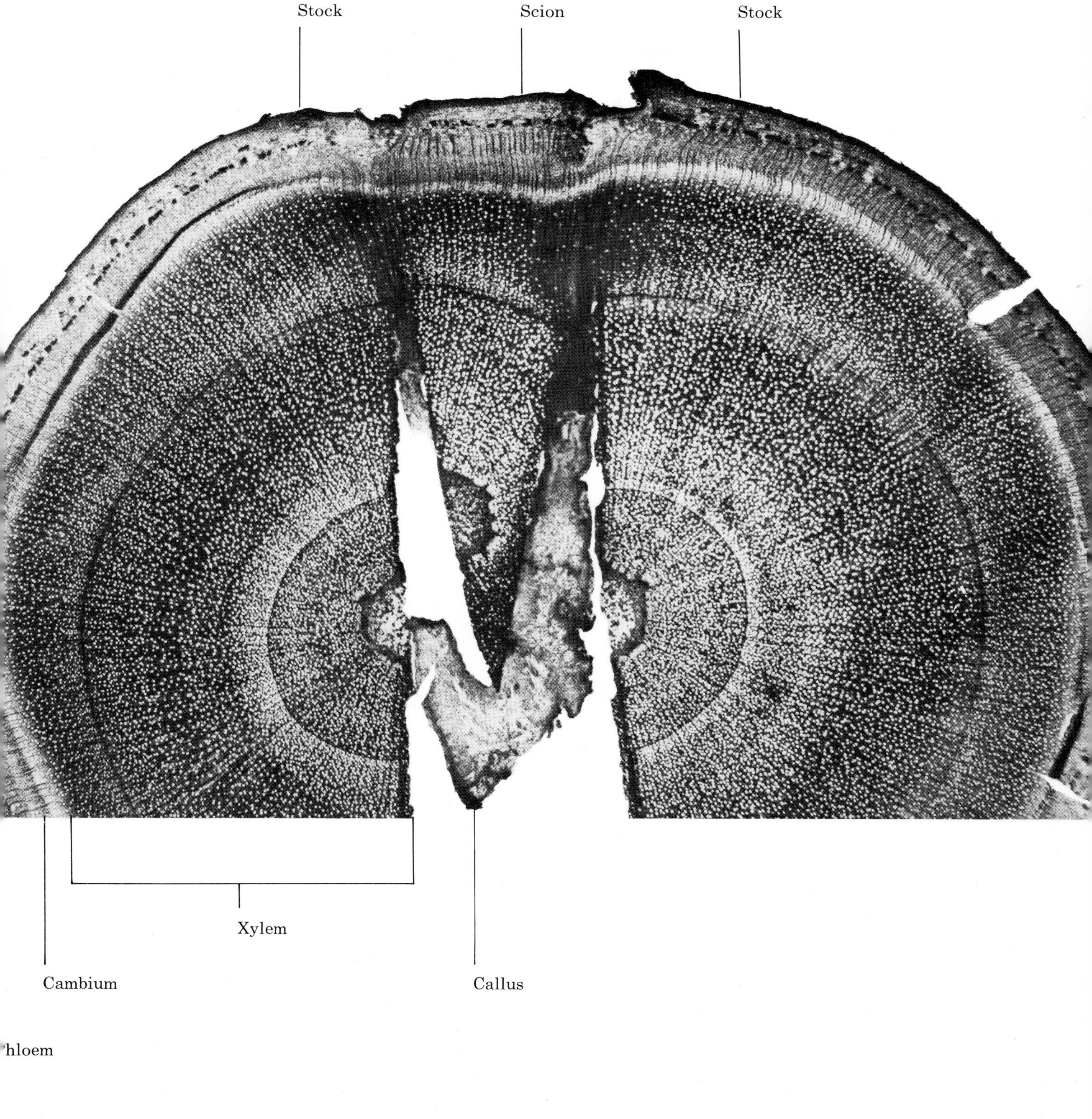

A section through a successful graft. Callus has formed and the cambial tissues have united, in spite of the fact that the cambium of the scion and the cambium of the stock were not precisely in line.

BUDDING

Budding is another form of grafting, mostly used for roses, in which the scion is a bud attached to a slither of stem, just big enough to include the vital cambium. There are obviously far more buds on a plant than there are shoots suitable for grafting, so this method is particularly valuable for a grower who wants to increase his supply of plants as fast as he possibly can.

There must be almost as many different ways of attaching the bud to the stock as there are methods of grafting, but in every case the aim is the same. It is vital that the cambium layers of both scion and stock are pressed closely together. The T-bud and the chip-bud are perhaps the most commonly used, and the simplest to do in the garden.

The garden plant most dependent on budding is the rose. Centuries have been devoted to breeding and cross-breeding, and it must by now be the hybrid *par excellence.* The only way to get another plant of a particular variety is by propagating it vegetatively, and because cuttings taken from hybrids can rarely be persuaded to root, budding has proved the best way.

Every rose-bush that you buy has been 'built' from a root-stock and a bud. The bud comes from another bush of the same variety, and the root-stock is a 'species rose' – something like a wild dog rose – so the combination of the two has the strengths of both, with the lovely flowers of the hybrid and the good roots of the species. You can see how the root-stock would grow every time you remove suckers from the rose bed. Suckers are the shoots which grow from dormant buds on the root-stock. It is important to remove them because they steal the nourishment needed by the cultivated hybrid and, left long enough, will swamp it completely. If this happens, the rose is said to have 'reverted'. If you want to try budding your own roses then you can usually find suitable root-stocks advertised in the gardening press, or you can be entirely independent by growing your own from cuttings, because the species roses will take more easily than hybrids.

The process of breeding a new rose is fascinating. The rose breeder chooses the parent plants, which are bushes from good breeding stock with characteristics that he would like to see in a new rose. He keeps them under glass, in an insect-proof house, and then acts the part of an insect himself, with a paint brush and a little dish of collected pollen, performing perhaps thousands of crosses each season. By about Christmas he has collected all the hips, each holding between three and twenty seeds, and planted the seeds under glass. The ones that germinate can be seen above the soil by early spring, and these grow until they flower for the first time between April and June.

'Pot O'Gold'. A fragrant gold rose, raised in Northern Ireland, that received the National Rose Society's Certificate of Merit in 1979.

Plant Varieties and Seeds Act 1964

This Act works for a plant variety as a patent does for an invention. It means that the breeder of a new variety of any plant species that is named in the order (and that includes roses) can register his new variety by name, and it is then illegal to take buds, grafts, cuttings or anything else from a plant of that variety and grow them on for sale, without a licence. This protects the breeder from 'pirates' who take buds from a new and successful variety and then sell their plants in competition with the breeder himself. The gardener, buying a new rose-bush for the garden, is not at risk because there is no doubt that the pirated roses are the variety they claim to be, but their producer is reaping the benefits from eight or nine year's hard work on the part of the breeder.

Budding a few roses at home, either for interest or to increase your stock, is not affected by the Act, which specifies that plants must be intended for sale.

Two methods of budding

Chip-budding

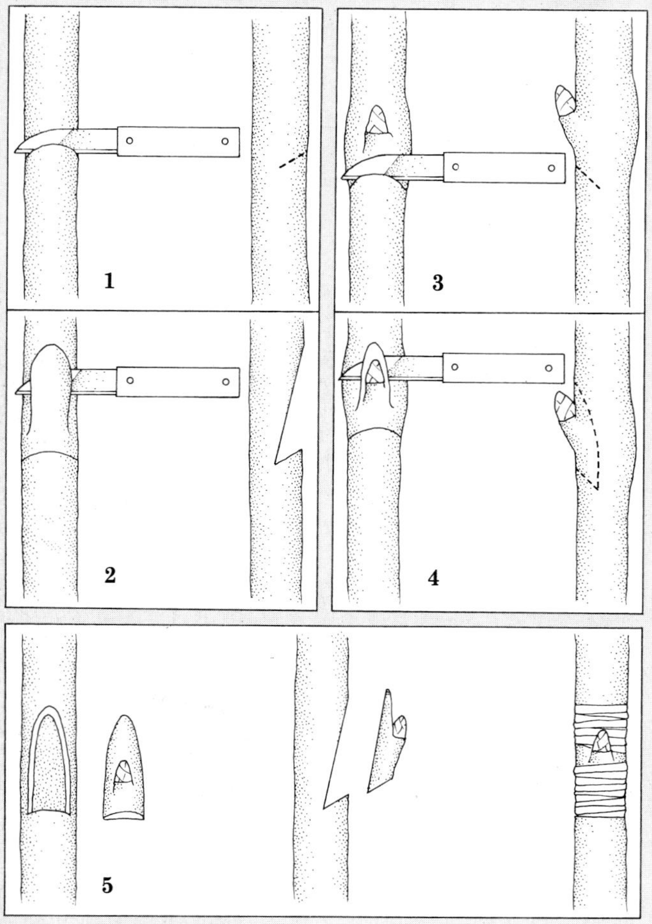

This is probably the easiest way to bud a plant. The cutting of the bud and stock are fairly easy but, even more important, this method provides a very good contact between the cambium of the bud and the stock. Chip-budding is used to propagate a wide variety of plants, including the magnolia and the rose, and can be used at any time of the year providing there are well-matured buds available. A temperature of 10°C (50°F) will ensure that there is a quick union between the bud and the stock.

Prepare the rootstock by making a slightly angled cut ¼ inch into the stem (1) and then making a sloping cut down to it from about an inch and a half higher up the stem (2). Remove a bud by making matching cuts below (3) and then above it (4). Fit the two together and bind firmly with raffia or grafting tape (5).

Once the bud grows, remove the binding and cut the rootstock plant back to just above the new bud.

T-budding

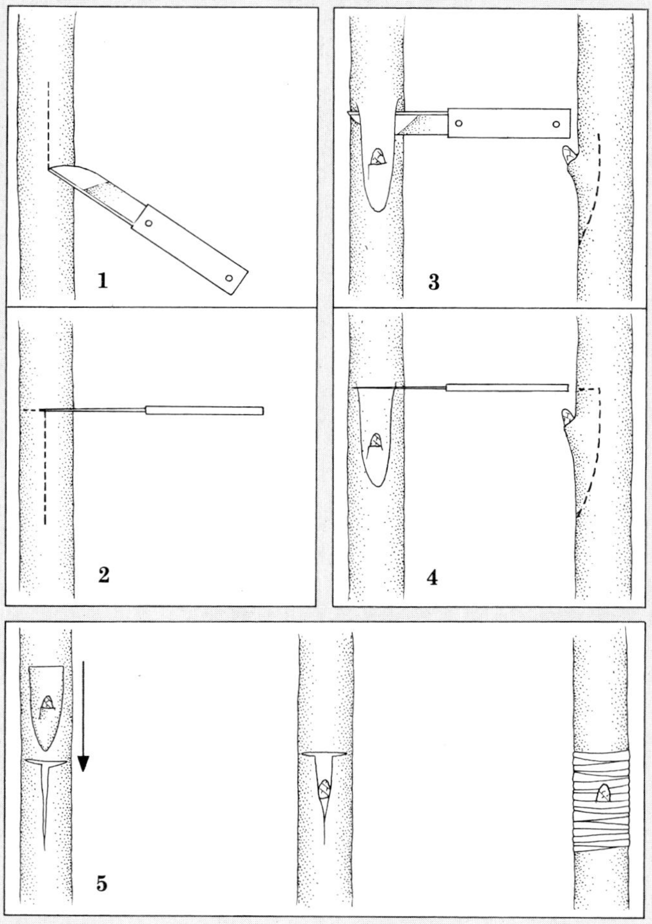

T-budding, or shield budding as it is also called, is the traditional way of budding a rose but it can be used only between May and August, when the bark on the stem of the root-stock can be lifted easily.

Prepare the rootstock by making a T-shaped cut in the bark (1 and 2). Slice beneath a suitable bud (3) and then cut into the stem above to remove it.

Loosen the bark (5) and slide the bud under it, trimming the 'shield' to fit. Bind the bud and stock firmly together.

When the bud grows, remove the binding and cut the rootstock back in the same way as for chip-budding. With roses, the removal of suckers, or buds growing from the rootstock, is particularly important.

From now on the skill of the rose breeder is in selection. He has to examine each of the seedling roses – and there may be hundreds – and begin to decide which of them might be best-sellers. The tiny plants do not look at all like rose-bushes, each one has little more than a single shoot and a flower, so picking out the possible successes of the future is a daunting task. The few that are chosen are then budded on to three or four root-stock plants and put out into the rose fields to see how they look as bushes, how much they succumb to disease and how well they cope with the weather through the changing seasons.

The next year the breeder has to choose again. An even smaller number make the grade this year, and these are budded again on to more root-stocks and the rest thrown out. A rose field is a lovely sight, with row upon row of bushes laden with flowers of every colour, shape and size, but a walk around with the rose breeder can be a depressing business. Standing waist-deep in roses that, to the untrained eye, look quite perfect, he explains that most of them will end up on the bonfire.

After several years of this continual weeding out, selection and reselection, only one or two of the hybrids from a single season remain, and these are the ones that are finally seen in the shops and in the garden. First, however the supply of plants must be built up to meet a possible large demand, and this, again, is done by budding on to root-stock plants. Every bush of a new variety that reaches the shops is directly descended from a seedling that was one of the chosen few in the first year of breeding. Each one is budded from a bush that was budded from a bush – and so on, back to that first plant.

Budding and grafting will work only if the scion and the stock are compatible. Broadly speaking, the more closely two plants are related, the more likely it is that a successful graft can be made between them. Varieties within a species will usually graft, although species within a genus are less reliable. Genera within a family can sometimes be grafted, but it is usually considered impossible to graft between families. However, when plants are compatible, when they can be grafted together, there is no reason to stop at two. 'Family trees' can be grown – or constructed, perhaps – by grafting together a plum, a peach and an apricot, or several varieties of apple or of pear. These are sold specifically for small gardens, but, whatever the space available, there is some excitement in being able to pick two or three different fruits or varieties of fruit from one tree and some achievement in using the natural responses of the plant to produce one of the wonders of the garden world.

CHAPTER SIX

THE GOOD EARTH

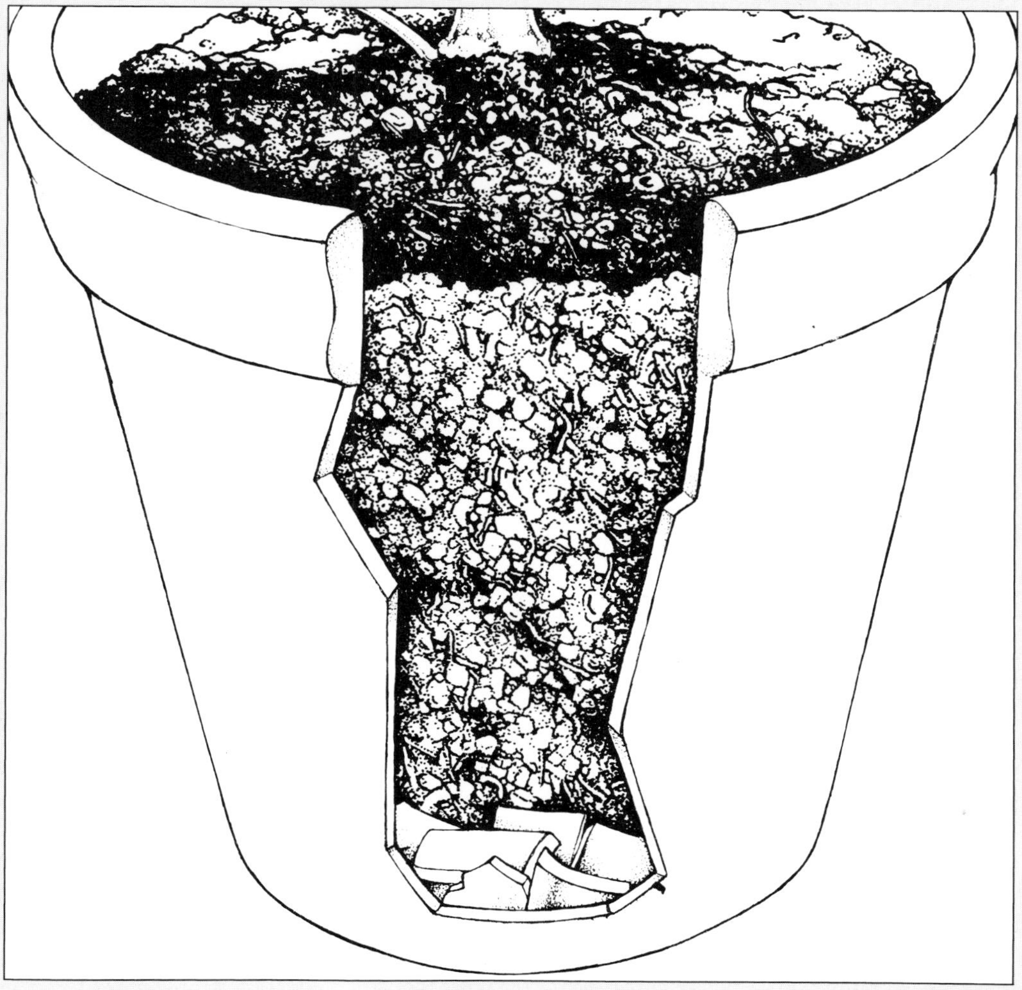

Soil is the raw material from which the dreams of a gardener grow into reality – or not, as the case may be. Every garden, however discouraging it looks, has a soil with a great potential, and with time and work most plants can be grown in it. However the soil also imposes limitations, and the individuality of a garden depends on exploiting the raw material to the best of its potential – on working with nature rather than against it.

Every soil is made up of two main parts. It contains organic material, called 'humus', and inorganic particles, and these two together make up a world which holds water, has its own soil atmosphere and supports an enormous population of both animals and plants.

The inorganic part of the soil is made from ground-up bits of rock. In some cases the character of these tiny rock fragments depends on the underlying geology, on the nature of the bedrock below the garden. In other cases they may have a different origin. Thousands of years ago major ice movements carried huge masses of smashed and broken rock across many miles of country. These glaciers came from the north, and reached down into Britain as far as a line drawn between East Anglia and the Bristol Channel. When the ice melted, the ground-up mixture of rock that it carried was just dropped and left where the glacier had stood, so if you live in the northern part of the country your soil may well depend on rocks transported in the glacial deposits.

Whatever its origin, the inorganic component of the soil makes a big difference to the garden. Soils on limestone, for example, are alkaline. They have a high pH value, and a soil like this will restrict the choice of plants that you can grow without some rather drastic treatment (see Chapter 1, page 18). In particular, the inorganic part of the soil affects the ease or difficulty with which you can dig. The important factor is the size of the particles. To a soil scientist there are three different sizes of soil particle – small, medium and large – defined as follows:
Small – less than 0·002 mm in diameter, called clays.
Medium – 0·002–0·02 mm in diameter, called silts.
Large – 0·2–2·0 mm in diameter, called sands.
Anything bigger than 2·0mm across is considered as a pebble and is ignored when assessing the sizes of the particles that make up a soil sample.

Predictably enough, a sandy soil is one that contains mostly large particles, and a clay contains mostly the smallest particles. A loam, which is the ideal soil for any gardener, has just about the right mixture of the two and some medium-sized silts as well. You can assess the particle mixture of your own soil quite easily – and, fortunately, without having to measure any particles – but what do the results mean for your garden and how can you alter your soil to give your plants the best conditions possible, for their growth and development?

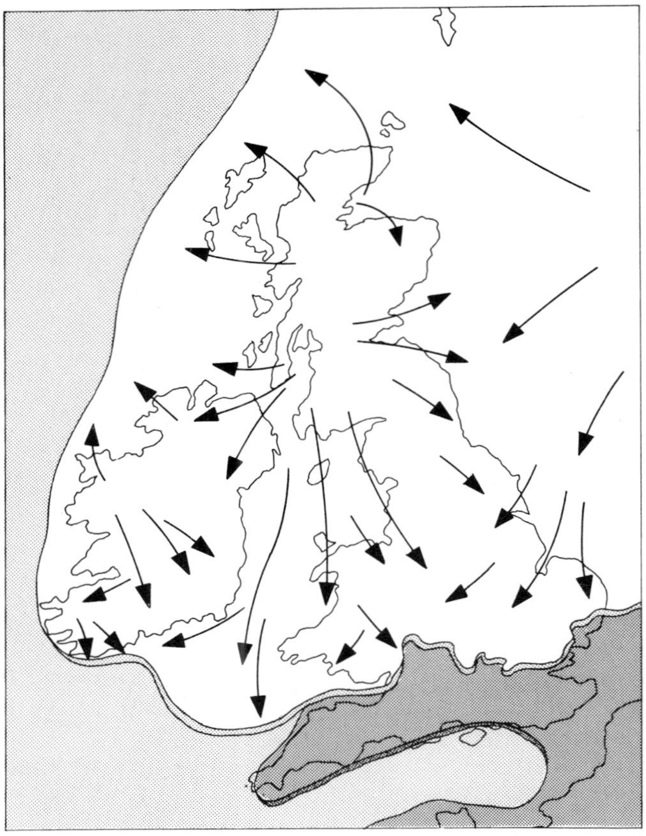

The extent of the ice in Britain. The soil in this area today may be a product of glaciation.

A CLAY SOIL

If you have a clay soil, you will not need telling that it is heavy to dig. However, most of the weight that you feel when you strain at a spadeful of clay is water. Water is held in soil in two ways. Firstly, it is held in small spaces between the particles that make up the soil; and secondly, it is held as a very thin film around every particle. The water in the spaces is called 'available water', and can be taken up out of the soil by the roots of plants; the thin film around each particle remains held fast by strong attractive forces between the water and the molecules of the particle. No matter how much a plant growing in the soil wilts, the water in the film around the particles remains unavailable, stuck in the soil and useless to the plant. Clay has a large number of small particles so it contains a lot of both available and unavailable water.

The tiny clay particles also carry minute electrical charges which attract them to one another, so when you dig a clay soil and it feels 'sticky', that is actually just what it is. The strong cohesion among the clay particles makes it very hard to break the soil up and get a good tilth.

Stereoscan pictures of soil. The two upper photos are × 24 and the two lower ones are × 240. The soil on the right hand side is a sandy loam and contains much larger particles than the soil on the left, which is a clay loam.

A SANDY SOIL

A sandy soil, by contrast, has particles which are either rounded or angular in shape and do not pack closely together. They are not, like clay particles, held together by any cohesive forces, and, because there are large spaces between them, drainage is good. Indeed, drainage is often too good, because the water percolates swiftly through the soil carrying the nutrients needed by the plants with it. The soil left behind has little fertility; it dries out much too readily, but it is at least light to work.

The gardener is not the only one to find a light, loose soil an asset. Plant roots have to grow between the particles of soil, and if the spaces available are narrower than the diameter of the root, then the root has to force its way between them. A compacted soil with small spaces resists growth and leads to stunted roots. Internally the growth and structure of the root is quite distorted, and externally the overall volume of the roots, the size of the root 'ball', is much too small and the roots may never get down to the water-table. Annuals suffer most, because perennials can apply the kind of slow but sure pressure that shifts paving stones over a number of years, but all plants do better if their roots can grow unimpeded through a loose, well-aerated soil.

The large spaces between the particles contain tiny pockets of air, and this soil atmosphere is very important. Roots need to breathe and, if there are not enough air spaces or (as easily happens in a clay soil) the spaces are flooded with water and the soil is waterlogged, then the roots will slowly suffocate.

The soil population – the millions of organisms that live in the soil and increase its fertility – also need air. The sheer quantity of life in a spadeful of good soil is quite astonishing, and loamy soils contain the most. Soil organisms need water and air, just like garden plants, so a very sandy soil, which drains so well that it holds hardly any water at all, and a clay soil, which has plenty of water but very little air, cannot support a large population of soil organisms any better than they would support a large population of garden plants, without the help of the gardener.

What kind of soil have you got?

Take a handful of top-soil, and shake it thoroughly with water in a large test tube or any other glass bottle or jar that has straight sides. If the soil remains in a stubborn lump and refuses to break up, either keep stirring until it does or try again, this time breaking up the handful of soil in a pestle and mortar or even with the back of a spoon, before putting it in water. After a good shake, leave the bottle of soil for a couple of hours to settle.

The heaviest particles fall to the bottom first, so any small pebbles in the sample make up the first layer, followed by the largest mineral particles and then all the others in order of size. The very fine clay particles will remain in suspension, making the water look milky, or just plain muddy, depending on how much clay you have. They will finally settle if left undisturbed for a few days. Organic matter usually floats on the surface of the water, or sometimes settles on top of the mineral particles. Once the sample has settled, you can look at the way the layers of particles have fallen and assess the make-up of your soil. (See colour photo on page 120.)

The centipede is one of the many beneficial animals that live in the soil.

THE SOIL POPULATION

In the soil you will find largish animals, like centipedes, millipedes, leather-jackets, springtails and an assortment of worms, along with an enormous number of much smaller organisms – mites, fungi and microscopic bacteria. Some of them are villains and pests, but the vast majority do far more good than they do harm in your garden, and some of them are essential to its well-being. Some of the bigger animals contribute to the porosity of the soil, keeping up the air content and easing root growth by their burrowing activities. Earthworm casts may be a nuisance when mowing a damp lawn, but they contain many soil nutrients and crumble to make a good top dressing when they are dry. Underneath the lawn, the activities of the worms more than compensate for their unsightly casts on the surface. Not only do they ease root growth by their burrowing, but they also pull organic matter down from the surface and more or less dig it in for you.

The multitude of microscopic animals and plants in the soil also benefits the gardener by working away at the organic matter, or humus. They break this down for their own food, but in doing so they release valuable nutrients that are locked up in the humus and that are needed by the plants. That is why humus disappears or is 'burned up'. The burning is nothing to do with the heat of the sun but with the activity of micro-organisms.

Somewhere between the two extremes of sand and clay there is the soil that every gardener dreams about. All soil management is directed towards building up a good, loamy soil which will retain water without becoming waterlogged, hold an atmosphere without losing its nutrient solution and support a large and healthy population of soil organisms. In fact, what we want is a soil which has the advantages of both clay and sand without any of their problems. It does not happen often, but, however difficult the soil you have, it can be improved. Strangely, the same treatment is best for both sandy and clay soils, although for different reasons. That treatment is the addition of humus, in the form of compost, manure, spent hops, anything you can get hold of, providing it increases the organic content of your soil.

In a clay garden, adding humus breaks down the electrical charges that hold the tiny particles together, causing them to 'clump' or aggregate together into groups. This improves the soil structure, increases aeration and gets rid of the 'sticky' feel that

Some of the many mites that benefit the soil by breaking down organic matter to release valuable nutrients. The photo on the left is × 50 while that on the right is × 100.

makes digging a clay soil such hard work. Gypsum (also called calcium sulphate) and lime have much the same effect, but compost and manure contain nutrients and so benefit the soil in two ways. The traditional practice of autumn digging also helps to break the bonds that hold the clay particles together by exposing them to the action of frost. The breakdown of clay soil is hindered when you walk on it; particularly if it is wet, you succeed only in packing the particles more tightly than ever. When a compacted, puddled clay soil dries out, it is like iron and absolutely hopeless as far as plants are concerned. A clay garden works best if you plan small beds with paths between them so that you do not need to tread on the soil at all.

The worst aspect of a sandy soil is its inability to retain water. This quickly drains through, carrying the soil nutrients with it. Humus helps to retain water – and therefore nutrients – and the manure or compost will also help replace some of the food already lost.

Adding organic matter to any soil is to mimic Mother Nature at her best. In a natural community of plants in the wild there is a constant recycling of nutrients, as dead material is broken down by microscopic organisms that live in the soil and eventually released for the benefit of the plants that grow there. The plants use just the amount of nutrient that is available from the continual weathering of the bedrock below as well as the recycling of waste material from above. There is a perfect balance.

As gardeners, we do not want to mimic this balance too closely, because it can be maintained only when nothing is taken away from the environment – and a vegetable garden in which nothing was ever picked would be foolish, to say the least. Every crop that is picked in the garden has taken something from the soil, and that 'something' has to be replaced if the quality of both the soil and the plants that grow in it is to be kept up. Chemical fertilisers can replace the soil nutrients used by the plants, but in the long run all soils benefit from the application of organic matter as well. The best way to do this is by means of the compost heap.

Some gardening writers manage to give the impression that building a compost heap is the prerogative of 'eco-freaks' and those wishing to become self-sufficient. According to them, all you need to keep your garden in the peak of condition is a sprinkling of this and a handful of that, all easily obtainable at your local garden centre. Nothing could be further from the truth. The Royal Botanic Gardens at Kew maintain a compost heap described by the curator as being 'as big as a house', and containing not only their own garden waste but also fallen leaves from other gardens and parks in London. They do buy chemical fertilisers, but they certainly appreciate the importance of recycling their own garden waste.

On an infinitely smaller scale, kitchen rubbish, together with clippings, prunings and plant remains can be used in a recycling process which benefits the whole garden. Compost enthusiasts grow all their crops without any chemical fertilisers at all, making up the discrepancy between what the plants need and what can be collected in kitchen and garden waste by getting hold of extra organic material, something like farmyard manure. Even the most urban gardener will find that a compost heap pays dividends, although it may not entirely eliminate the need for chemical fertilisers.

In nature, the build-up of dead, organic material on the soil is part of the maintenance of a stable soil system, but in the garden, any progress that may be made towards such a system is completely destroyed each autumn when the garden is dug. A lot of people now believe that the usual practice of digging the garden annually does more harm than good. As this digging is one of the most arduous tasks of the entire gardening year, any theory that calls upon us to abandon it has its appeal, but devotees argue that there is more to it than letting you off some hard work and a stiff back. When you dig the soil you undoubtedly increase aeration and expose a good area of soil to the crumbling action of frost. On the other hand, you destroy the burrows painstakingly channelled by the earthworms, which would have aerated the soil just as well if left to themselves, and when you put a good layer of humus on top of the soil you improve its surface texture just as much as the frost would. In addition, digging redistributes nutrients in the soil, perhaps burying them beyond the reach of the plants that need them, and it must play havoc with the routine of all the other soil organisms, some of which live only in the top few centimetres of soil. When they suddenly find themselves buried at three or four times that depth, they probably give up altogether.

In agriculture, much has been made of the comparison between crop yields from land that has been ploughed and then sown in the conventional way, and land that has been sown by 'direct drilling' without ploughing. The argument still continues but it seems that, on clay soils at least, the results from direct drilling are just as good as those from ploughed land, and the crops cost less to grow because the time and expense of ploughing are saved. When a field is to be drilled without being ploughed, the stubble is burned off and any weeds that germinate later are killed with a chemical herbicide.

Building a compost heap

There must be almost as many ways of building a compost heap as there are compost heaps, because no two gardeners seem to agree on the best possible way. At one end of the scale the relationship between gardener and compost is reminiscent of that between nurse and invalid, with thermometers and constant attention, whereas at the other end there is a pile of garden rubbish in a corner which will, eventually, rot.

Organic waste materials are decomposed by the action of bacteria, and these bacteria need air, water and nitrogen, so these are the conditions that you need to provide within the compost heap. The bacteria live in the soil, so the heap should be built on to bare earth. This will also allow earthworms to crawl up into the heap and keep it well mixed. It is easier and tidier to keep the compost in some kind of bin but, whether you make or buy one, there must be plenty of holes in the sides to allow ventilation. Some gardeners always start their compost heaps with a layer of branches and twigs, which helps to keep air circulating underneath. However you start, you should then add the material for composting until you have a level layer about 6 to 10 inches deep. At this point opinions vary about the best steps to take. If you cover the first layer with an inch of garden soil you will be introducing more bacteria, and this will speed up decomposition. You can also help the bacteria by adding a layer of something rich in nitrogen – manure is best, or bonemeal, or a commercial 'compost activator', or a handful of an inorganic fertiliser. If you have an acid soil, you can keep the compost sweet by including a little lime, but do not add nitrogen and lime at the same time.

Continue building the compost heap with layers of waste and layers of soil or an activator until you get to the top. Do not add a huge layer of any one thing, like lawn clippings, because this will form a waterlogged, airtight mat, but try to keep the compost material within each layer thoroughly mixed. The heap should be kept moist but not soaking wet. It needs to generate heat, both to speed up the breakdown of the waste and to kill any disease spores and weed seeds it contains. A very small heap will have a large surface area by comparison with its not very large volume, so it will tend to lose too much heat. Somewhere between three and five feet is about right for the length, width and depth. If you have a small heap which will not get to a very high temperature, then you should burn the seeding heads of weeds and the rhizomes of plants like bindweed which may survive the compost and need pulling up all over again. When you get to the top of the bin, cover the compost with a final layer of soil or manure and then with either black polythene sheeting or a piece of carpet. Leave it for between three and six months and you should have compost fit for a king – and certainly ideal for the garden. If you build two, or even three bins, then you can use them in rotation and will always have compost ready.

Almost anything of organic origin will eventually rot, but animal waste, fish bones and the like will take longer to break down, smell horrible and will probably make your garden a Mecca for every cat in the area. The best material for a compost is healthy, green vegetation. Plants which have been sprayed with persistent chemicals should be left out, and it is as well to avoid anything that is diseased, in case the virus or spores survive to infect another crop. In particular, potato foliage with blight, Brassicas with clubroot and onion with white rot are all a bad risk and should be burned, although the ash can go on the compost after the bonfire.

The same green waste that goes on to the compost heap would be decomposed by the same bacteria with just the same beneficial effect if it were dug straight into the soil. The problem is that when the bacteria make the compost they use a lot of nitrogen, and if they are doing this in the soil, they are using nitrogen that would otherwise be available for the plants. In the long run, the nitrogen is released and returned to the soil when the bacteria die, but, meanwhile, the plants suffer a deficit of a very important nutrient.

1 A simple bin of wire netting.
2 A converted oil drum, with both ends knocked out and ventilation holes cut in the wall.
3 A plastic bin, with sliding panels so you can hope to use compost from the bottom while still adding raw materials at the top.
4 A frame of wooden planks keeps the compost warm and gaps between them provide ventilation. A double bin allows you to make compost in one side and use it from the other.

1

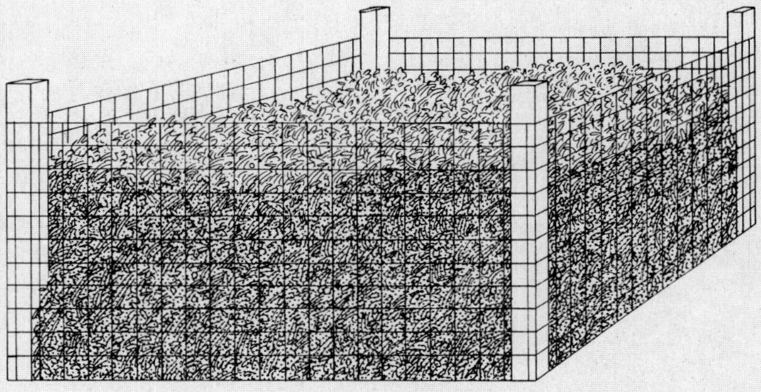

2

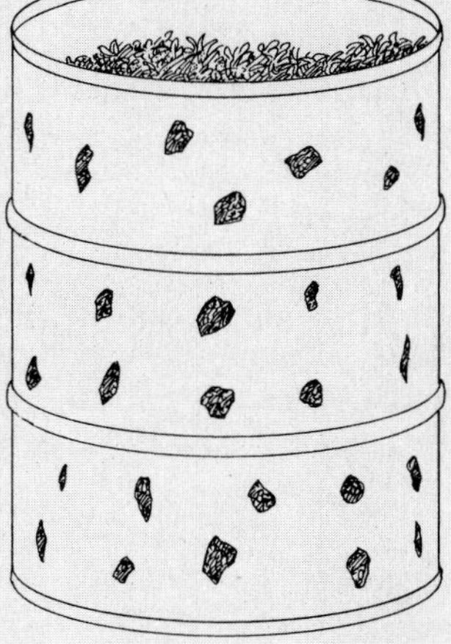

3

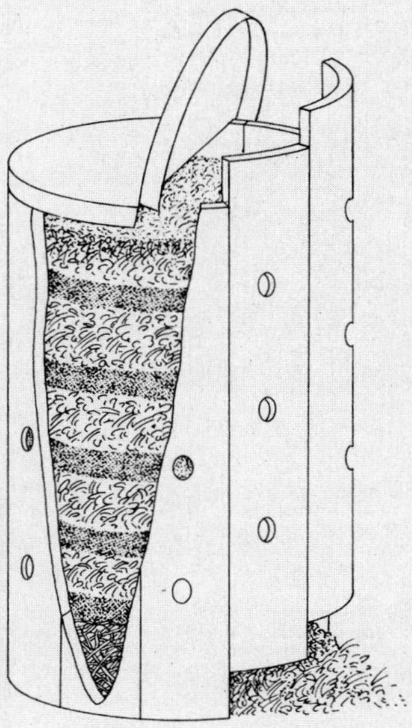

4

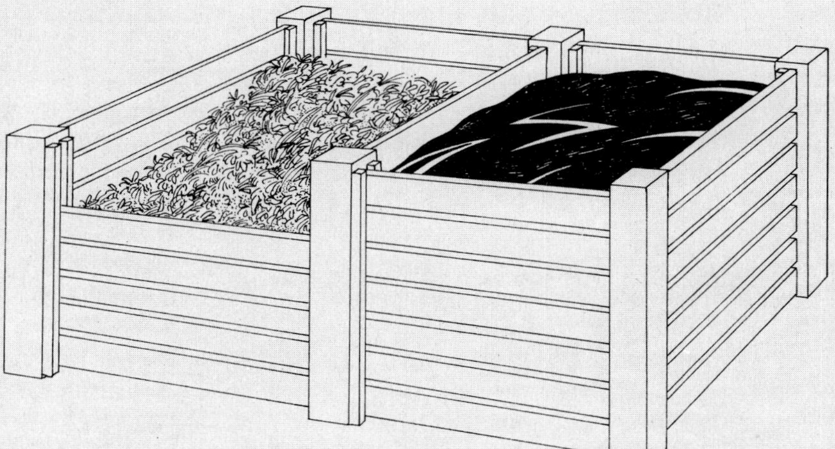

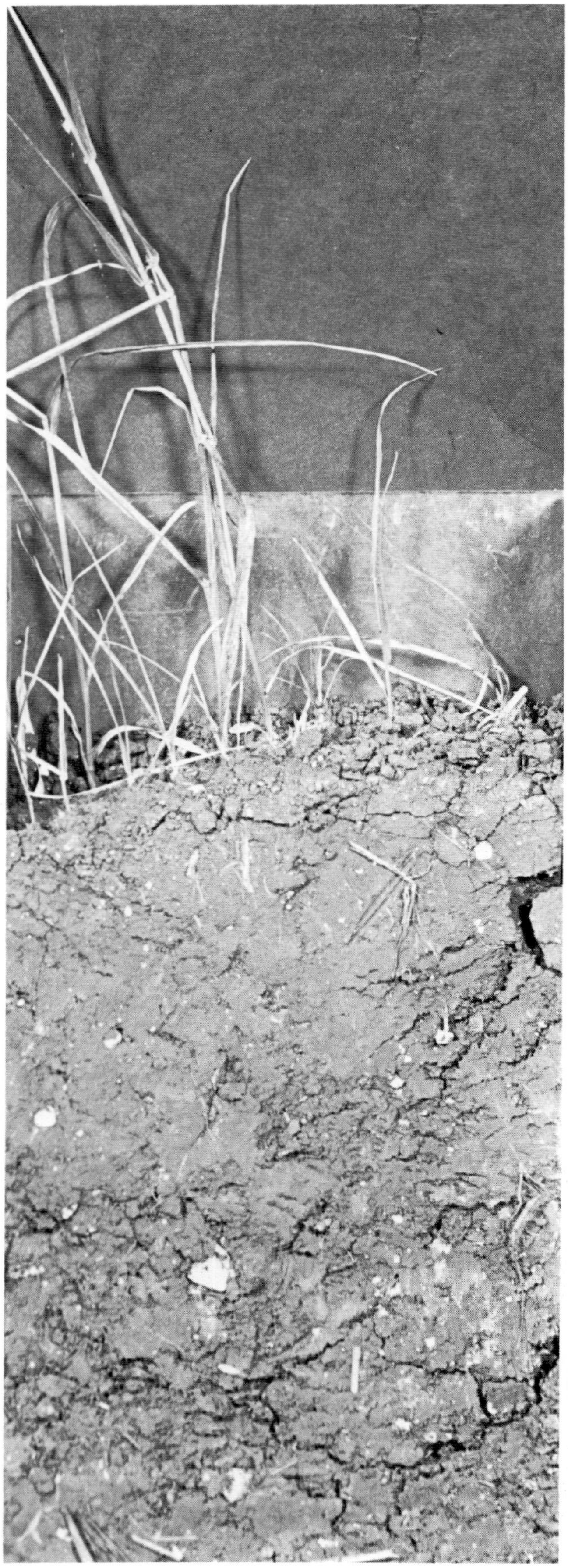

(Opposite page.) An experiment performed at the Rothamsted Experimental Station to demonstrate the way in which the burrowing of earthworms facilitates root growth. Two containers of soil were sterilised, so that all the organisms living in them were killed. A few earthworms were then added to one of the containers and both were planted with a cereal. The results are dramatic. The plants in the pot on the left, which did not contain worms, are very small, with hardly any roots visible. The pot on the right did contain worms, which have aerated the soil and allowed extensive root growth, making the plants in this pot much larger and healthier.

(This page, below.) A earthworm on the soil surface. (Right.) An earthworm pulling surface debris down into its burrow. This 'digging' greatly improves the organic content of the soil.

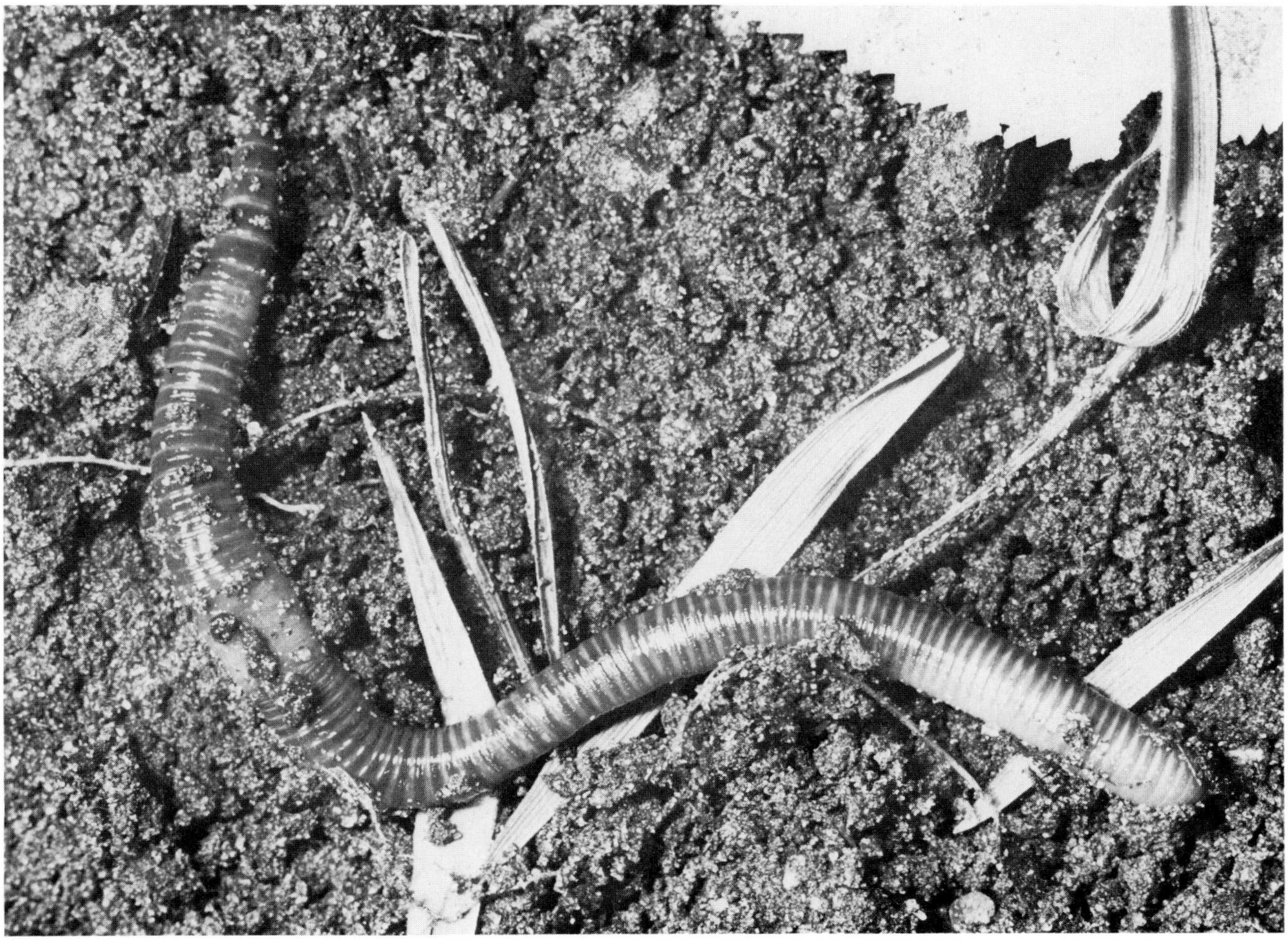

TO DIG OR NOT TO DIG?

This controversy continues into the garden. Supporters of a 'no-dig' philosophy maintain the fertility and structure of their soil by adding a layer of humus to the top-soil, just as would happen in nature. The key to success is that the beds are never trodden down or compressed in any way. The point is that although the annual dig does some damage, it does at least loosen the soil and allow decent root penetration. If you are going to rely on the work of earthworms and other soil animals to maintain the structure of your soil, then it is vital that you keep your feet off their burrows. If you crush their burrows and compact the soil by walking over it, the soil will not be aerated and the garden is doomed.

One way of managing a garden, without digging, is by using 'deep beds'. These contain very loosely packed soil with a lot of humus which gives them a large volume and raises them above the level of the surrounding paths. If you can construct small beds with paths right around each one and then keep yourself and everybody else strictly to these paths, your deep-bed garden could be very successful. Because the soil is soft and crumbly, root growth tends to be straight down rather than spread out around the plant, so plants can be grown closer together than usual. This obviously increases the crop, particularly with root vegetables, and certainly compensates for the growing space lost in building all the paths. Plants like tomatoes and peas that need an enormous amount of light cannot be planted too closely, whatever their roots are doing, because it increases the shade around them, so these do not show any change in crop yields. Interestingly, even the plants like Brassicas, which are normally trodden very firmly into the ground, do well in deep beds. It seems to be enough to plant deeply and to firm the soil around the stem when the plants go in.

(This page.) A well established deep bed garden.
Opposite page. (Top left.) Two carnations, one standing in water and one in ink, to show the 'veins' through which water is transported. (See page 111.)
(Centre left.) Ripening fruit exudes a minor growth substance called ethylene. When a single ripe tomato is shut in a closed box with unripe fruit, the ethylene it gives off will speed up the ripening of the rest. (See Chapter 4.)
(Bottom left) A natural soil profile in a heathland area. (See pages 95–96.)
(Top right.) A grafted ornamental, copper-leaved cherry, with green-leaved branches growing from the rootstock at ground level. (See pages 83–87.)
(Bottom right.) The Monstera, *or Swiss cheese plant, only flowers and fruits when it reaches a height of about sixty feet, so you are unlikely to see your house plant in this condition!*

Starting a deep-bed garden

The first step in converting a garden to deep beds is to plan their size and position. The width of each bed must be no more than twice the distance that you can reach from the path, so that you can get at every inch of it from one side or the other. That means that the maximum is about five feet. The length can be whatever you like, bearing in mind that you will have to walk right around the bed every time you need to cross it, so long beds mean a lot of walking.

The initial digging is hard work, so it may be easier to convert one bed at a time, rather than tackling the whole garden. The first step is very like the 'bastard trenching' that many people use each year when doing the autumn digging, but for a deep bed it is vital to incorporate a good layer of manure and to loosen the subsoil a little, by poking a fork into the bottom of each trench and shifting it about.

If you collect all the stones in the soil as you dig, they can be used to 'pave' the paths that run between the beds. The width of these paths is a matter of taste. The narrower they are, the more room there is for vegetables, but if you use a barrow regularly then they will need to be wide enough to accommodate that – say, about eighteen inches.

Over the years the beds get deeper and deeper as compost and manure are added to them, and the paths begin to look like little valleys between them. If your garden is on a hill, it is a good idea to dig the beds and the paths across the slope rather than down it, in the same way that a farmer ploughs around a hill rather than over it. This helps to cut down soil erosion in heavy rain.

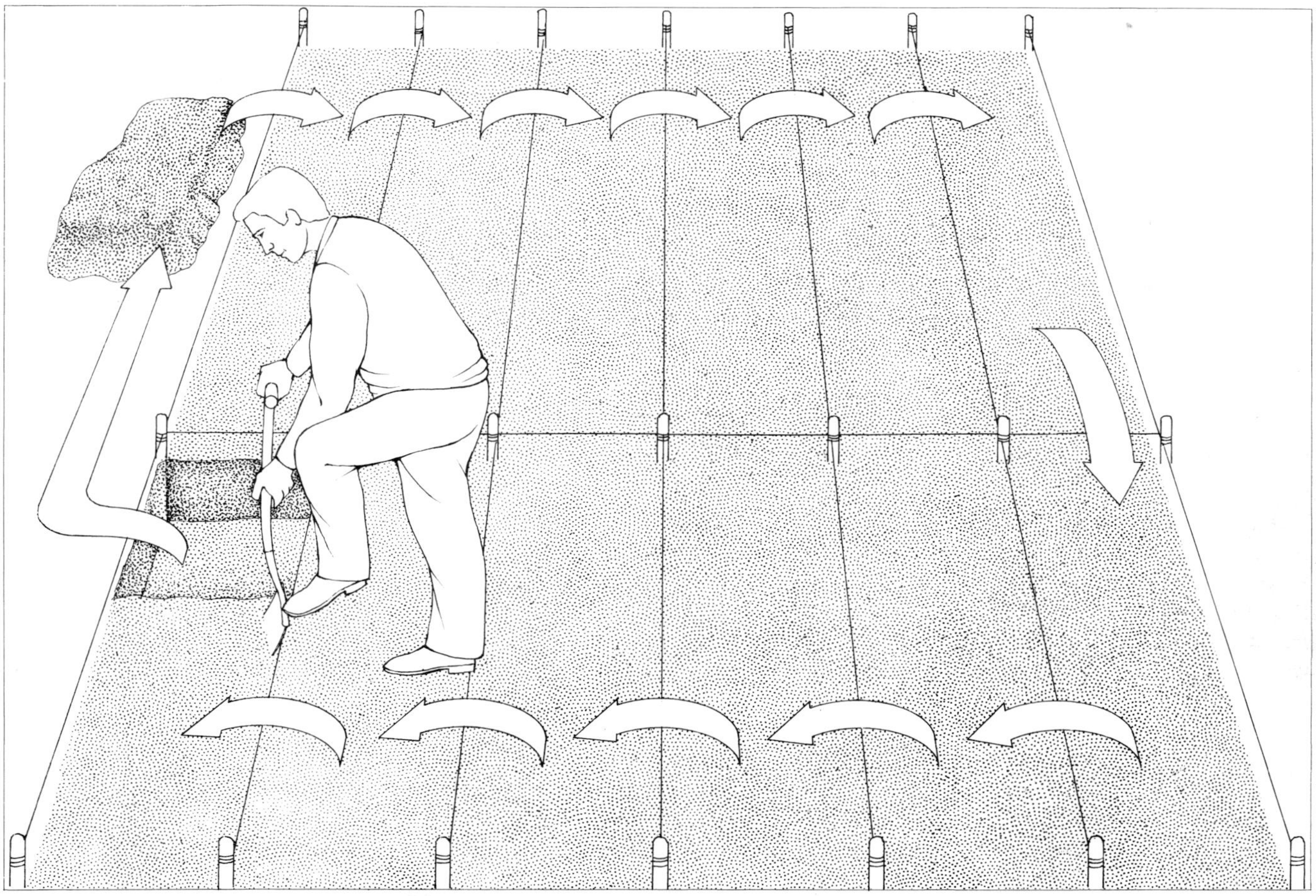

(Above.) Bastard trenching. Start by digging one trench and then fill it with soil from the next, so that all the earth is circulated around the pilot.
Opposite page. (Top and centre left.) The leaves of these trees are not all the same shade of green, but they do all contain chlorophyll and photosynthesise in order to feed the plant. (See Chapter 9.)
(Top right.) The white shaggy cap fungus does not contain chlorophyll and cannot feed itself.
(Bottom.) Two parasitic plants that do not contain chlorophyll and are dependent on their hosts for food. On the left, the lesser dodder, which is twining around ling, and on the right, broomrape, which is parasitic on an ivy. (See page 140.)

Deep beds are an attractive proposition for the gardener, because the yields are impressive and the labour they involve is rather less than a conventional garden, once the beds are established. Conversion to a deep-bed demands one very heavy, deep dig to start it off, but from then on it is much less work than usual. Because the plants grow closer together, their leaves shelter the earth from evaporation, so watering is less. There is less room for weeds because of the close planting – and any that do grow can be pulled out with ease because of the loose, crumbly texture of the soil. (Incidentally, they too will have impressive roots.) Another attraction – less practical, perhaps, but an attraction all the same – is that deep beds are much closer to the natural and continually developing soil profile. They narrow the gap, just a little, between the unnatural garden and the world outside.

Maximising planting space

You can sow seed straight into a deep bed, but, because you need to plant very accurately in order to make the maximum use of space, it is generally easier to grow seeds in boxes or a seed bed and transplant the seedlings. The best way to get close spacing in deep beds – as in any other type of garden – is by planting in diagonal rows rather than right-angled ones. This leaves the same amount of space between the plants in every direction, and cuts to a minimum the ground that is wasted.

If you need to walk between rows to weed or look after the crop then you cannot plant like this, but for deep beds, as there are paths to walk on at all times anyway, it is ideal. Using this arrangement, deep beds have been successfully cultivated with three or four times as many plants as could have been grown in rows in a conventional bed. A density as high as that needs a lot of good compost, and in your first year, when the deep beds are new and have had only one dressing of compost, it might be better to compromise with only twice as many plants as usual. Even that is a much better return for labour than a garden cultivated in the conventional way.

In a closely planted single row the plants have to share the water and nutrients within their reach and their growth is limited (1). They grow best if they have sole possession of the area penetrated by their roots (2). Planting several parallel rows like this (3), wastes an enormous amount of space, but this empty ground can be minimised by planting in diagonal rows (4).

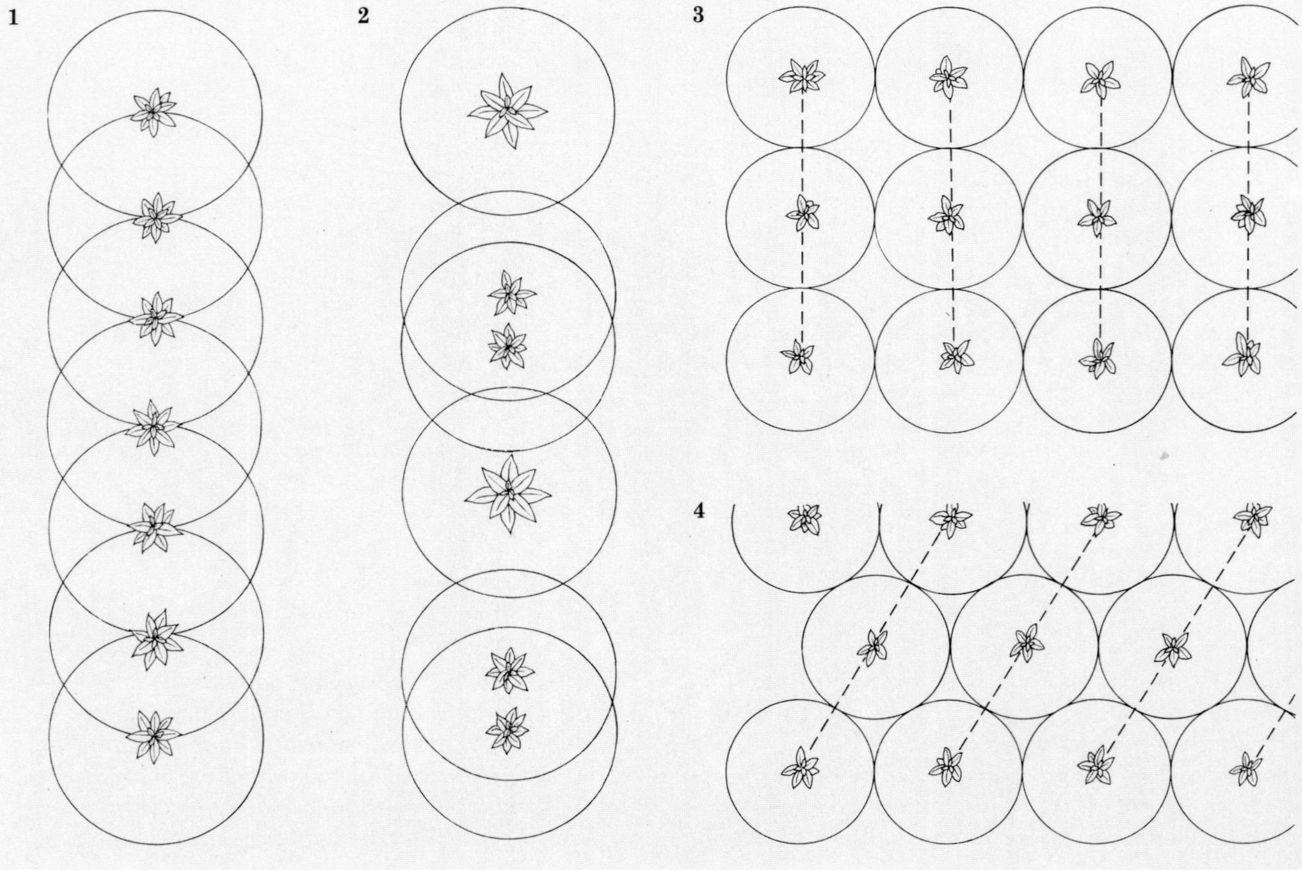

CHAPTER SEVEN

PIPES AND PLUMBING

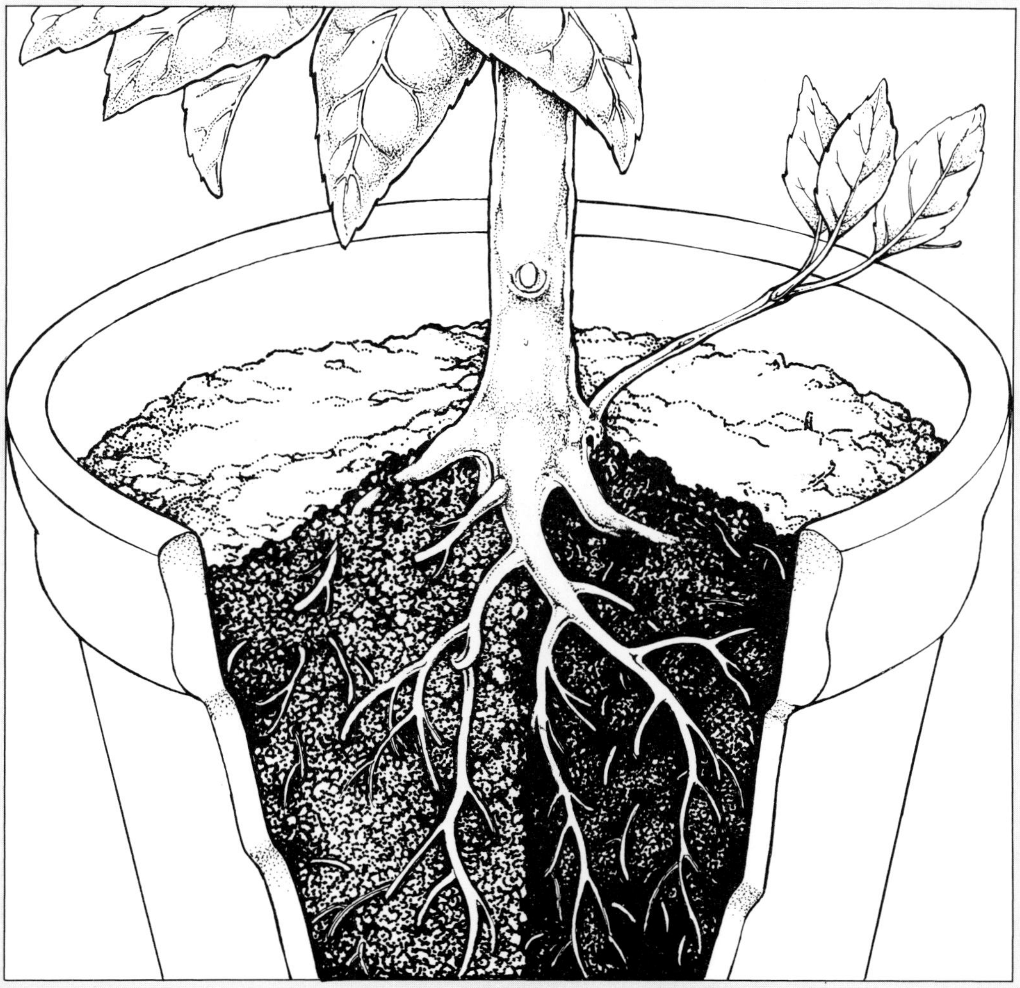

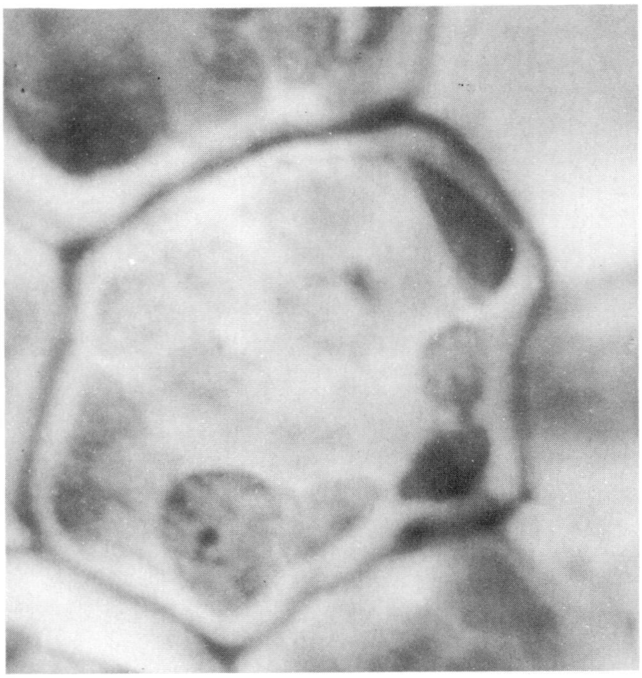

(Above.) A typical plant cell.

One of the most important things taken by a plant from the soil in which it grows is water. The amount that each plant uses varies a great deal. A tomato plant, in the course of a hot, sunny day, will take up about half a gallon. That sounds a great deal, particularly when you are struggling with a brimming watering can to cope with the demand, but it pales into insignificance beside the needs of a mature oak, which, on the same day, could get through fifty gallons in a single hour and two hundred gallons during the day.

Unlike human beings, who can rush to the tap to quench their thirst, plants are firmly anchored, so water loss is a real threat. The most vulnerable plants are the herbaceous ones, and that includes most of the garden plants, because as much as nine-tenths of their weight is made up of water. Most of this is contained in the plant's cells. The life of the plant depends on these cells – small units which, like building blocks, make up the plant. As it grows and expands, its cells become differentiated or specialised to perform all the processes and functions that it needs, so the mature plant contains cells of many different kinds.

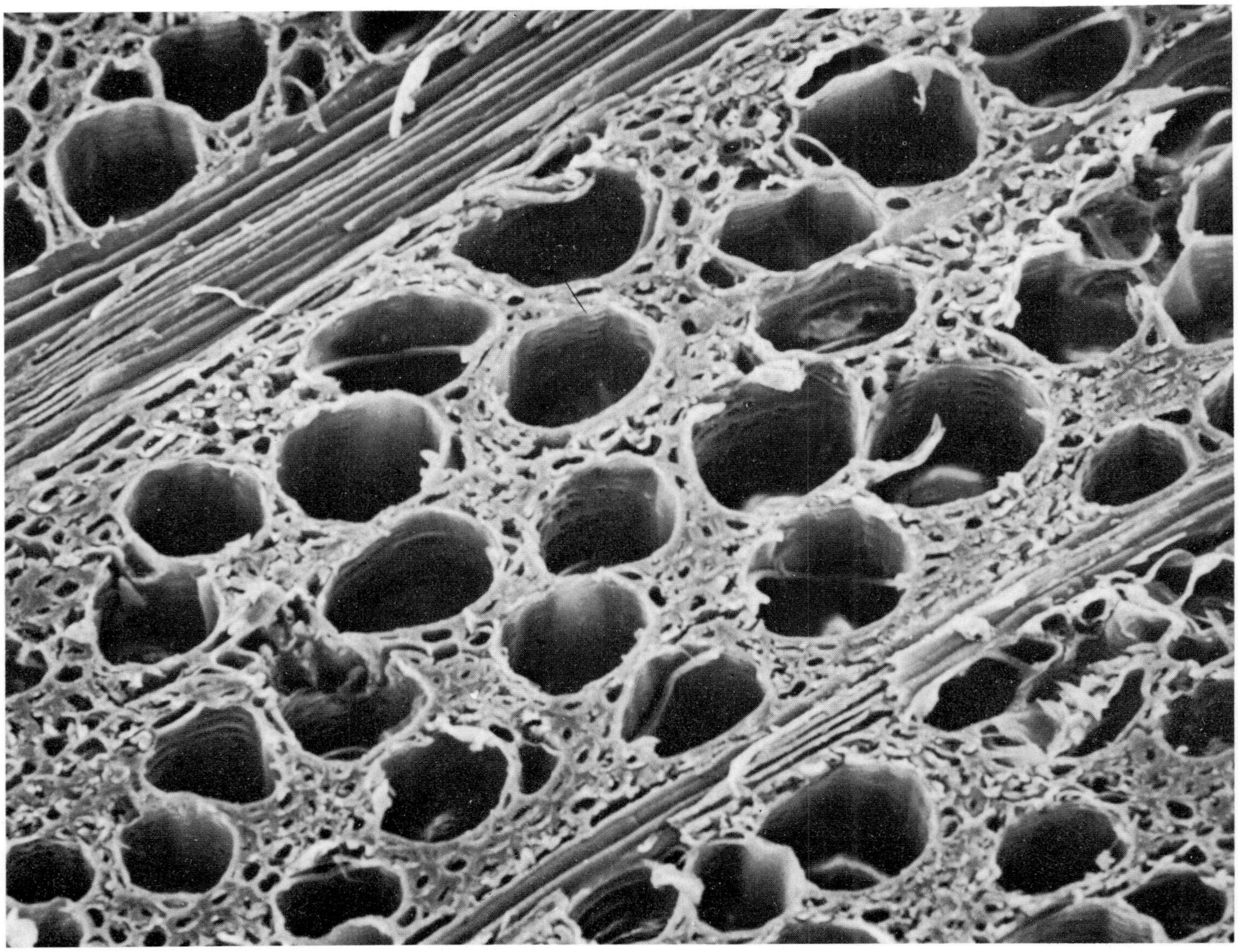

Some of the cells become specialised to provide a pathway through the plant for water and dissolved nutrients. These cells are actually dead. Their walls are thickened with a substance called lignin, which makes them fairly rigid and very strong and woody. Great trees contain relatively little living tissue. Most of the cells in their trunks and branches are dead, but that does not by any means make them useless. These dead cells make up continuous tubes right around the plant, a massive plumbing system that carries water and soil nutrients from the root in the soil right to the top of the tallest tree. This tissue is called xylem.

Herbaceous plants, on the other hand, show much less differentiation during their shorter life cycles. Most of their cells remain alive, with a large water content, and the effects of this difference between woody and herbaceous plants can be seen at the first signs of drought. The differentiated xylem tubes that make up wood act as a kind of skeleton that supports the plant, so that although the leaves may wilt, the plant itself will remain upright. Herbaceous plants do not have enough xylem tissue to provide this kind of support, so when water is short the whole plant droops. The plant actually uses water to keep itself upright.

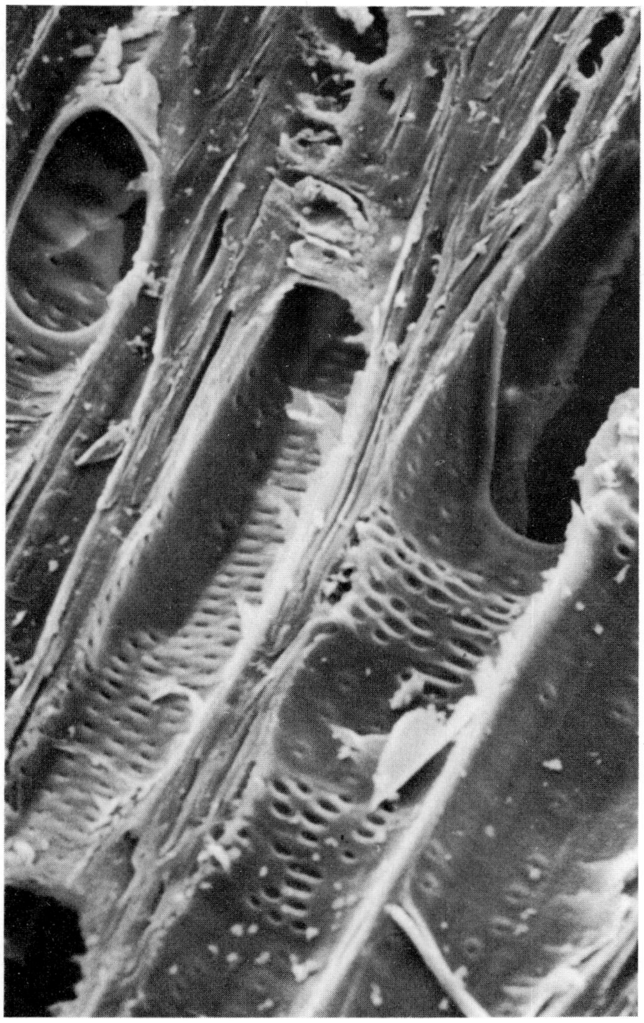

The explanation of this phenomenon lies in the structure of the living cells that make up the plant. The cell is surrounded by a wall which is made of cellulose fibres, woven into a tough little net and lined with a membrane. This wall does have some rigidity and does give a little support to the plant, but nothing like enough to keep it upright. Inside the cell, and sticking to its walls, there is a thin layer of cytoplasm. This is the living entity of the cell, and it contains a number of chemical systems, rather like tiny factories, that keep the cell – and therefore the plant – alive and functioning. The cytoplasm also contains the nucleus of the cell – which is, in a manner of speaking, in charge of all these vital chemical activities. It directs and regulates the life of the cell and also contains the genetic template of the plant on its chromosomes.

However, the part of the cell responsible for keeping the plant upright is the hole in the middle, the vacuole. This contains some sugar and mineral salts, dissolved in a variable amount of water.

Water passes very easily both in and out of the cell and the vacuole, because the cytoplasm and the cell wall are both permeable, but any substance which has molecules larger than those of water has much more of a problem. The membrane lining the cytoplasm is permeable to water which has small molecules, but impermeable to things like sugar and proteins with their much larger molecules. Membranes like this, which let some things through but not others, are called 'semi-permeable membranes', and they are vitally important in maintaining the water balance of plants and, indeed, of every other living organism. They are important to the plant in this case because water will always pass across such a membrance from a weaker to a stronger solution, as though it were trying to dilute the stronger solution. This is called osmosis. Cytoplasm is a very strong solution, containing all sorts of salts and sugars, so living cells take up a lot of water, all of which swells the vacuole. The cells take up so much water that they become inflated, like balloons, and each one pushes against the other cells around it. The pressure of these inflated cells inside the stem makes the tissue rigid, which keeps the stem upright and supports the plant. When water is short, the cells in the stem deflate and shrink away from one another, making the stem lose its rigidity and collapse. The plant is said to have wilted.

(Opposite page.) A stereoscan picture of xylem tissue, with the tubes through which water passes looking like great, dark tunnels. × 360.

(This page.) Another stereoscan, showing the 'ribs' of lignin that support the xylem tubes. × 450.

Water is taken from the soil by the roots, but most of it passes swiftly through the plant and is lost from the leaves. If you cover a plant with a glass jar on a sunny day, the water that it loses will very soon coat the walls of the jar with a mist, a phenomenon painfully familiar to anybody who has started a bottle garden and then found the whole thing totally obscured by condensation. You can show that it is the leaves themselves that are responsible by securing a small plastic bag over a single leaf and watching the water accumulate.

The water gets out of the leaf with such ease because its surface is perforated with tiny holes called stomata. (One of these pores is called a stoma, but the plural is 'stomata'.) Each stoma is surrounded by a pair of crescent-shaped cells, called guard cells. The inner wall of each crescent is much thicker and less flexible than the outer wall, so when the cells fill with water and become turgid, the outer wall stretches more than the inner wall, causing the thickened area to cup inwards. This makes the guard cells more curved in shape and opens the stoma. When the cells lose water and become flaccid, they straighten, and this closes the pore and prevents water loss.

The rest of the surface of the leaf is covered with a waxy, waterproof layer, called the cuticle, and the stomata are the only route by which water can escape from the leaf. So, to a certain extent, the plant can control the amount of water that it loses by opening and closing its stomata. It is true to say, in general, that the stomata are open for the latter part of the night and during the morning, but, as the temperature rises on a hot, sunny day, they close. If they were to remain open in the heat of the afternoon, the plant would lose a great deal of water and be in a state of considerable stress by evening. As the day draws on and the temperature drops, they open again, but they close as night falls. This regime is ideal for maintaining the water economy of the plant, but also gives rise to a considerable problem.

The paradox is this. The stomata are the route by which water gets out of the leaf, but they are also the pathway into the leaf for carbon dioxide, a gas that is vital to the plant when it makes food, by the process of photosynthesis. When the sun is up and the temperature is high, the water balance demands that the stomata shut down and conserve moisture. However, at precisely the same time the plant's need for carbon dioxide is at its greatest, because it is under these conditions that the plant can best use the chemical works in its leaves to manufacture carbohydrate food. The plant, therefore, has a finely divided need, and the complexity of the interaction between water economy and food manufacture is immense. But it can safely be said that when water is short the stomata close and this not only cuts down water loss, but also slows down the vital synthesis of carbohydrate. Vegetables can be very badly affected by a check in their early growth, so watering the garden to prevent any signs of wilting can pay dividends in increased growth and increased crops.

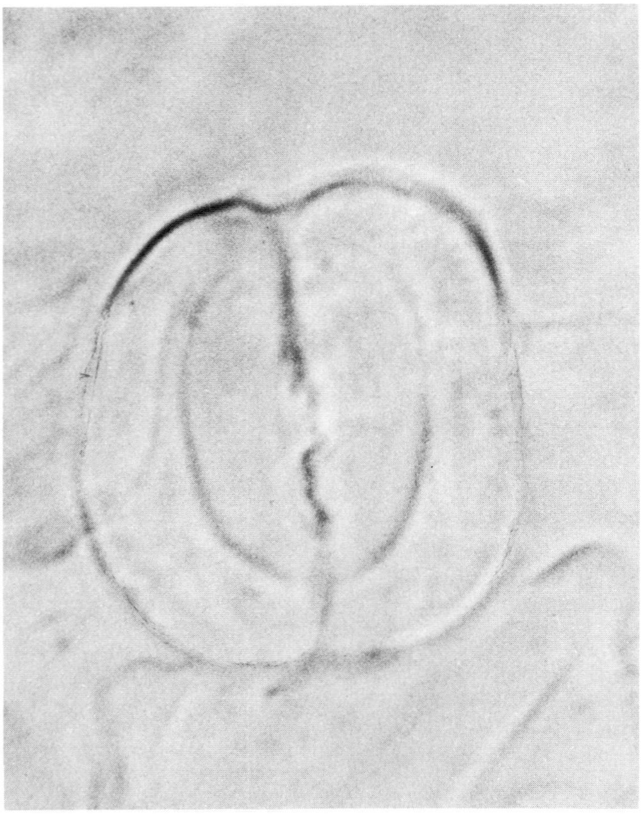

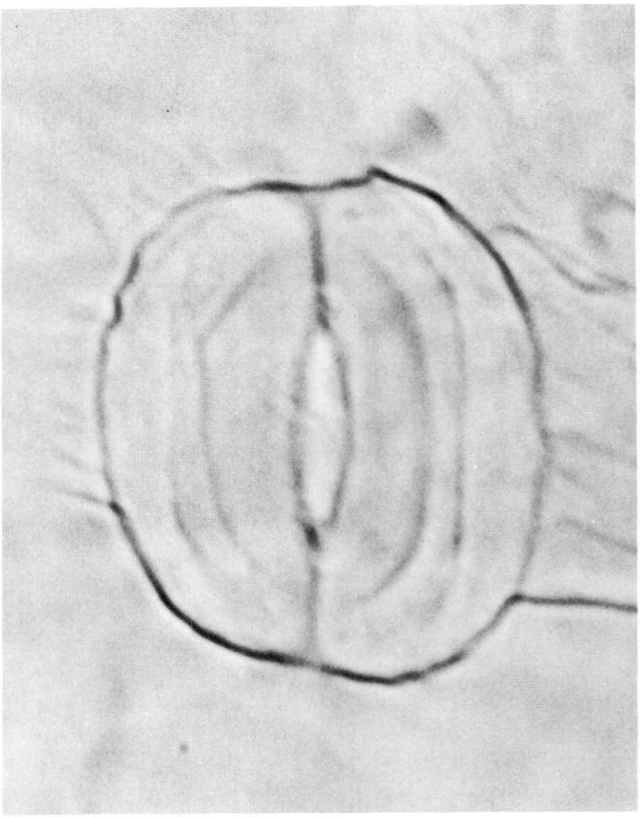

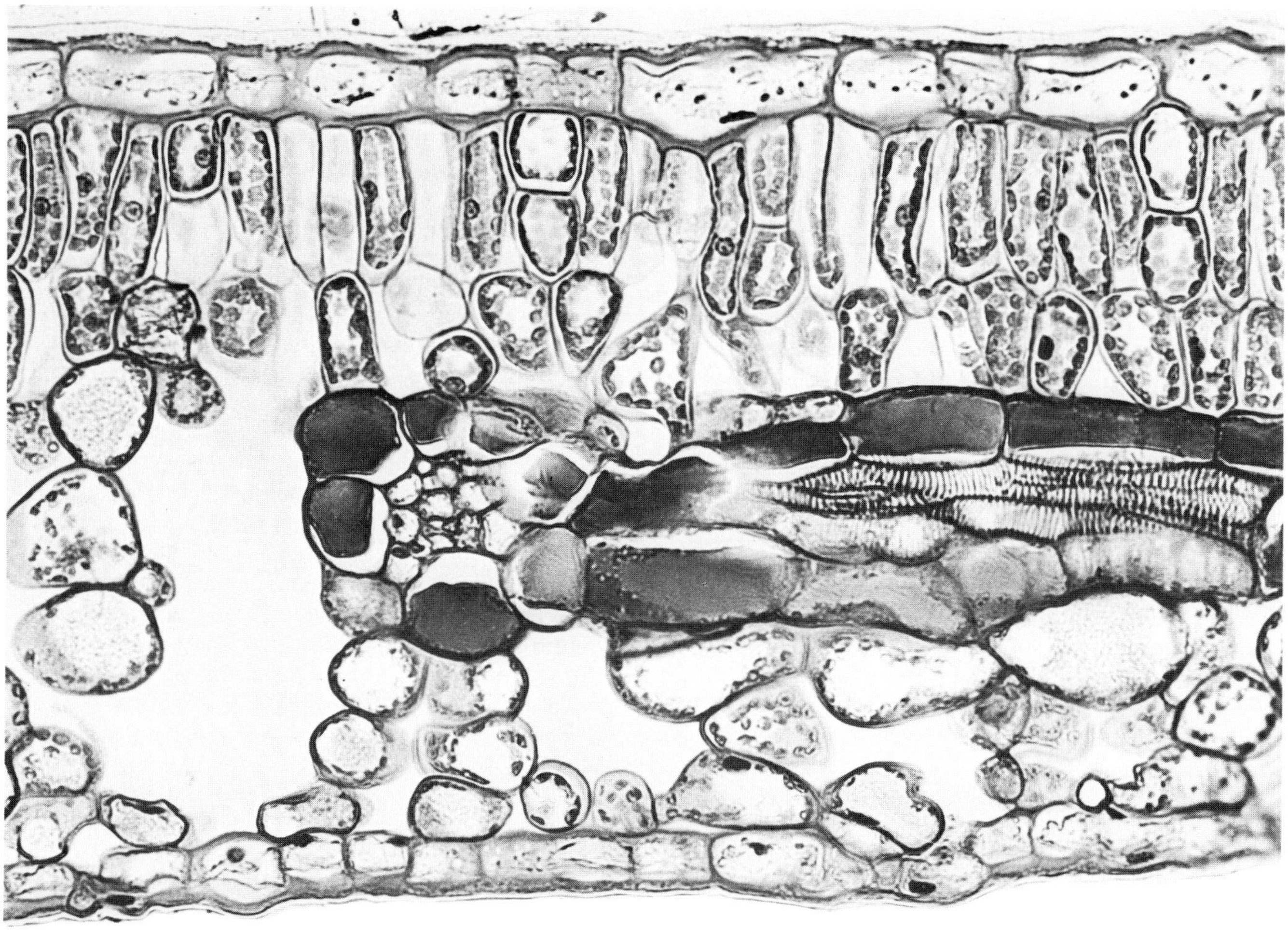

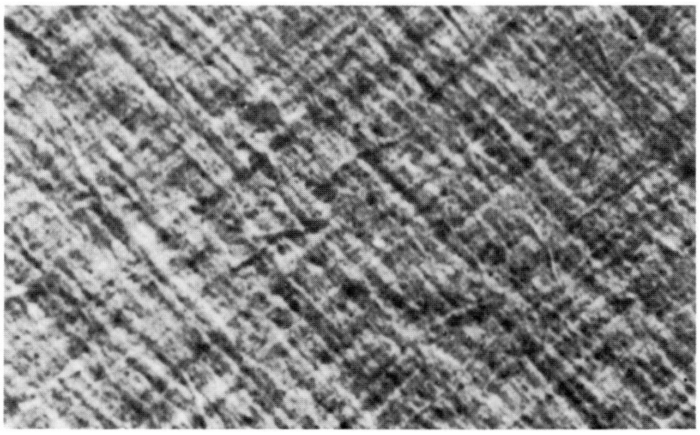

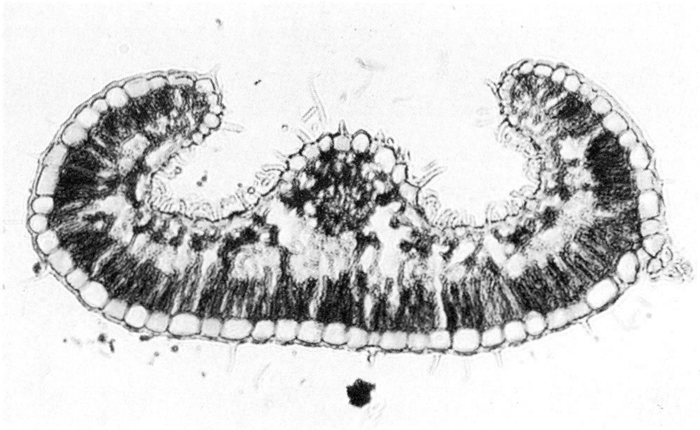

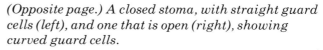

(Opposite page.) A closed stoma, with straight guard cells (left), and one that is open (right), showing curved guard cells.

(Above.) A section through a leaf, as seen under a microscope, showing one of the many veins, with lignified xylem cells. Water passes from the vein to the stomata through the cellulose walls of the cells between.

(Centre.) A stereoscan picture of the cellulose wall of a plant cell. There are minute spaces between the fibres that make up these walls, along which the water passes.

(Below.) A section through a heather leaf. Some plants, like heathers, protect their leaves from water loss by sheltering their stomata from drying winds. The leaves of heather are curled, with the stomata to the inside, and this enables the plants to survive in windy, bleak locations.

Secondary thickening and annual rings

The stems of trees and shrubs increase in girth – they grow outwards as well as upwards. This increase in girth is caused by the production of new tissue, called secondary tissue, and the growth of the stem is called secondary thickening. The new growth includes many cells with strengthening tissue, which imparts rigidity to the stem or trunk and allows the tree to grow to a great height.

The cells that produce secondary growth are called cambium. They arise in the vascular bundles, between the two kinds of conducting tissue, the phloem and the xylem (1). As the plant matures, the vascular cambium joins up to form a complete ring within the stem (2). Once the ring is formed, the cambial cells divide, both to the inside and the outside of the circle. The cells formed on the inside are xylem cells, while those on the outside form phloem (3).

The function and form of these secondary tissues is much the same as that of the primary tissue. Xylem cells carry water and nutrients up the plant, become impregnated with lignin and die, making the strong and rigid wood of the tree trunk. The phloem, which carries food and metabolites both up and down the stem, is not lignified or strengthened and the cells remain alive. As growth proceeds, the oldest phloem cells become disorganised and are eventually destroyed. In addition to producing xylem and phloem, the cambium produces another kind of tissue, called ray parenchyma. These cells remain alive and conduct materials across the stem.

The annual growth of the tree increases its diameter or girth. As secondary xylem is laid down, the cambium is pushed outwards and adds more cells to the ring to cope with the increase in girth. The amount of phloem does not increase as the tree grows. Phloem cells are not strengthened and they are crushed as the secondary xylem and the cambium press outwards. The ring of cells on the outermost part of the stem cannot increase its circumference to accommodate the increase in girth as the tree grows, so, to protect the surface of the trunk, another secondary tissue is formed. This is produced by division of cells in a second cambium, the cork cambium. Like the vascular cambium, this lies in a ring around the trunk and produces cells to both the inside and the outside, but in the case of the cork cambium, the outer cells are more permanent, and form a protective coat, called bark.

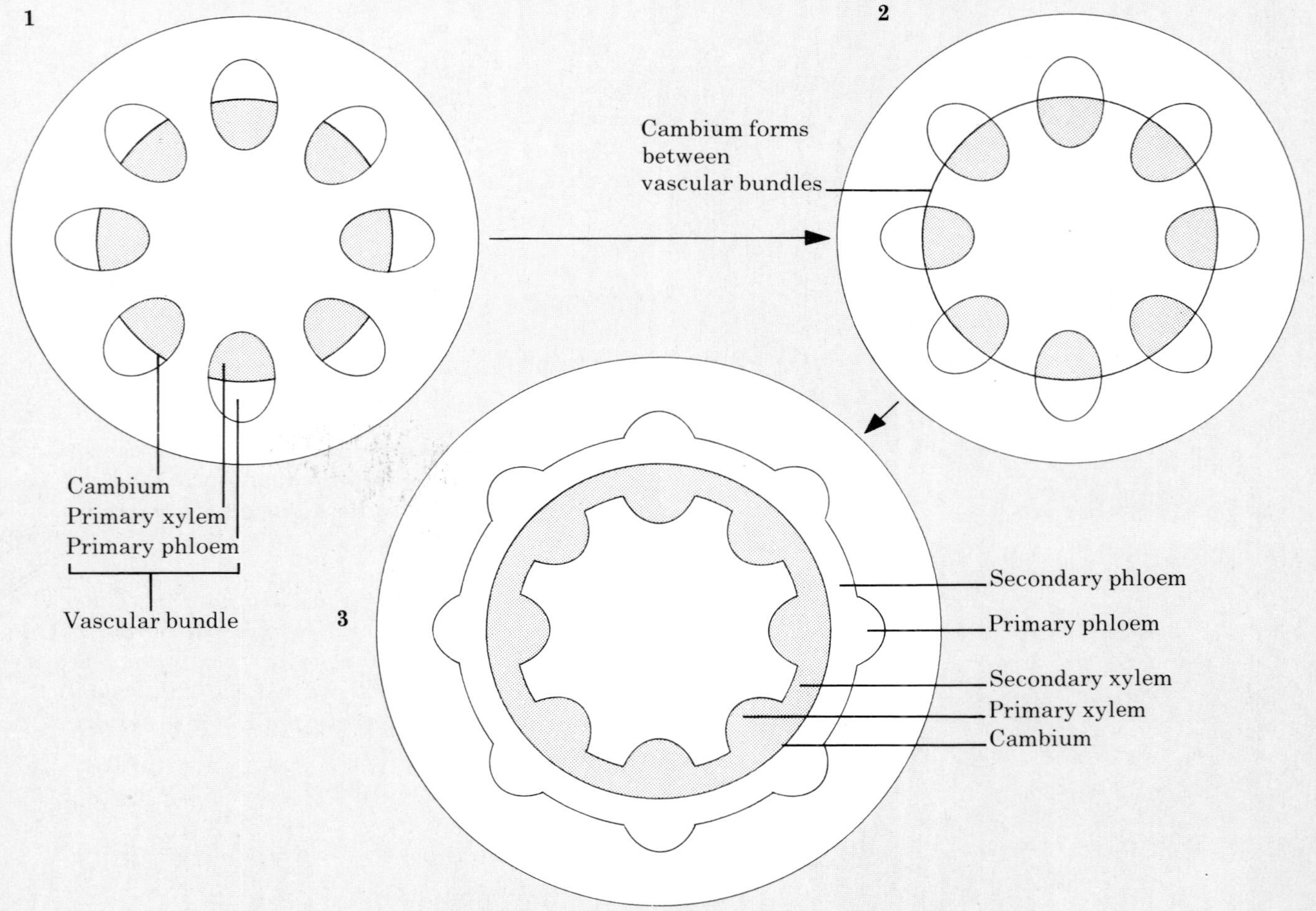

Cork cambium is relatively short lived. As the girth of the tree increases new cambial cells arise, inside the older ring, so that, in time, the cork cambium lies in the older, disorganised phloem cells. When botanists use the term 'bark' they generally mean all the tissues outside the vascular cambium, which means that bark is a mixture of different tissues including the normal, functioning phloem, the cork cambium and the cork itself. These tissues form quite a thin layer, in comparison with the woody xylem, which is why 'barking' can be used to stop the flow through the phloem when air layering (see Chapter 5, page 81) and why rabbits and deer nibbling at the bark of trees can do so much damage. The detailed formation of the cork varies from species to species and this is why the bark on each kind of tree looks different. With practice, most trees can be identified by their bark.

In the flush of early growth in spring, there is a need for lots of water and nutrients to be passed up through the stem. Many trees respond to this need by producing xylem cells with a particularly large diameter. As the season progresses, the need for water lessens and the diameter of the xylem cells produced lessens accordingly until the division of new cells stops altogether in late autumn. Each season this cycle is repeated and this leads to the production of annual growth rings within the stem. Each annual ring contains the xylem tissue laid down in one year's growth. The rings can be seen because of the way the xylem cells change in size as the season progresses.

A section through the trunk of a young lime tree. The woody xylem tissue shows annual growth rings and, once a tree has been cut down, these can be counted to discover its age.

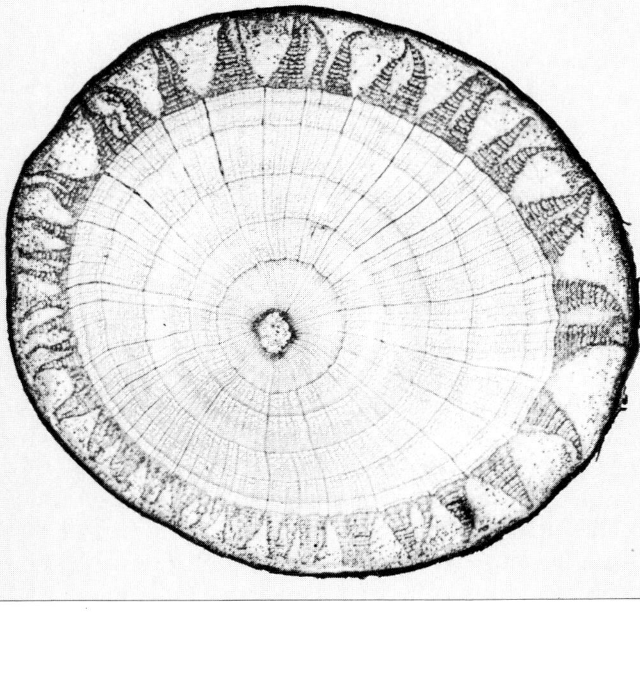

WATER CONSERVATION

Because of the fragile balance between 'water out' and 'gas in', many plants have developed modifications that minimise the loss of water without the plant taking the final step of shutting up shop and closing the stomata. A leaf with open stomata loses water or dries in just the same way as washing on the line, by evaporation. They both lose water most quickly when the sun is hot and the wind is blowing, so these are the factors from which the plant needs to protect its stomata. Most stomata are on the underside of the leaves, a position which protects them from the worst effects of the sun. Wind protection is achieved by a variety of means. A covering of scales or hairs on the leaf cuts down the wind speed over its surface by trapping a layer of still air, and this lessens evaporation. In some species the hairs are so tiny that they are hardly noticed, but in others they are very conspicuous and make the leaves attractive enough to be a feature in the garden. Some of the common names given to these plants, like 'pig's ear' and 'lamb's tails', indicate the furry feel of the leaves; their silver foliage remains through summer and winter when all the flowers have gone.

WATER MOVEMENT

In some plants it is quite easy to see the xylem tissue forming a continuous pathway between the roots, where the water gets into the plant, and the leaves, where it returns to the atmosphere as water vapour. The best way to do it is by taking another look at the childhood trick of leaving a white or pale-coloured carnation standing with its stem in a pot of ink. (See page 101.) After a few hours, the flower petals show a delicate tracery of countless tiny veins, all darkly stained by the ink, but if you cut through the stem and look at it with a magnifying glass you can see a circle of inky tissue. This is made up of the tubes that carry water up the stem of the plant. Having seen the route that water follows through the plant, the question that puzzled and fascinated botanists for years was this: how does the water get up the tree? What motive force can shift as much as fifty gallons an hour to the top of the tallest oak?

Early experiments tried to explain this as a function of the root. This model proposed that the root generated a pressure, and that this pushed the water to the top of the tree and out through the leaves. The evidence was the fact that, if you cut the top off some plants, the stump will weep. The forces responsible for root pressure are not fully understood, but they result from the continuing movement of water and dissolved soil nutrients out of the soil, through the root tissue and into the xylem. Soil nutrients cannot just diffuse into the root; they are, as it were, 'pumped' into the root, and it is this 'pumping' that generates root pressure. Scientists attached a gauge to a cut stump and measured the pressure generated, but found that it was not enough to account for the movement of water to the top of even a moderately sized tree. There had to be another explanation.

The xylem vessels have an extremely small internal diameter, equivalent to some of the most finely-drawn glass capillary tubing. Water in very fine tubes like this has great cohesive properties. The molecules stick to one another and to the sides of the tube, and it can take an enormous force to break them apart. This makes the fine column of water in the xylem vessel very strong, and, if it is moved upwards, it exerts a tension, a pull that is strong enough to drag more molecules of water up into the tube behind it.

This means that the pull from the top that is needed to keep the column of water in the xylem tubes moving up the tree is not very large. The tubes are so fine that the water will, as it were, stick together at all costs. The tension exerted on the column by the loss of water from the leaves is enough to keep it moving. Water is not, as was first thought, pushed up the tree: it is pulled.

The system works in much the same way as an oil lamp. The water in the soil is like the reservoir of oil in the lamp – the continuous tubes of the xylem tissue are like a gigantic wick, and the loss of water through the stomata is the equivalent of the burning flame at the top of the lamp that drags the oil up the wick. It works only because the column of water, or oil, is continuous. From the very tip of the root in the soil to the very cell from which the water finally evaporates there must be no break in the chain. The combination of water tension through the xylem and evaporation from the stomata in the leaves is now widely accepted as the force that moves water and soil nutrients through the plant.

This continuous column of water, stretching between the outside world at the root and the outside world at the leaf, explains why so much of the water that is taken in by the plant travels straight through and out again without being used in any way. Most of it does not even enter a living cell. The living cells that lie along the pathway between the root and the leaf can take water from the xylem tissue at any point, through their semi-permeable cell membranes. There it can be used for some metabolic process or to keep the cell turgid and the plant upright, but this transfer of water can also be reversed. If water is being lost from the leaves more quickly than it can be taken up by the roots, the continuous tube of water in the xylem tissue is maintained by taking water from the living cells. The cells are no longer turgid, and the plant wilts.

IN THE WINTER

The heat and the drying winds of summer are not the only conditions in which plants feel water stress. Winter brings its own problems. The deciduous trees lose practically no water and suffer no stress because their leaves fall in autumn, but the evergreens, which retain their foliage, continue to lose water through their stomata. In the colder months water becomes more viscous and is harder to move around the plant. It may even freeze in the soil, in which case it is not available to the plant to replace water lost from the leaves. Evergreens that are to survive in the cold of winter must have mechanisms to combat these threats.

Conifers cut down water loss by having stomata that are sunk in deep, protective grooves along their leaves. They also conserve water by making food, or photosynthesising, more slowly than usual, but in particularly cold weather these measures are not enough. When garden conifers turn brown in the cold winter winds, it is a sign that the plant has lost more water than it can replace in the circumstances and has become 'dried out'. Very cold winter weather may even freeze the water that is inside the plant. If ice crystals form within the cytoplasm, they will destroy the living cell membranes and kill the plant, so all evergreens need a way to stop this happening. As the temperature falls, they transfer water from the living cell contents into the walls of the cells and the intercellular spaces. This causes the cell contents to shrink and the cytoplasm to become more concentrated. The concentrated cytoplasm then behaves like anti-freeze in a car. Because it contains a high concentration of salts, it lowers the freezing point of the living cell contents and prevents the formation of the destructive ice crystals.

This ability, to move water out of the living tissue very quickly, is one of the mechanisms that all evergreens must have if they are to survive in parts of the world that experience winter cold. Equally important is the ability to reverse the process just as fast. The early morning sun, which thaws the ice in the intercellular spaces and the cell walls, also starts up the process of photosynthesis and begins to evaporate water from the leaves. If the water does not get back into the living cells as the ice thaws, the results can be disastrous.

The so-called 'sensitive' evergreens – generally the ones that evolved in warmer climates than our own – should always be planted out of the reach of morning sunshine in winter. They lack the ability to 'put their house in order' at speed after a freezing night. They cannot cope with the rapid change of temperature they experience when a cold winter night is immediately followed by early morning sunshine, and they will dry out and turn brown.

Watering the vegetable garden

Watering the garden is one of the chores of summer; the penalty we pay for having enough sunshine to sunbathe. But watering must be undertaken with care, because, although in a really hot summer like 1976, everything in the garden needs watering regularly, in a more average season it is easy to do damage by watering too much.

Roughly speaking, watering a plant encourages the production of a lot of leafy growth. This means that vegetables which are grown for their leaves, like cabbage and lettuce, need ample watering throughout their lives, but vegetables that are grown for their swollen roots, like carrots and turnips, are a different matter. If these get too much water they develop a great deal of leaf but the roots are neglected, so root vegetables never need a great deal of watering. Vegetables grown for their fruits and seeds, like peas, beans or tomatoes, need different amounts of water at different times in their lives. When they are growing leaves, but before the flowers form, they are better left without too much water for the same reason as root vegetables – they will put all their energies into growing leaves and not much else. Once the flowers form, however, there is a tendency for the plant to cut down on root development, and this may lessen its ability to take up water from the soil, so watering at this stage can increase the yield considerably.

It makes sense to water as little as possible, partly because it is hard work, but also because continually pouring water into the soil washes the soil nutrients downwards, beyond the reach of the plant's roots. The important thing is to give the plants as much water as they need, but to do everything you can to make them need less.

For example, plants which grow close together compete for the available water in the soil around them. In a small garden you have to accept this – put your plants close together and do the rounds with the watering can. If, however, you are lucky enough to have all the space you need, you can cut down on watering by planting further apart and allowing each plant access to a larger volume of soil. Weeds also take water, so weeding cuts down the competition and leaves all the available water for the important plants in the garden – the vegetables.

The amount of water that is available for your plants depends on the soil structure, and that can best be improved by adding bulky organic material, like compost or manure. A study at the National Vegetable Research Station showed that, after digging in ten pounds per square yard of stable manure before each crop for six years, the amount of available water held in the top eighteen inches of soil had increased by twenty-five per cent, although the amount in the top six inches had gone up by a staggering seventy per cent. So it really does reduce the need for watering.

Large scale commercial irrigation of potatoes.

Another way of increasing the amount of water available to the plant is by increasing the amount of soil that its roots can penetrate in their search for water, and you can do this by loosening the soil below the usual one-spit depth of garden digging. When the plant roots are growing downwards, rather than out at the sides, it is possible to put the plants closer together. Followers of the deep-bed method of gardening have found that they can plant so tightly that there is hardly any bare soil left, which greatly reduces the amount of water that can evaporate from the ground surface.

Mulching also helps to reduce the amount of water lost from the surface of the soil. For the best effect, put the compost, peat or leaves around the plants after rain or after watering. Some people leave hoed weeds on the soil surface as a mulch. These will reduce water loss by covering the soil, but they will also leave a legacy of seeds for years to come. If you do intend leaving weeds lying on the surface, it is best to hoe early in the morning so that the weed roots get thoroughly dried out and killed by a day in the sun.

The time of day that you choose to water can also affect the amount that you need to supply. Less water is used in the cool of the evening, because there is plenty of time for the water to sink into the earth; whereas, the bright, hot sunshine of the earlier part of the day will evaporate some of the water on the surface before it is soaked up. On the other hand, leaving plants wet overnight may encourage disease (for example mildew in lettuce starts on wet leaves), so there are some problems, whatever time of day you choose.

In this country we grow a lot of evergreen vegetables – plants like the winter cabbage and Brussels sprouts – and these too have to cope with periods of cold and frost. In bad weather they look droopy and wilted, but that is their defence, their protection against water loss. Once the temperature rises, they generally recover.

It is not possible, in winter or in summer, actually to see a plant wilt before your very eyes. The movement of water within a wilting plant is not fast enough to cause a visible change. But the same sort of process – the transfer of water from one cell to another in the plant to produce changes in water pressure – can be done much more quickly in some plants, and when that happens it can produce some quite spectacular plant movements. The 'sensitive plant', *Mimosa pudica*, is a good example. When touched, the leaflets of this plant fold together, and, if the shock is great enough, the petiole, or leaf stem, also collapses. In nature this is a response to high temperatures, and ensures that as small an area of leaf as possible is exposed to damage from the sun. You can stimulate the response by touching the plant or by exposing it to some heat, like a cigarette end held close to a leaf.

A striking feature of this response is the way that the stimulus is conducted through the plant. If a pair of leaflets at the end of a leaf is gently touched, then, starting from that point, the leaflets will fold together back down the leaf to the petiole. The stimulus may then pass both up and down the stem to affect other leaves. This stimulus is generally conducted at a rate of between 4 and 30 mm per second, but following a larger stimulus, like a hefty knock, rates as high as 100 mm per second have been recorded, and this is approaching the speed at which the slower animal impulses can be conducted.

It is not clear just how this stimulus is moved by the plant, but it is well understood that the actual folding of the leaf blades and the petiole is caused by changes of water pressure within certain strategic cells. These cells are at the base of the leaf blades and at the junction of the petiole and the main stem. When stimulated they lose a lot of fluid very quickly and collapse, which produces the 'sensitive' response. Recovery time is about fifteen or twenty minutes, and by the time this has elapsed the cells are 'pumped up' and turgid again, which raises the petiole and the leaflets back to their normal upright position.

The other fast movers of the plant world are the insect-eating or carnivorous plants, especially the well-known Venus fly trap. This has leaves that are modified to make traps that snap shut if an insect walks through them. They shut astonishingly fast, in about 0·01 to 0·02 seconds. This imprisons the insect very firmly, and several weeks may pass before the leaf opens again. The quick movement of the initial response is brought about by a flood of water into certain cells on each side of the mid-rib or 'hinge' of the trap. This causes the cells to expand very rapidly and force the trap to shut. Once the insect is caught, it is digested by enzymes that are secreted by the leaf, and it is believed that the presence of these chemicals keeps the trap shut until the gory meal has been completely devoured.

The uses that a plant makes of the water that it takes from the soil are astonishingly varied. It is used for support, for movement, in innumerable chemical reactions and for all kinds of transport throughout the plant. But the water that the plant takes from the soil contains other things as well: it holds the nutrients that are vital to the growth and well-being of all living plants.

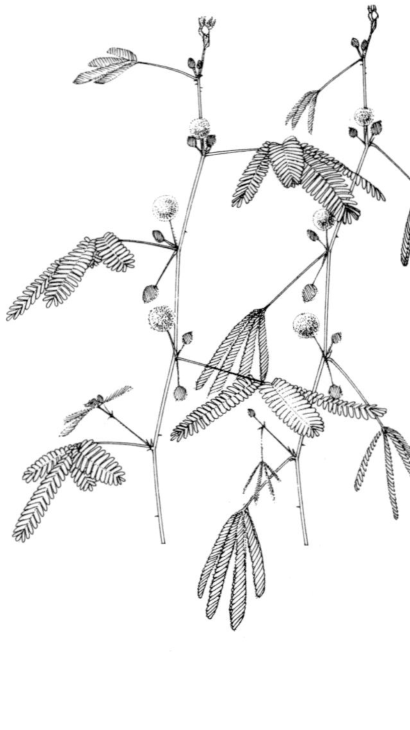

(Left.) Mimosa pudica.
(Below.) The Venus fly trap.
(Right.) Detail of one of the traps. The trap only shuts when three of the small hairs are touched. When more than three hairs are moved, the speed of closing increases.

CHAPTER EIGHT

NUTRIENTS FROM THE SOIL

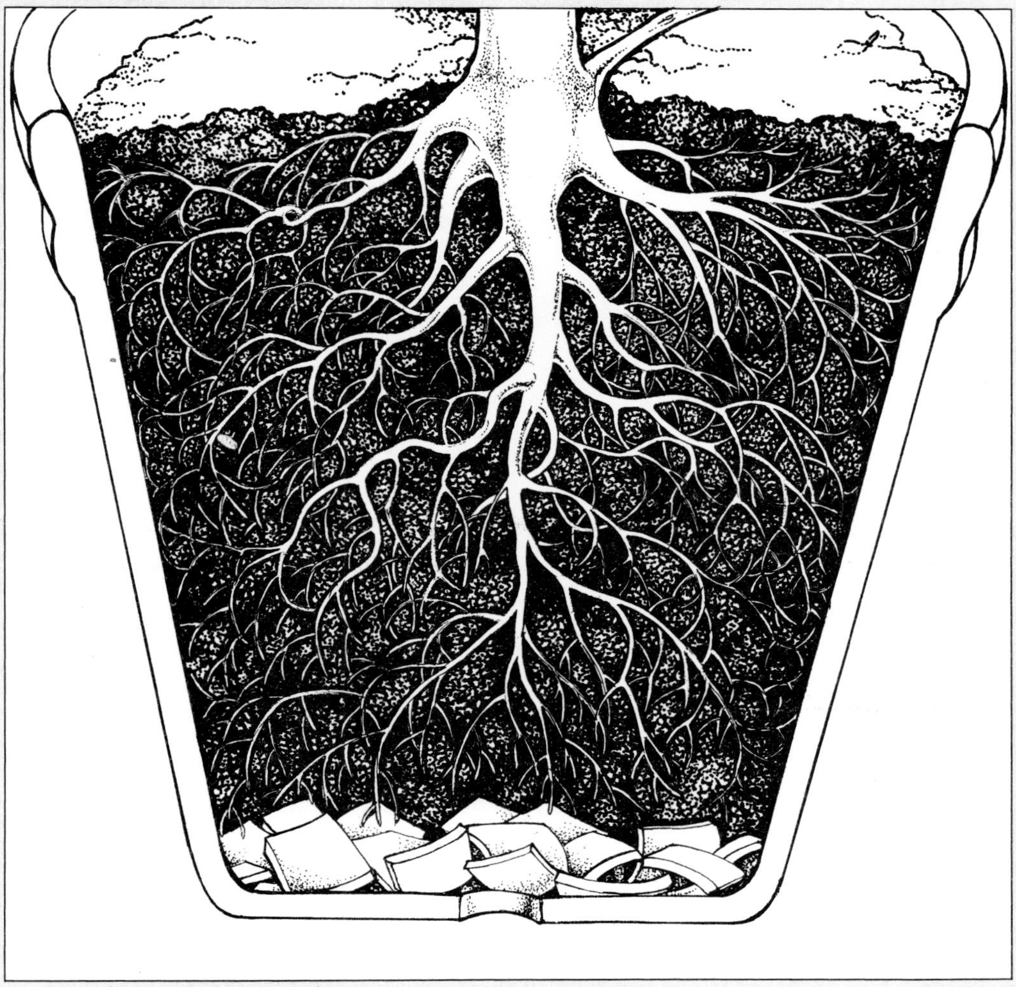

It is, perhaps, a surprise, considering the importance of the nutrients that the roots take up from the soil, to find them in such small quantities within the plant itself. If a plant – almost any plant – is broken up and subjected to a detailed chemical analysis, it is found that over ninety per cent of its weight is made up of carbon, hydrogen and oxygen, which do not come from the soil, while the remaining small percentage contains as many as sixteen or seventeen other chemical elements, all of which are taken up in an aqueous solution from the earth. It is these nutrients that are contained in fertilisers and in chemical 'plant foods'.

Six of these nutrients are used in relatively large amounts, and the remainder are needed in absolutely minute quantities and are, in consequence, known as the 'trace elements'. In the following list of nutrients, the chemical symbols are included, in brackets, because they sometimes appear on packets of fertiliser.

Major nutrients	**Trace elements**
Nitrogen (N)	Iron (Fe)
Phosphorus (P)	Manganese (Mn)
Potassium (K)	Boron (B)
Calcium (Ca)	Copper (Cu)
Magnesium (Mg)	Molybdenum (Mo)
Sulphur (S)	Zinc (Zn)
	Chlorine (Cl)

The list of these trace elements is by no means complete and closed. Their existence and function became evident only when chemists developed techniques that were able to reveal such tiny amounts, and, as chemical analysis advances, the list of trace elements grows longer. Sodium and cobalt have now been found in plant tissue, and botanists are currently working to establish their precise role in the plant's metabolism. No doubt other elements will follow.

The amount of the trace elements required is so small that some seeds actually contain enough to supply the developing plant right through to maturity. In this case a plant will show a mineral deficiency only if the seed that it grew from was inadequately supplied by its parent.

Each element that the plant takes from the soil plays a part in the life and growth of that plant, so a shortage of any of them will show as slow, weak or stunted growth. Moreover, in addition to this general malaise, many nutrient deficiencies cause clear symptoms, and spotting these in your plants can provide a valuable guide to the soil's fertility.

There are, however, a number of problems in assessing the soil in this way. Although, some symptoms are very clear, others can be confusing and can vary from crop to crop. Because nutrients get into the plant through its roots, any damage to those roots can slow down water and nutrient uptake, and can retard growth. Some virus diseases have symptoms that look much like nutrient deficiencies, and these may cause confusion. Lettuce mosaic virus, for example, and a shortage of magnesium both produce similar marbling patterns on the leaves.

In addition, there are a number of reactions which occur among the nutrients themselves that can seriously affect the performance of the plant. Glasshouse tomatoes are generally given a good dose of a potassium-rich fertiliser because potassium promotes strong flowering and fruit growth. But potassium also reduces the ability of the plant to absorb magnesium, so plants growing in a soil that contains a perfectly adequate supply of this nutrient nevertheless begin to show the yellowing of the leaves that is characteristic of a magnesium deficiency. A one per cent solution of magnesium sulphate (Epsom salts), sprayed on to the leaves, will repair the damage but it can generally be prevented by using a ready-mixed tomato fertiliser that is rich in potassium but that also contains some Epsom salts.

The acidity, or pH, of the soil does not affect the actual quantity of nutrient it contains but it can drastically alter its availability to the plant. On chalk or limestone, for example, where the soil is alkaline and the pH is high, iron, manganese and boron become insoluble. Because the plant can take up its nutrients only in an aqueous solution, this often causes trouble. At the other end of the pH scale, an acid soil inhibits the plant's ability to absorb molybdenum and calcium, but so increases the solubility of manganese and aluminium that the plant may actually suffer from an overdose.

A calcium deficiency in the plant but not in the soil can be cured by spraying the foliage with a one per cent solution of calcium nitrate, from the chemist. The only difficulty is that the spray must be applied where the plant is damaged by the deficiency, because the plant can only transport calcium in the xylem – which means that it can move it only up the plant, not down. The phloem tissue, which normally transports materials down the plant, cannot carry calcium, so a calcium deficiency in the lower leaves can be remedied only by a foliar spray on those leaves. A spray aimed any higher is wasted.

Genuine shortages of trace elements in the soil are fairly rare. If your plants show the symptoms of a trace element deficiency, it is probably caused by the acidity of the soil. Most plants grow best on soil with a pH of between 5·5 and 6·5, and almost every soil can be treated until, eventually, it reaches this level (see Chapter 1, page 18).

Nutrients, their functions and symptoms of deficiency (colour photographs on page 52)

NUTRIENT	FUNCTION	DEFICIENCY
NITROGEN (N)	Constituent of many substances in the plant, including proteins, amino acids and chlorophyll. Of particular importance in leafy growth.	Poor growth. Leaves around the base of the plant turn pale yellow and die. In the Brassica family these leaves are sometimes reddish-orange in colour.
PHOSPHORUS (P)	Used in building cell membranes, nucleic acids and enzyme systems. Very important in good root growth.	Sometimes no obvious symptoms, other than slow growth. Lower leaves can turn a dark blue-green colour.
POTASSIUM (K)	Activates enzymes, including those that make protein, so it is a vital 'turn-key' in making many important cell constituents. Particularly important in flowering and fruiting.	Older leaves turn yellow – become 'chlorotic'. Growth is slow, and some leaves show brown mottling and 'scorch' around the leaf margins.
MAGNESIUM (Mg)	Used in building chlorophyll, the pigment that makes plants green.	Older leaves become chlorotic between the veins, giving them a marbled appearance. Leaves then fall off.
CALCIUM (Ca)	Important in the structure of cell walls and as a carrier, transporting other elements across living membranes.	Stunted growth, particularly in younger leaves and around growing points.
SULPHUR (S)	Important component of protein.	Younger leaves become chlorotic, especially between veins.
IRON (Fe)	Essential as an enzyme activator in many reactions, and used in making the pigment chlorophyll.	Younger leaves become very badly chlorotic between the veins.
MANGANESE (Mn)	Important part of enzyme systems.	Older leaves become chlorotic between veins and spots of dead tissue appear.
COPPER (Cu)	Used as an electron carrier in the food making process, photosynthesis.	Younger leaves darken or turn grey green.
MOLYBDENUM (Mo)	Used as an electron carrier in photosynthesis.	Leaves do not develop and remain 'strap-like'. Older leaves become chlorotic, and the growing point is distorted. 'Whip-tail' in cauliflowers.
BORON (B)	Used in the movement of sugars around the plant.	Stunted younger leaves and distorted growing points.
ZINC (Zn)	Part of a number of enzyme systems.	Older leaves become mottled with curled, yellow leaf margins. Young terminal leaflets form rosettes.
CHLORINE (Cl)	Part of a number of enzyme systems and the chlorophyll molecule.	Leaves turn yellow and wilt. Root growth is stunted, and the young roots thicken.

SOIL TESTING

Another way to find out how fertile your soil may be is to test it with one of the various kits available commercially. The usual procedure is to shake a small sample of soil with water, and then use either a sensitive paper or an indicator solution. These react to produce a colour that can be compared with a standard to show whether a soil contains ample, enough or too little of the major soil nutrients. These tests can give a general idea of the quality of your soil, but they are unfortunately not nearly as accurate as the pH tests. More precise tests are available for the commercial grower, but they are so expensive that they are not generally offered to the gardener at home, for the moment at any rate.

A rather clever, new way of testing for nitrogen in the plant is the sap test. This assesses the quantity of the element in the plant stem rather than in the soil, which is a neat way of getting around any side effects of acidity or antagonistic reactions among elements. The test is beautifully simple. You just snap the stem of a young plant, press the sappy end against a test paper, then compare the colour this produces with a standard chart.

Rhizobium *nodules on the roots of a lupin.*

THE ORIGIN OF NUTRIENTS

In a natural environment, before the gardener steps in to organise and control, the bulk of each nutrient is produced by the weathering of the bedrock that lies below the subsoil. This is why soils lying over rocks that weather easily are generally richer in nutrients than soils on very hard rocks, like granite, which only yield their nutrients slowly. However, there is one very interesting exception, nitrogen, which is vital to the plant as it is used to build up amino acids and protein. Nitrogen is one of the gases that makes up the air around us. Indeed, the atmosphere we breathe is about seventy-eight per cent nitrogen, and this acts as the major source of the element for the plants that need it. But nitrogen as a gas is no use at all to a plant, because it is insoluble and plants can only take up nitrogen in soluble compounds, like the nitrates and ammonium salts. There are, however, a few bacteria living in the soil that trap nitrogen and convert it into suitable compounds. This is called 'nitrogen fixing'.

Some of the nitrogen-fixing bacteria live in the roots of plants, where they cause swellings that are called 'root nodules'. Both bacteria and plant benefit from this liaison. The bacteria get a home and some food out of the root, and the plant gets a plentiful supply of nitrogen in a suitable, soluble form. This symbiotic, or mutually beneficial, relationship can occur in a number of plants, including the alder and bog-myrtle trees, but for the gardener the important nitrogen fixers are the *Rhizobium* bacteria that live in nodules on the roots of the leguminous plants, the pea and bean family.

A fairly large number of different species of *Rhizobium* form nodules on the roots of runner beans and peas, and the plants readily use the nitrogen that is fixed by the bacteria. The 'odd man out' is the French bean, where the situation is rather different. Very few of the bacteria that are generally found in the soil, either of this country or other parts of the world, invade the roots of the French bean. To complicate matters still further, different strains of *Rhizobium* live in different varieties of French bean, so, even if a particular crop is invaded and nodules form, there is no guarantee that another variety, sown the next year, will benefit in the same way. All in all, it is better to assume, for the moment at least, that French beans are not getting nitrogen from the activities of *Rhizobium* and will need a nitrogen fertiliser when the young plants are growing fast and developing foliage.

(Above.) Rose of Sharon and (below right) Convolvulus tricolor. *Both these attract hoverflies, which eat aphids. (See page 144.)*
(Below left.) Plum leaves showing silver leaf. The symptoms increase in severity from left to right. (See page 151.)

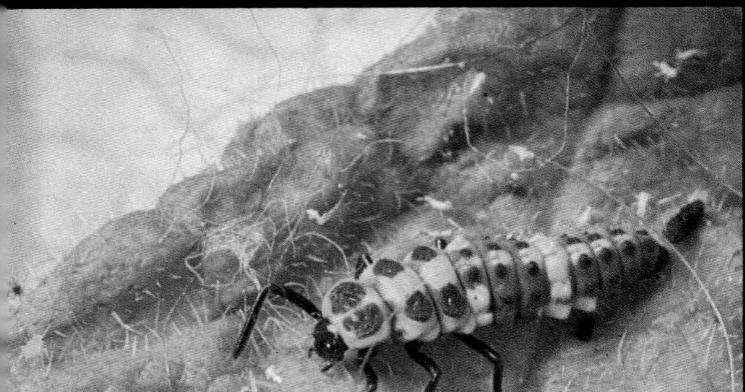

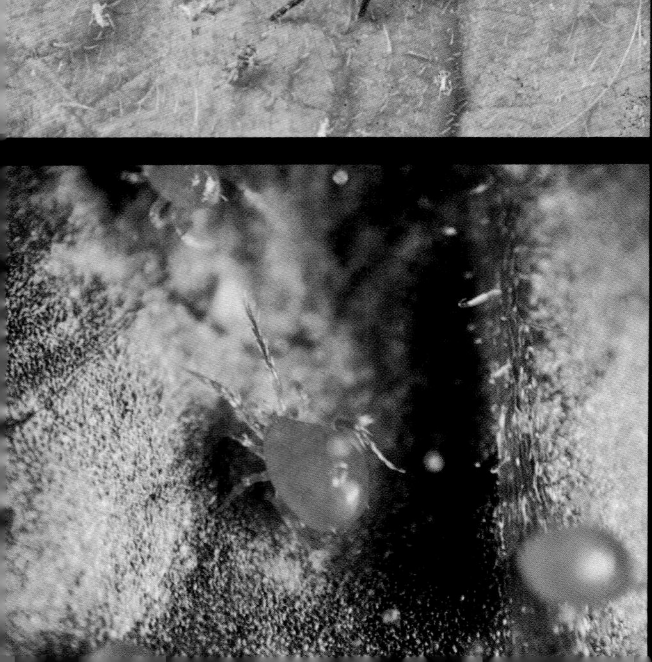

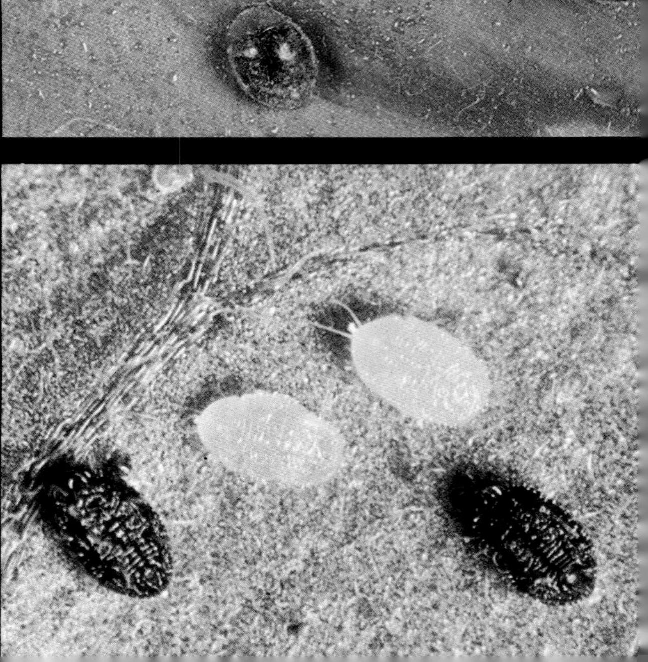

Recent research has shown that once the strain of *Rhizobium* that invades a particular variety of French bean has been identified, it is possible to enclose the seed inside a 'packet' of peat that contains the live bacteria. When treated seeds like this are planted, nodules will form and the plants will be supplied with nitrogen, just like other Legumes.

When you have picked all your peas and beans, you can maximise their effect on the soil by cutting the plants off at soil level, rather than uprooting them. If you grow the same crop in the same place the following year, *Rhizobium* remaining in the soil will be able to invade the roots of the new plants very quickly. If the next crop is not a Legume, it will nevertheless benefit from the residual nitrogen contained in the nodules. This is one of the reasons that most vegetable rotation cycles put a heavy nitrogen feeder, like one of the cabbage family, after a crop of peas or beans. A 'green manure' crop of a leguminous plant, like lucerne, or one of the vetches or clovers, fixes nitrogen in just the same way, increasing the fertility of any unused patch of the garden, ready for the next crop to be grown there.

Available nitrogen also gets into the soil from animal remains. Animals obtain their nitrogen from the plants they eat – and so, indirectly, from the soil – and they return it to the soil either in the load of manure that the gardener forks in or, more slowly, when they die and their bodies decay and decompose. Dead plants return their nitrogen to the soil in the same way, when they are broken down and decomposed by bacterial action, and this nitrogen can be recycled in the garden by using a compost heap.

A rather odd and extremely unreliable source of nitrogen is found in lightning. A flash of lightning fixes atmospheric nitrogen, which is then carried to earth in a rainstorm that is not water but a weak solution of fertiliser. A nice bonus, but not something to count on!

On the debit side, nitrogen is the nutrient most easily leached from the soil, especially when heavy rain hits cultivated, well-drained soil. Bare earth suffers the most, so keeping your garden as full as possible helps to cut losses, as does growing a green manure crop when you are not growing vegetables. Some bacteria can also reverse the good work of *Rhizobium* by releasing nitrogen from its compounds as a gas, but these bacteria thrive only in waterlogged and airless soils – yet another reason for working to improve the structure of your soil.

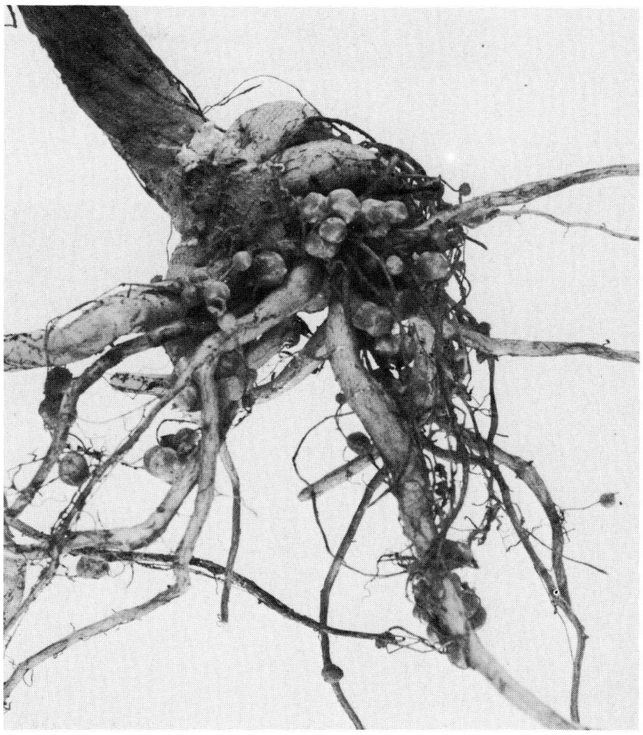

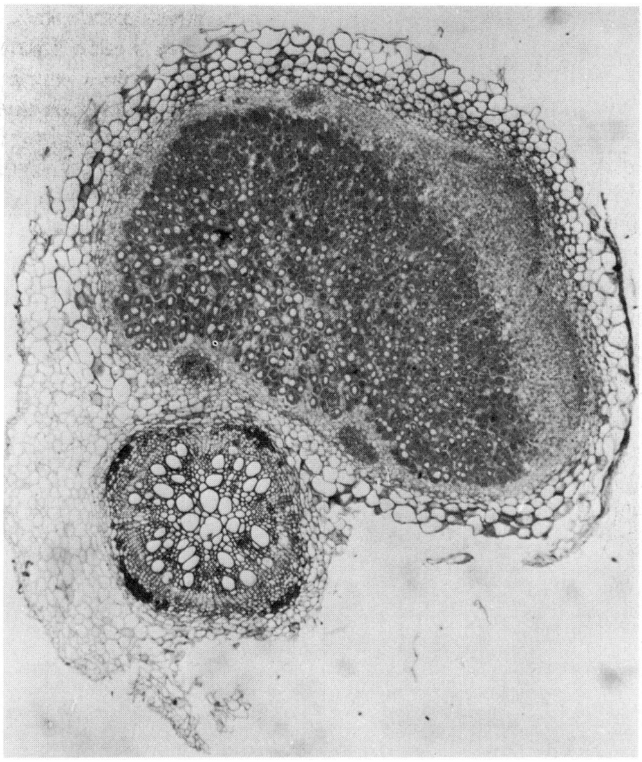

(Opposite page, top.) Three soils, tested to determine their inorganic components. From the left, clay, loam and sandy soil. (See page 94)
The other photos are of predators or parasites on garden and greenhouse pests. (See pages 143–144.) (Centre left) The ladybird larva with aphids. (Centre right.) The larva and adult Cryptolaemus.

(Below left.) Phytoseiulus. *(Below right.) Healthy white and parasitised black scales of the whitefly. (This page, top.) Nodules on the roots of a runner bean. (Above.) A section through a root and its nodule. The vascular tissue of the root is in the lower left hand corner, and the cells of the nodule are packed with the bacteria* Rhizobium.

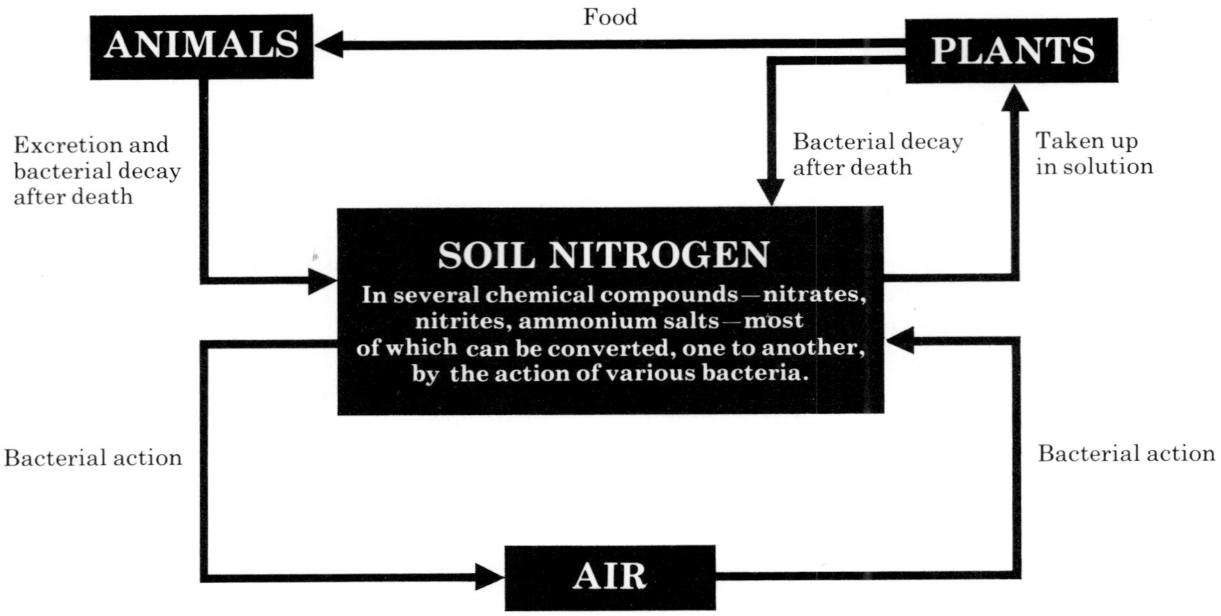

The nitrogen cycle.

A diagram showing how nitrogen is cycled and recycled in nature looks rather like a mass of magic bacteria all busily converting something into something else, but there are a couple of things worth noticing. The first is that all the useful bacteria live in well-drained soil with a good soil atmosphere and plenty of humus, whereas the 'villains' do well in a waterlogged soil with no air at all. The second is that this picture does not include the biggest influence of all in the garden, the gardener.

CHOOSING A FERTILISER

Gardeners harvest crops. They take plants from the natural cycle and eat them or put them in vases, and if the circulation of nitrogen between animals, plants, the soil and the air is to be maintained, then the nitrogen – and all the other nutrients that these crops contained – must be returned to the soil to benefit plants grown the following year.

There are two ways that a gardener can go about this. The first is by adding organic matter like manure, spent hops or compost, and the second is by adding the inorganic fertilisers that can be bought. These can be purchased either as individual chemicals, each containing one nutrient, or as mixtures containing several. Whatever kind you buy, the amount of actual nutrient will appear somewhere on the packet as a percentage of the total weight. For example, sulphate of ammonia, which is a common nitrogen fertiliser, contains twenty-one per cent nitrogen. The important thing about this figure is that it refers only to the nutrient that is in a form that the plant can take up. With nitrogen fertilisers, in particular, the chemicals that you can buy are absorbed by the plant at different speeds. Any 'nitrate' fertiliser will act very quickly, because nitrates are highly soluble, so this sort of fertiliser makes a good boost for leafy vegetables.

The most important soil nutrients – the ones that need to be added to the soil in the largest quantity – are nitrogen, phosphorus and potassium. Many gardeners like to buy a number of chemicals, each rich in one of the nutrients (say, ammonium sulphate, superphosphate and sulphate of potash) and retire to the potting shed with a pair of scales and a recipe book to prepare the compound fertiliser that best suits them, their gardens and the crops they plan to grow. As an alternative, there are any number ready mixed and on sale. The advantage of preparing your own is that if you are sure of the requirements of your soil, you can mix a fertiliser that fulfils them exactly. On the other hand, the compound fertilisers are easy to use and are often granular, which makes them easy to distribute.

The best known of the mixed fertilisers is 'growmore', which was first sold as 'National Gromore' during the 'Dig for Victory' campaign of the Second World War, and seems to be holding its own in the new enthusiasm for gardening that has risen along with the price of vegetables in the shops. It is a good general fertiliser, containing equal amounts of nitro-

Mustard is commonly used as green manure. When the plants are mature, they are dug into the soil to increase its organic content.

gen, phosphorus and potassium – seven per cent of each. Mixed fertilisers are generally labelled with a series of three numbers. These are the percentages of nitrogen, phosphorus and potassium that the compound contains, in that order. So 'growmore' is a '7:7:7' fertiliser whereas a compound labelled '10:5:20' would contain ten per cent nitrogen, five per cent phosphorus and twenty per cent potassium. If the labels on fertiliser packets talk about 'N, P and K' they refer to the chemical symbols for those three vital nutrient elements.

As well as the general fertilisers, like growmore, there are many mixed fertilisers that are made for specific purposes or to suit specific crops, like roses, lawns or tomatoes, and these, like many general fertilisers, also contain enough of the trace elements to eliminate any possibility of deficiencies.

Most fertilisers are either dug in or dissolved in water and poured on to the soil. They are usually placed alongside the plant, close enough to give the roots easy access but far enough away to prevent scorching or other damage from over-concentration. Foliar sprays are useful if there is enough of a particular nutrient in the soil but for some reason the plant is unable to absorb it. This happens most often because the pH of the soil renders a nutrient insoluble and therefore unavailable to the plant. The long-term solution is to alter the acidity of the soil, but this can be a slow job, particularly when the soil is too alkaline rather than too acid, and a foliar spray will sometimes help the crop that is actually in the ground and suffering.

Any organic matter that you add to the soil has a double function. On the one hand it increases the humus content and greatly improves the texture of the soil, and on the other it is a source of N, P and K in just the same way as an inorganic fertiliser. The debate between the followers of these two approaches, inorganic and organic, sometimes becomes heated. Inorganic fertilisers are expensive. Their manufacture uses quantities of oil-based chemicals at a time when the end of the oil boom is in sight. There is also a profound danger of falling into the habit of thinking that you can cure every ill of the garden with a shake of some patent chemical, without considering the over-all health and condition of the soil.

On the other hand, there is no doubt at all that inorganic fertilisers are a much more concentrated source of the nutrients that the garden needs. If you grow crops in the garden without adding any organic material at all, but using plenty of inorganic fertilisers, you will probably get excellent results for the first few years. However, these will inevitably deteriorate along with the texture of the soil. The basis of good organic gardening is not just to take as big a crop as possible this year but to treat the earth with respect, as the best long-term investment we have, maintaining its fertility into a future when the oil-based chemicals will cost goodness knows what. For the gardener with a small plot, particularly in a town when manure may be impossible to find, a completely organic garden is hard to keep up – but why throw organic waste into the dustbin (and give the council the trouble of burning it), when it could be enriching your own garden?

PLANTS WITHOUT SOIL

One of the side effects of all the research into plant nutrients over the last few decades is an increasing tendency to grow plants without any soil at all. That sounds something of a paradox. The function of the soil is to support the plant, which anchors itself by its roots, and to supply the plant, by way of those roots, with nutrients in solution and with air. If we can perform those functions some other way, we can manage without any soil at all. The 'soil-less composts' that you see in every shop and garden centre, are usually based on peat – that is, on humus – which is only one part of a complete soil. It seems a bit of a cheat to describe a compost made from the organic fraction of soil without the inorganic as 'soil-less', but that is what these composts usually contain, mixed with a little sand to improve the drainage. This makes a growing medium with a lovely texture but hardly any nutrients at all, so the needs of the plants are met by adding specific concentrated chemicals.

The composts used for growing and pricking out seedlings avoid high nutrient concentrations that might burn the sensitive, developing plants, but contain the nutrient in a form that is readily available to ensure sturdy growth. Composts that might be expected to support plants for much longer contain nutrients that last longer and that dissolve and become available to the plant more slowly. 'Growing bags' generally contain enough nutrients to feed the recommended number of plants for about six weeks. After this the compost will continue to support the roots of the plant, providing air and water but absolutely nothing else, so heavy feeders – like tomatoes, which are often grown in these bags – need substantial feeding after this first few weeks.

If you want to grow plants in bags you can prepare your own by mixing a well-sieved peat with some sand and damping it thoroughly with a strong solution of a mixed fertiliser. This can cost substantially less than buying ready-made bags, but you will need to add more nutrients right from the start and not just after six weeks.

Early experiments to determine just which elements were essential for healthy plant growth were generally conducted by growing plants in a nutrient solution. The contents of a culture solution like this could be measured exactly and the nutrient uptake of the plants precisely controlled. The plants were supported with sticks and string, and aeration was kept up by a pipe bubbling air through the solution. The plants thrived, providing they got the right nutrients, and the science of hydroponics was born. Nowadays, many of those early, experimental techniques have become acceptable, even conventional, alternatives to soil and soil-less composts, particularly for the commercial growers.

One method, called the nutrient film technique, or NFT, is commonly used for glass-house tomatoes and lettuce. There are small-scale versions of this technique on the market, for use in the domestic greenhouse, but they must be regarded as a curiosity for the enthusiast rather than an economic way of keeping the family in tomatoes. The big worry is pump failure. If the pump breaks down on a Friday

night, just after you have set off for a week-end away from home, then the plants will have been without water for two days by the time you get back on Sunday. They will be lucky to survive, and the crop that you get will certainly be drastically reduced. On a commercial scale there is an army of alarm bells ringing and spare pumps standing by to avoid a disaster, and even then they sometimes happen. At home, this kind of breakdown is a real risk, however well maintained the equipment.

There are claims for enormously increased crops using hydroponic techniques, but many of them have been disputed, and, without doubt, the major advantage for the commercial grower is that without soil there is no need for the annual soil sterilising treatment. This gets rid of the pests and diseases that would otherwise accumulate but is heavy on fuel and, as a result, very expensive.

Hydroponic systems have also been useful in places where water is available but there is not enough top-soil to cultivate in the usual way. During the Second World War, troops stationed on coral atolls grew themselves vegetables using hydroponics, and since then various schemes have pumped water and nutrients into desert areas with some success.

(Opposite page.) A large commercial greenhouse, growing tomatoes using the nutrient film technique.
(This page, above.) The plants grow in closed plastic troughs, through which the nutrient solution flows.
(Below.) The nutrient solution is pumped from a reservoir tank around the glasshouse and through all the troughs. When it returns to the tank, it is aerated, its nutrient strength is tested and chemicals are added, as necessary, to keep it at the right strength. All this is done automatically, to ensure that the roots of the plant can obtain the air and nutrients they need, as well as water, from the solution that flows over them.

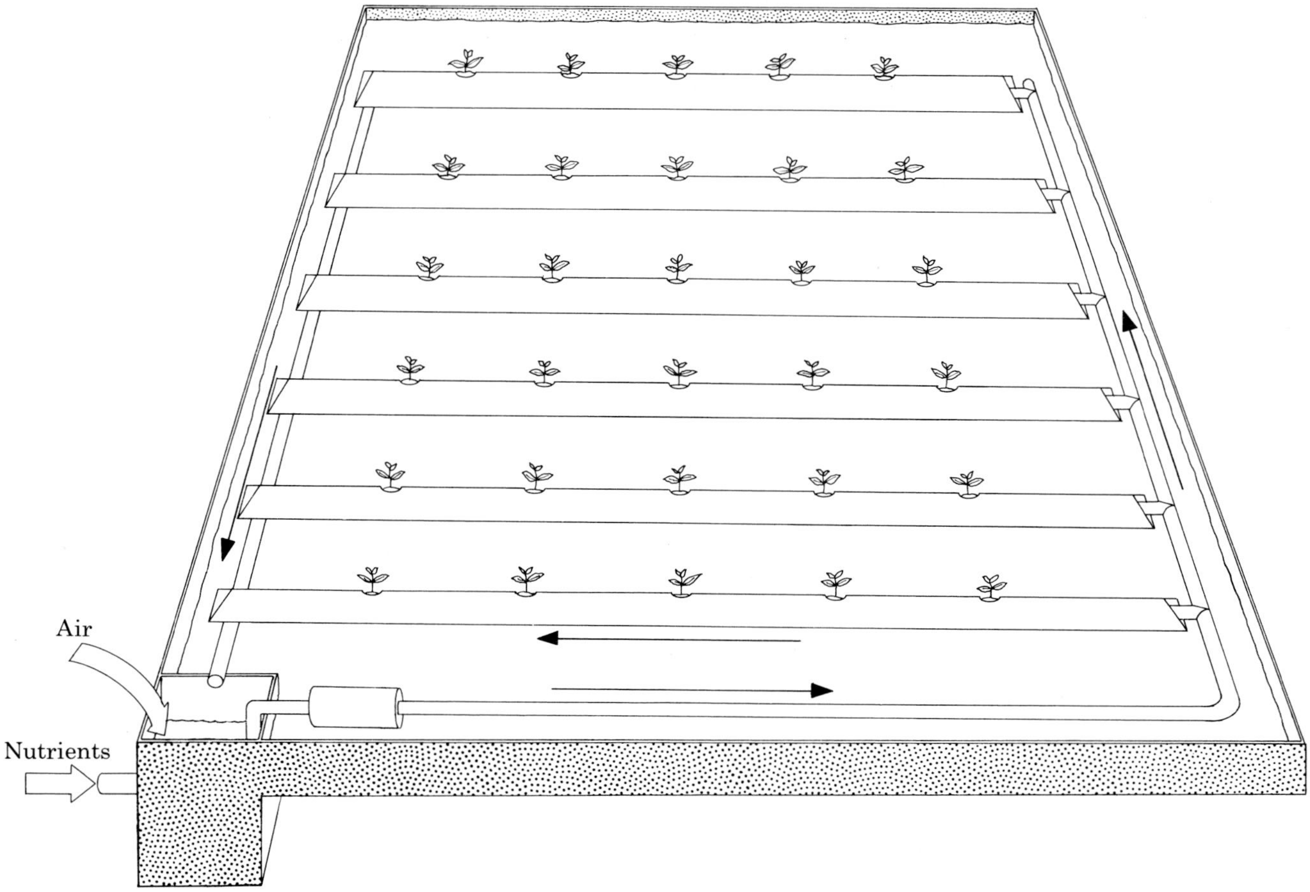

In the home, there are now any number of ways of growing house plants without soil, particularly the large displays found in offices and commercial buildings. The key to success lies in the structure of the medium that is used to support the plant. This must be able to hold and supply the plant's roots with both water and air. The system most commonly seen uses hard, reddish-brown pieces of porous clay aggregate, but new versions appear in the shops every year. The advantages are clear. Nutrients are supplied in a slow release form and given to the plants once or twice a year, and a floating indicator is used to show when they need water. Maintenance is almost foolproof.

(Above.) A house plant, grown without soil in a pot of clay aggregate.

HOW NUTRIENTS GET INTO THE PLANT

Whether a plant gets its nutrient solution from the latest product of the laboratory or from deep in the earth, the same process is involved in getting the vital elements into its roots. Water is taken up into the root hairs and the surface cells near the apex of the root. From this point, until it reaches the xylem, the water travels by one of two routes. The first route is through the cells that lie between the root hair and the xylem. This complex method involves the water passing in and out of the living cell contents of each of these cells, and depends on the many other processes that are going on inside them.

The second pathway is essentially very simple. Water diffuses along the walls of the cells and through the intercellular spaces without ever entering the living contents of the cells. This path is blocked, however, by a cylinder of cells that lies towards the middle of the root and is called the 'endodermis'. A band of impermeable, waxy material runs through the radial and horizontal cell walls of each of the cells in the endodermis, and this band, which is called the Casparian strip, stops water passing through the cell walls. All further movement inwards, towards the xylem, has to take place by way of the living contents of the cells in the endodermis.

(Below.) At one side of the pot is a tube which contains a small float. The position of the marker on top of this float indicates the level of water in the pot. The plant is held within an inner pot, made of netting (dotted line), so that it can be transplanted.

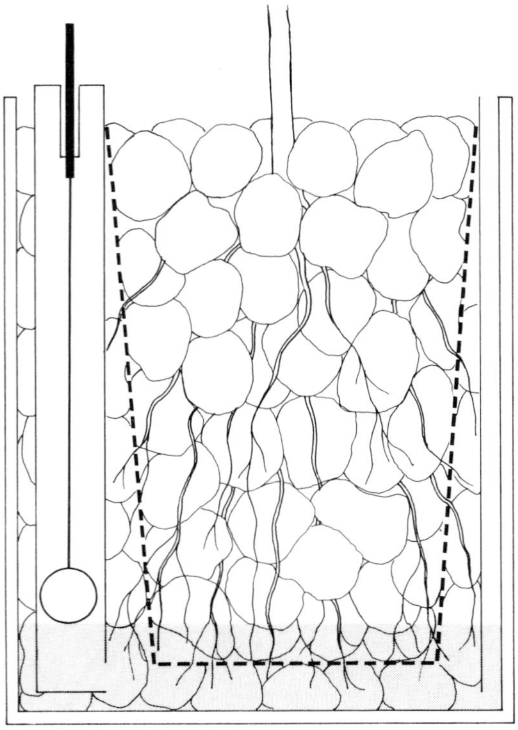

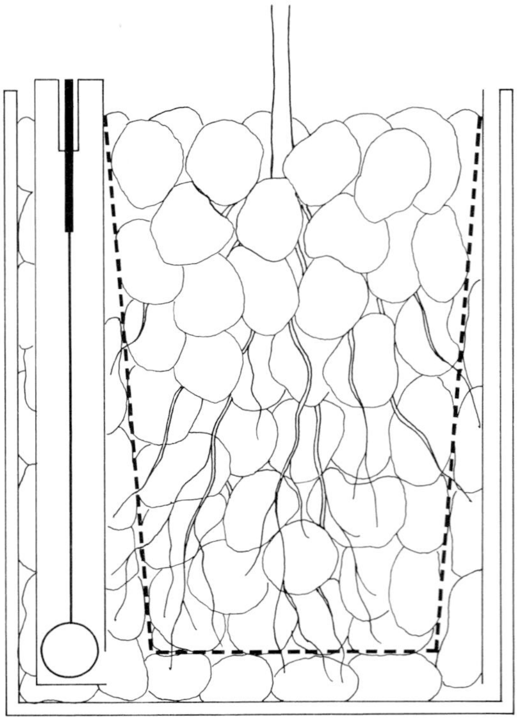

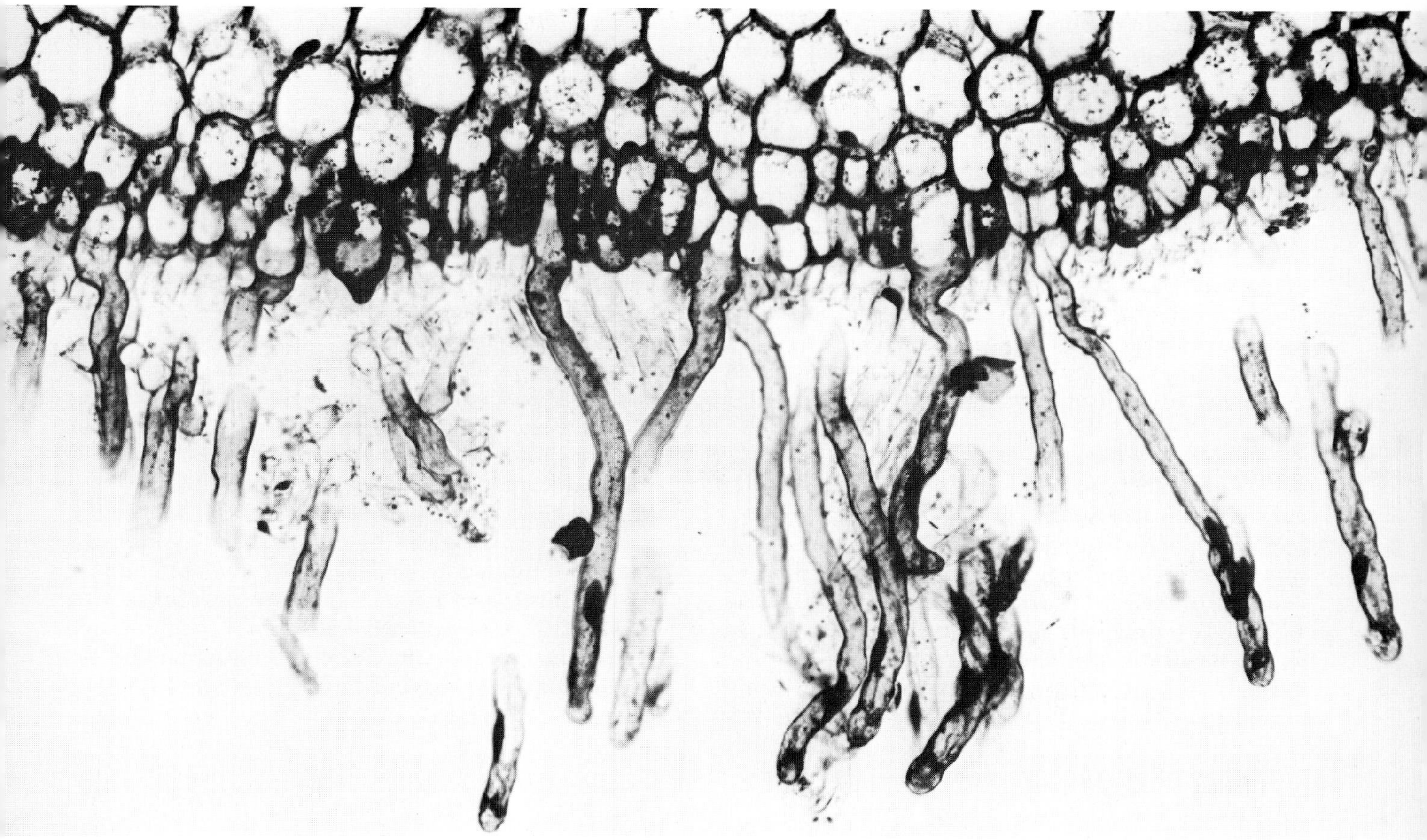

(Above.) A section through a root, showing the root hairs. These are not real hairs, but small projections of the epidermal cells which increase the root's intake of water by increasing its surface area.
(Below.) Water gets into the root through the cells between the root hairs and the xylem, or through the walls of these cells and the intercellular spaces. This second route is blocked by the Casparian strip, so all the water and nutrients entering the root must pass through the living cells of the endodermis.

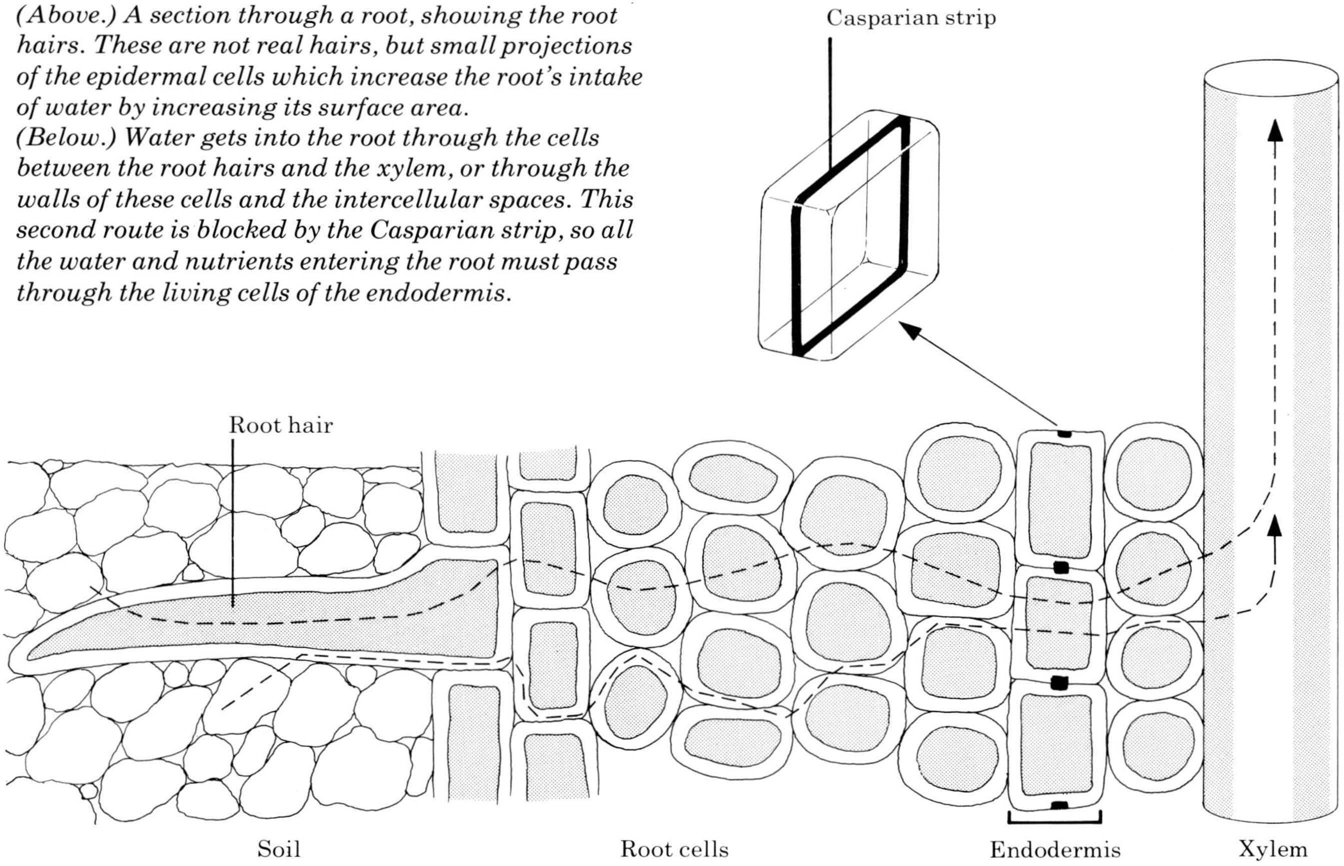

At this point the plant may be selective about what it takes in. Certain nutrient salts are needed in larger quantities by some plants than by others. Other salts, less essential ones, are carried in with them, and both become concentrated within cells to the inside of the endodermis. We know that water is the medium in which the nutrients are carried, and we know that energy is expended by the plant at this time but the exact mechanisms by which the uptake of nutrients is controlled are not yet fully understood, although many and varied explanations have been proposed.

One theory, which receives wide support, is that nutrients enter the endodermis on a kind of molecular piggy-back. Some substance, possibly an enzyme, carries the nutrients through the cell wall and membrane and into the cell, drops it and goes back out for some more. This needs energy on the part of the plant; and, indeed, if the rate of respiration goes up (which is a measure of energy expended), then the rate of nutrient uptake rises as well. Only living cells can take up nutrients in this way. If a cell is killed, then the nutrients it contains diffuse out until the cell contents are in equilibrium with the solution in the surrounding soil. Root pressure, which sometimes causes sap to exude from a cut stump, is a kind of 'over-flow' from this active uptake of nutrients.

Some nutrients – phosphorus in particular – are also helped into the root by a symbiotic association between the plant and a fungus. The body of the fungus consists of a mass of long thread-like filaments, the hyphae, which live partly in the root of the plant and partly in the surrounding soil. Some fungi that enter plant tissue do a great deal of damage, but this type, a *Mycorrhiza*, does quite the opposite. The millions of hyphae act like a network of pathways that can be used by the soil solution, passing from the soil into the root. The fungus is so extensive that it provides access to areas of soil which would otherwise be beyond the reach of the root system, and this increases the amount of nutrient that is available to the plant. As in every symbiotic relationship, the plant has to pay for the benefits of living alongside the *Mycorrhiza*. The price in this case is a food that the fungus takes from the plant. The food is carbohydrate, as good a source of quick energy for a fungus as it is for a human. This carbohydrate is made inside the plant by a process called photosynthesis.

The root of a Scots pine, covered with a white mat of hyphae.

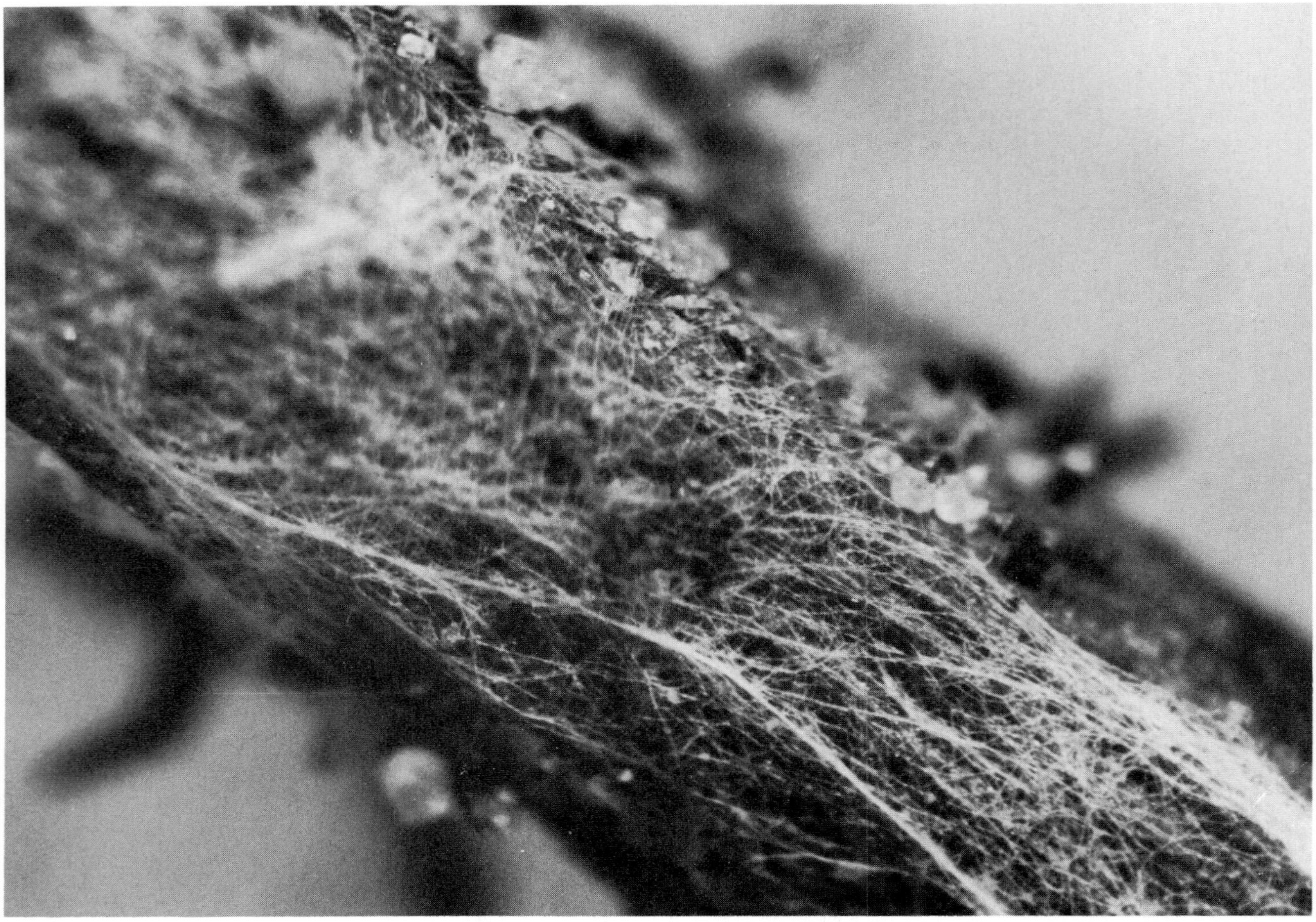

CHAPTER NINE

THE FOOD MACHINE

All living organisms need a supply of energy, and plants are no exception. We get our energy from the food that we eat, but what about plants? Plants do not munch their way through breakfast, and they cannot uproot themselves and go off hunting to find their dinner, but they do have an ability unique among living things. They can make their own food. They do something that no insect, bird, fish or brilliant scientist has yet managed. They take the simple raw materials around them and, using the energy in sunlight and the pigment that makes them green, they manufacture sugar.

This wonderful process is called 'photosynthesis', and, in the long run, every scrap of food that we eat depends on it. Every plant that we eat has trapped the energy from the sun to make its food, and every animal that we eat has either eaten a plant itself or fed on another animal that has. The food chain – the plan that links an organism both to its food and to its predators – always has a plant at the bottom because all food depends on the ability of the plant kingdom to make its own food by photosynthesis. Fossil plants continue to store the energy they trapped, and we release it when we burn fossil fuels like coal, gas and oil. The light from the fire in the grate is the light of the Carboniferous sun, trapped by a plant and imprisoned in fossil coal for more than three hundred million years.

A typical food chain

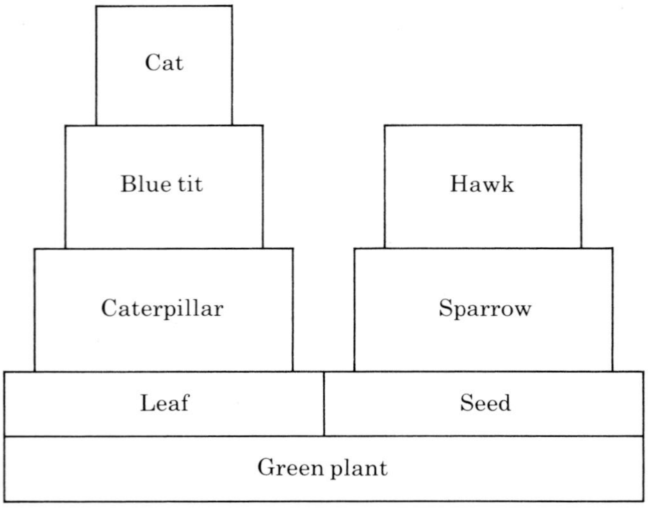

THE RAW MATERIALS

The raw materials for photosynthesis are carbon dioxide and water. The energy to power the reaction comes from the sun, and the tiny 'factories', where the whole process takes place are found in the green parts of the plant, particularly in the leaves. They are called 'chloroplasts' and are green in colour because they contain a green pigment called chlorophyll. Many facets of the structure of plants have evolved specifically to ensure that the raw materials necessary for photosynthesis are in the right place at the right time.

Water is the first requirement. This comes from the soil by way of the roots and the plant plumbing system, the xylem. The midrib and veins are part of this system and carry water into every corner of the leaf. From the tiny vein endings the water can diffuse into the cells where the chloroplasts lie and where photosynthesis takes place.

The importance of water to plants and their food has been accepted, although rather misunderstood, for hundreds of years. As long ago as the seventeenth century a Flemish scientist, Van Helmont, carried out experiments in order to investigate its role. He grew willow cuttings in a pot that contained a weighed quantity of soil, and for five years

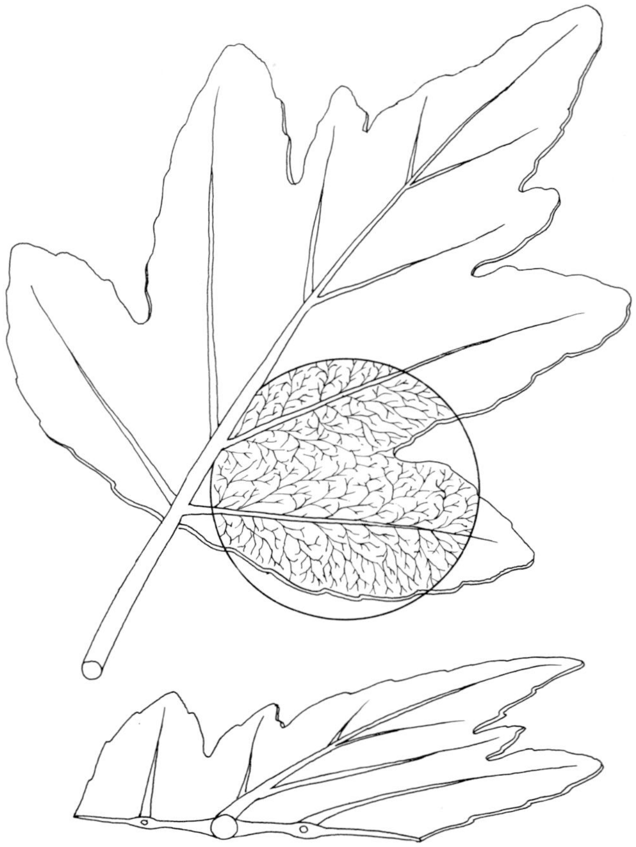

he watered them regularly but added nothing else to the pot. At the end of that time he weighed both the plants and the soil. He found that the soil had lost a tiny amount – about two ounces – whereas the willow cuttings, now young trees, had gained a staggering 161 lbs. He concluded that 'all vegetable matter immediately and materially arises from the element of water alone'. It sounds plausible, indeed convincing, but of course he was wrong. He made his mistake because he thought that his plants had had access only to water and forgot that they were surrounded by air. Air contains carbon dioxide, which is the second of the raw materials needed before a plant can photosynthesise and grow.

Later in that century, a Royal Society lecturer got a little nearer the mark when he proposed that plants were 'nourished and increased by a double food; the one an impregnated water, the other an impregnated air. These do initially mix and coalesce.' It was not for another couple of hundred years that the importance of carbon dioxide was fully understood.

All living organisms produce carbon dioxide as a waste product during respiration. It also exists in vast quantities in the sea, both as a gas, which is dissolved in the water, and trapped in carbonates, the chemical compounds which make up the shells of many marine animals. Only about 0·03 per cent of the atmosphere around the earth is carbon dioxide – which sounds very little but, for the purposes of the green plants on the planet, is enough.

Carbon dioxide gets into the plant by the same route that water vapour gets out – through the tiny pores on the leaf surface, the stomata. The ability of the plant to take in carbon dioxide and photosynthesise depends on the stomata remaining open as much as possible, and this depends – in part, at least – on the water that the plant contains. Only the stomata of well-watered, upright plants with turgid cells remain open. Wilting can threaten a plant with starvation (see Chapter 7).

(Opposite page, right.) Water is carried to every part of the leaf through a network of tiny veins, which branch off the larger veins. These in turn branch off the central midrib.

(Below left.) The vein network through a microscope. The distance between veins can be as little as 0·13mm.

(Below right.) A vein ending.

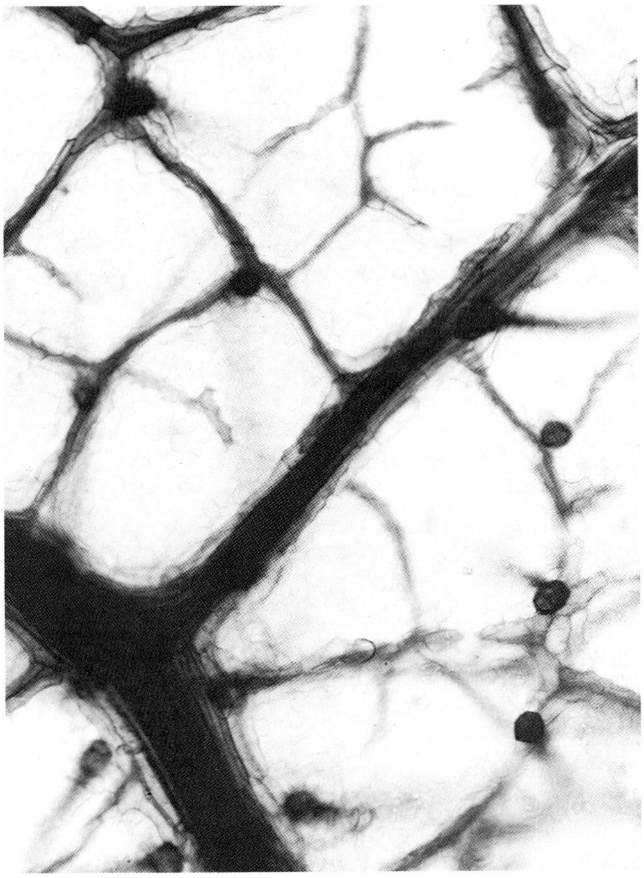

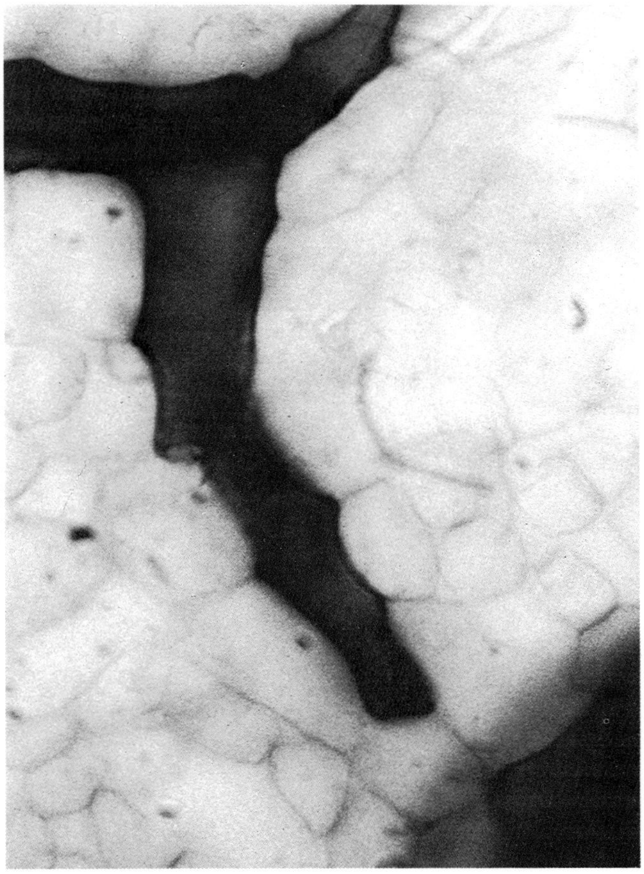

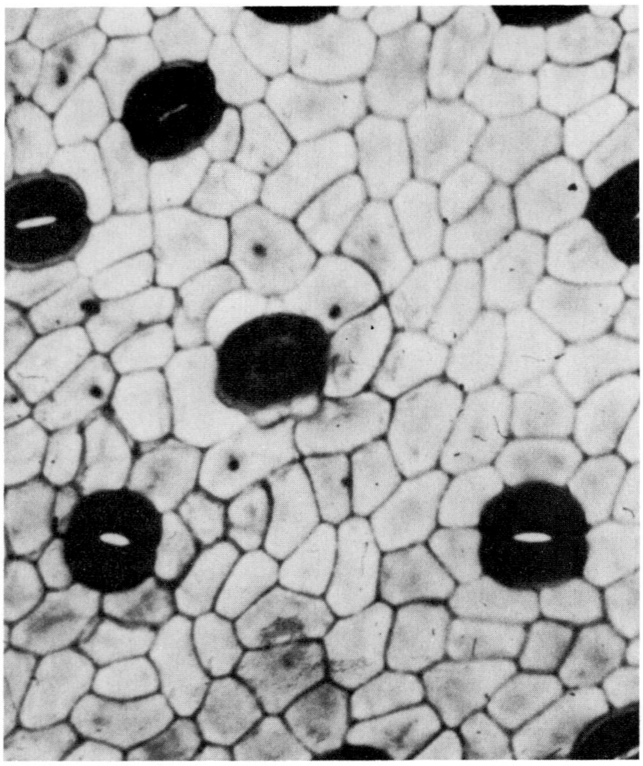

The stomata are scattered in greatest numbers on the underside of the leaf.

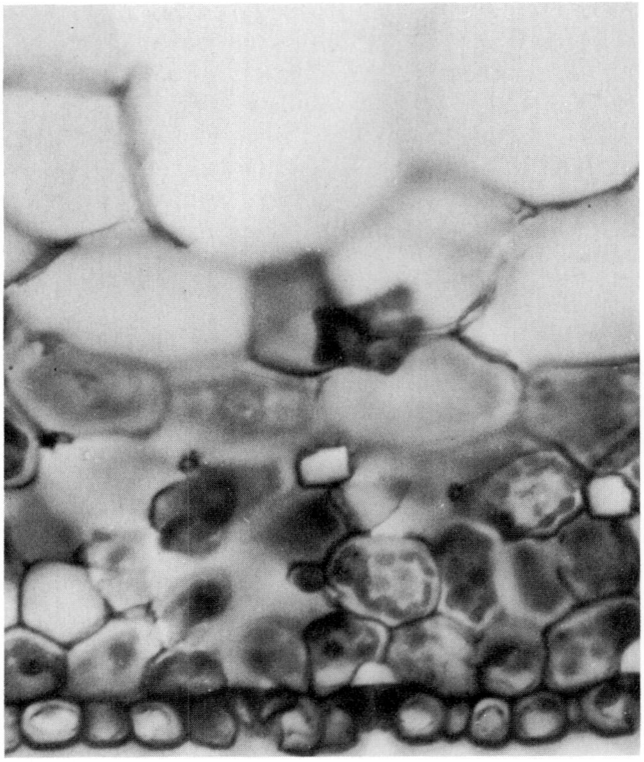

A section through a leaf, showing a stoma and the air space above it.

Stomata are found all over the plant, but the greatest numbers are on the undersides of the leaves. There is plenty of carbon dioxide here, but the stomata are sheltered from the strongest sunlight, which cuts down the evaporation of water vapour. Their frequency varies between ten and four hundred per square millimetre. Behind each stoma is a space, part of a spongy layer of cells with many gaps between them. The carbon dioxide passes through the stomata and into these spaces and then diffuses through the walls of the cells, where it dissolves in the water that they contain. Once it is in solution it can pass from cell to cell until it reaches the cells where photosynthesis takes place.

The sunlight that powers photosynthesis is absorbed by the chloroplasts, but they do not take up every part of the sunlight. White light, like sunlight, is made up of a spectrum of different colours – all the colours of the rainbow. You can see the colours by shining a narrow beam of light through a triangular glass prism. The glass splits the light into its seven component colours. But if you shine a beam of white light through a green leaf and then through a prism, there are some colours missing. There are dark bands in the part of the spectrum that showed red and violet, which indicates that it is red and violet light that is absorbed by the leaf.

This simple experiment implies that only part of the light spectrum is involved in photosynthesis. The truth of this was demonstrated by a nineteenth-century botanist, called Engelmann, towards the end of the last century. He took a long filament of a green alga, a water plant, and shone lights of different colours at different sites along its length. He then took some bacteria and added them to the tank. Before starting the experiment, Engelmann knew two things: that a plant which is photosynthesising gives off oxygen, and that his bacteria needed oxygen to survive. When he found that the bacteria had all swum to the part of the alga that was bathed in red light, he concluded that it was this part of the light spectrum that was vital for a plant during the process of photosynthesis.

The position and structure of the chloroplasts is designed to expose them to as much light as possible. Most of them lie in cells towards the upper surface of the leaf, and many plants can actually alter the angle of their leaves to follow the light of the sun. The chloroplasts need just the opposite position to the stomata; the stomata lie on the underside of the leaf where they are sheltered from some of the drying effects of the sun, whereas the chloroplasts, which need as much sun as possible, are mostly in cells on the upper surface.

The chloroplasts are oval in shape and usually lie with their long axes at right angles to the light, which exposes as much of the chloroplast as possible. Some plants can even shift their chloro-

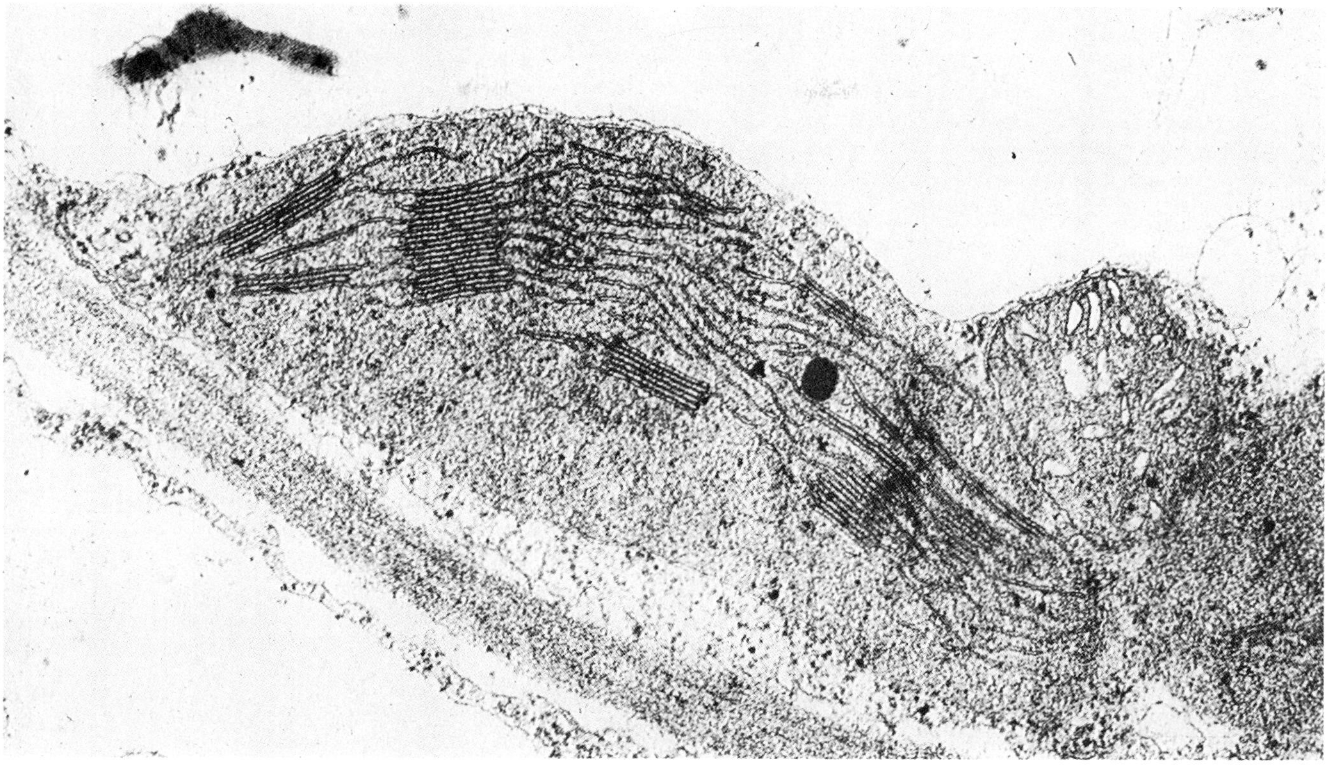

Photomicrograph of a chloroplast, with its parallel stacks of membranes or grana.

plasts about, to follow the movement of the sun. Inside the chloroplast there are stacks of membranes, the grana, and these stacks lie parallel to the line of the chloroplast – which again exposes as much of the membrane as possible to the light. It is molecules of the pigment chlorophyll that actually absorb the light. These lie on the membranes and even they are precisely spaced and oriented to trap as much of the light energy as possible.

The chemical reactions involved in photosynthesis are many and complex, but the over-all synthesis can be summarised by, single equation shown below.

What actually happens is that each of a long chain of reactions sparks off the next in line. Year by year biochemists sort out and add to the details, but the important fact is this: in the presence of chlorophyll and light, the plant synthesises sugar from carbon dioxide and water with oxygen as a waste product.

The efficiency of photosynthesis

In spite of nature's meticulous design, not all the light that falls on a leaf is used. Plants absorb about 83 per cent of the light that falls on them. Of this, only about 4 per cent is absorbed by the chloroplasts. A botanist with a mathematical bent has worked out that a maize crop uses only 1·6 per cent of the light energy that reaches it, and that a mere 0·13 per cent is converted into a form that is useful to man. So the sun certainly supplies a lot more energy than the plant uses, but of the light energy that is actually absorbed by the chloroplasts a staggering 90 per cent is converted into chemical energy, or food. This is the most efficient conversion of one form of energy to another that we know. Certainly the efficiency of energy conversion in photosynthesis makes the oil-to-electricity conversion of a power station look very poor.

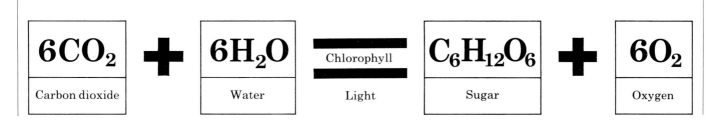

$6CO_2$	+	$6H_2O$	= Chlorophyll =	$C_6H_{12}O_6$	+	$6O_2$
Carbon dioxide		Water	Light	Sugar		Oxygen

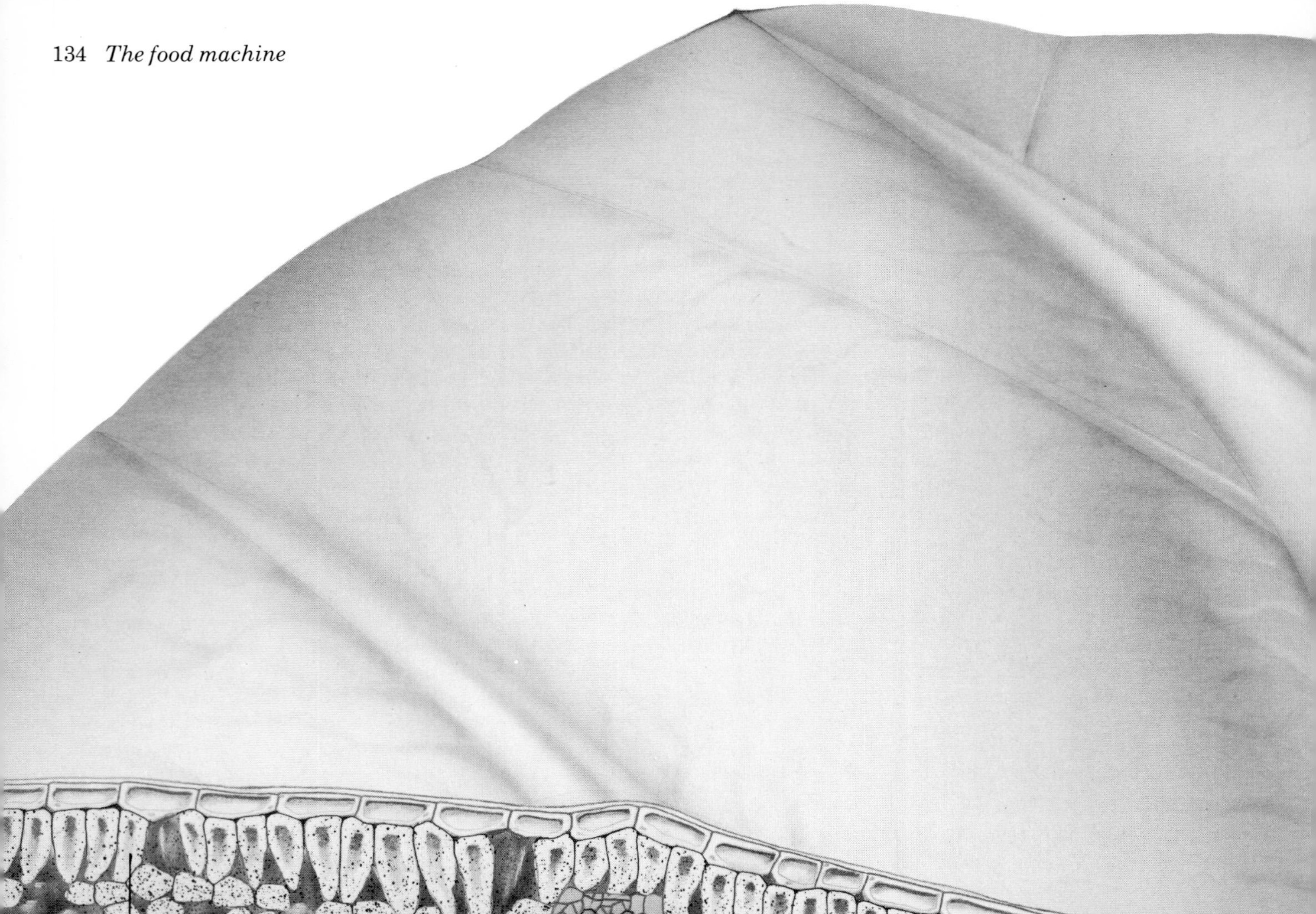

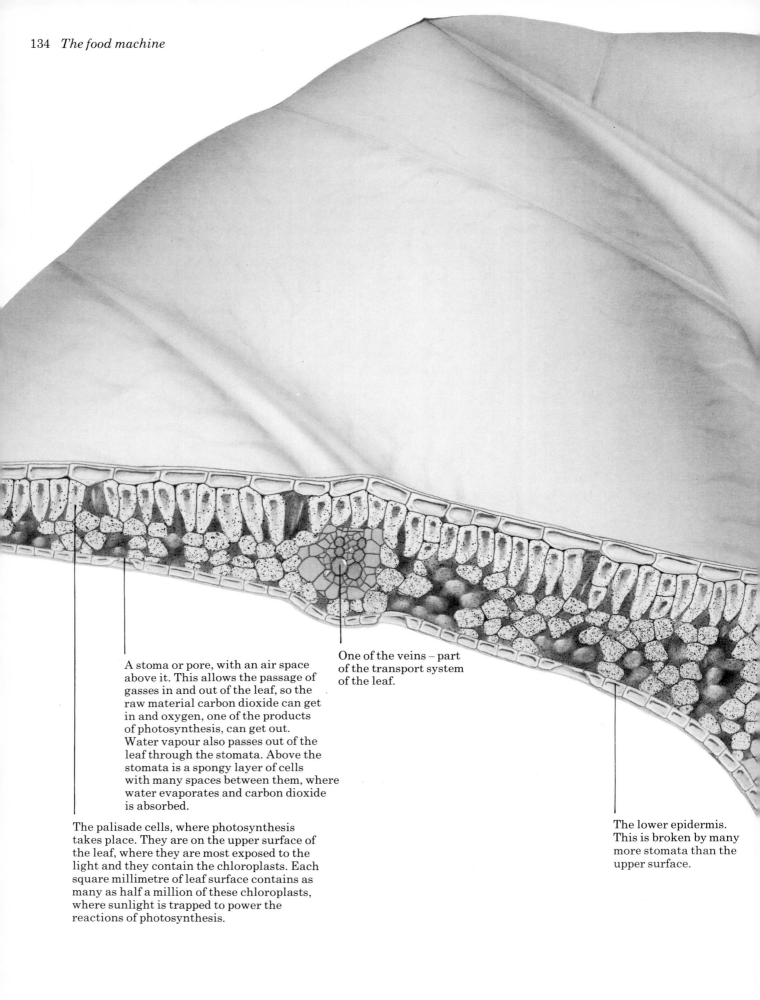

A stoma or pore, with an air space above it. This allows the passage of gasses in and out of the leaf, so the raw material carbon dioxide can get in and oxygen, one of the products of photosynthesis, can get out. Water vapour also passes out of the leaf through the stomata. Above the stomata is a spongy layer of cells with many spaces between them, where water evaporates and carbon dioxide is absorbed.

One of the veins – part of the transport system of the leaf.

The palisade cells, where photosynthesis takes place. They are on the upper surface of the leaf, where they are most exposed to the light and they contain the chloroplasts. Each square millimetre of leaf surface contains as many as half a million of these chloroplasts, where sunlight is trapped to power the reactions of photosynthesis.

The lower epidermis. This is broken by many more stomata than the upper surface.

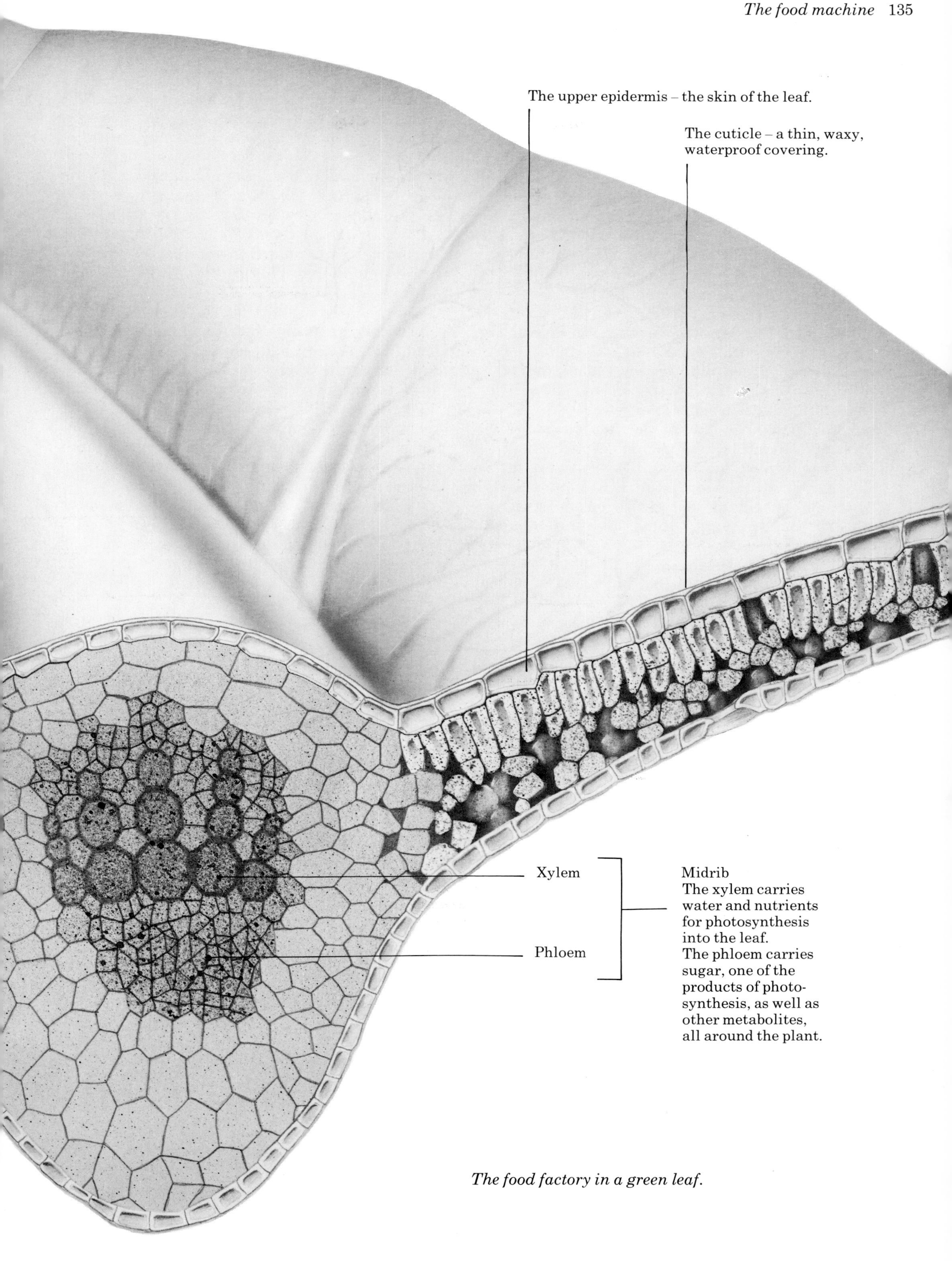
The upper epidermis – the skin of the leaf.
The cuticle – a thin, waxy, waterproof covering.
Xylem
Phloem
Midrib
The xylem carries water and nutrients for photosynthesis into the leaf.
The phloem carries sugar, one of the products of photo-synthesis, as well as other metabolites, all around the plant.

The food factory in a green leaf.

Some of the oxygen is used by the plant in respiration, but the rest of it passes out through the stomata and into the atmosphere. All living organisms need oxygen. We all need to breathe, to take in oxygen so that the food we eat can be 'burned' and produce energy, and it is an astonishing fact that all the oxygen in the atmosphere around this planet is produced by photosynthesising plants. Not only are we dependent on the plant kingdom for every mouthful we eat, but we also owe to them our very existence – for, without photosynthesis, there would be no oxygen and, without oxygen, life as we understand it could never have evolved.

In spite of the importance of oxygen to us and to the rest of the world, it is the sugar that the plant is really after. A very small amount is immediately converted, in the leaf, into starch, but most of it remains in solution and is transported to wherever it is needed. From the sugar the plant can make all the organic compounds that it needs and that are found within its tissues. Some of them, like starch, are carbohydrates – that is, they contain the same elements (carbon, hydrogen and oxygen) that are found in sugar. Others – like proteins, fats, hormones, vitamins and, indeed, chlorophyll itself – contain one or more other elements, and it is here that the soil nutrients are so important. The plant produces practically all the food that we take from the garden entirely by itself, almost in spite of the gardener, but plants can make the most of their ability to photosynthesise only if they are rooted in a soil that provides them with all the mineral nutrients they need.

If a plant needs to store food, to see it through the winter and to fuel the first spring growth the next year, it generally keeps its stores in the form of starch. Unlike sugar, starch is insoluble. If the plant stored sugar, the cells that contained it would be filled with a strong solution, because sugar is soluble, and this would exert an osmotic pressure which would 'pull' water into the cells (see Chapter 7 page 107). Because starch is insoluble it does not exert an osmotic pressure and can be stored safely. It is also more compressed in molecular structure than sugar, so it takes up less space in the plant. Starch is chemically quite close to sugar, so the plant can easily convert one into the other.

Many of our food plants, particularly the ones we call root vegetables, are the storage organs of plants. The term 'root vegetable' is actually rather misleading because some of them are not really roots at all. The potato, for example, is actually a swollen stem, complete with leaf buds in its 'eyes'. The carrot, on the other hand, is a genuine root, and when it is pulled from the ground you can see that it has fine lateral roots growing from its sides just like any ordinary tap root. A carrot is a typical example of a biennial plant. In its first year it grows from seed (A) into a plant with many green leaves (B), which photosynthesise and make sugar. This is stored as starch in the carrot root, which is swollen and modified for the purpose (C). What generally happens then is that the gardener takes advantage of the plant's winter stores and eats the carrot. However, left to itself, the plant would use the stores to grow in the second year, flower and produce seed (D), starting the two-year cycle all over again. Seeds themselves also contain some stored food, enough to fuel germination and the growth of the seedling until it develops leaves and begins to photosynthesise and feed itself.

Although photosynthesis is arguably the most important process on the whole planet, let alone in the back garden, there does not seem to be a great deal you can do to help it along. It is not possible for the gardener to intervene in the complex chain of reactions that eventually leads to the production of sugar. All we can do is make sure that the environment in which the plant lives is as favourable as we can possibly make it.

Take temperature. In the temperate zones of the earth, plants function best between 10 and 35 °C (50–95 °F). Within this range, photosynthesis increases as the temperature rises up to about 25 °C (77 °F) and after that it declines.

The life story of a carrot.

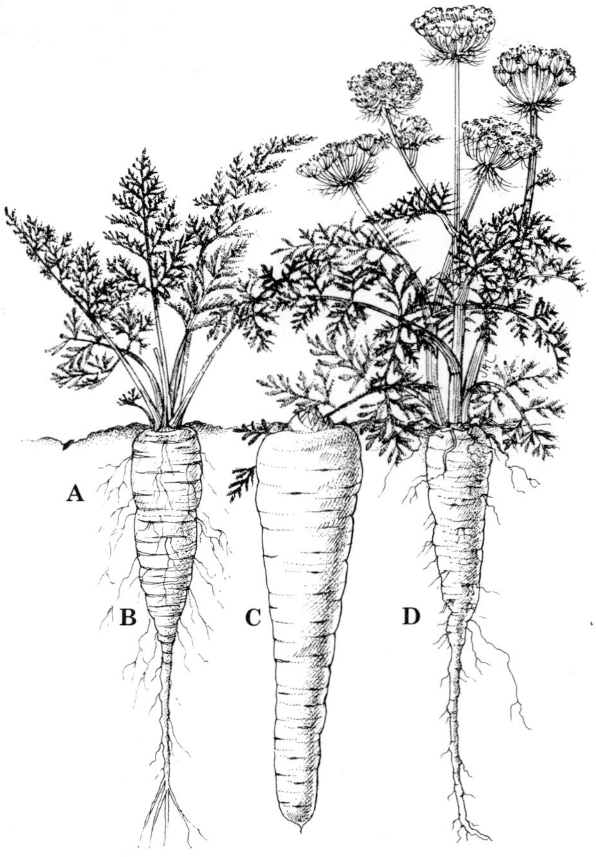

Testing leaves for starch

All leaves that photosynthesise produce sugar and some of that sugar is converted into starch, so where starch is found in a leaf it indicates that photosynthesis has been going on. Testing a leaf for starch can be done fairly easily in the kitchen.

Pick a leaf and dip it in boiling water for half a minute or so to kill all the enzymes and prevent any further chemical reactions from taking place. Then remove all the chlorophyll from the leaf by boiling it in methylated spirits until it is white (1). **This absolutely must be done with extreme caution,** and using some kind of water bath. To put a pan of meths on to the direct heat of a kitchen stove would be very dangerous.

When you take the leaf out of the meths it will be more or less white but rather brittle and hard to handle. It can be softened by dipping it once more into the boiling water. Then spread it out carefully on an old plate or ceramic tile – a white one if possible, because the rest of the test involves colour changes, and they will show up better against a white background.

If you now pour a little iodine over the leaf, the areas which contain starch will turn a dark blue-black, and where there is no starch it will turn brown. If you chose a leaf that had been photosynthesising successfully in the sunshine then the whole leaf will be blue; but if you try the test on a variegated leaf (2) then only the parts that were green will turn blue, proving that it is the green pigment they contain that is essential for photosynthesis.

A leaf from a plant that has been kept in the dark for a few days or a leaf that has been covered with something light-proof, like cooking foil, will not turn blue at all. The leaf needs light to photosynthesise, and you can use this, with the starch test, to 'draw' leaf pictures. Make a stencil from foil – a simple shape or even your initials – and tape it firmly to the top surface of a growing leaf. Leave it there for a couple of days and then test the leaf for the presence of starch.

You should get your initials in blue (where light got through the stencil, the leaf photosynthesised and starch was formed) against a brown background (where the darkened leaf remained inactive) (3). You can even get a picture of sorts by using a black-and-white photographic negative instead of a stencil. For the best results, tape the negative to the upper side of the leaf, and cover the lower side with foil to exclude unwanted light.

1

2

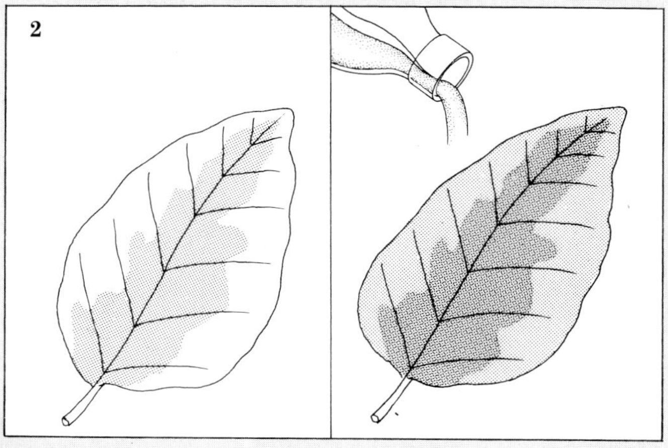

3

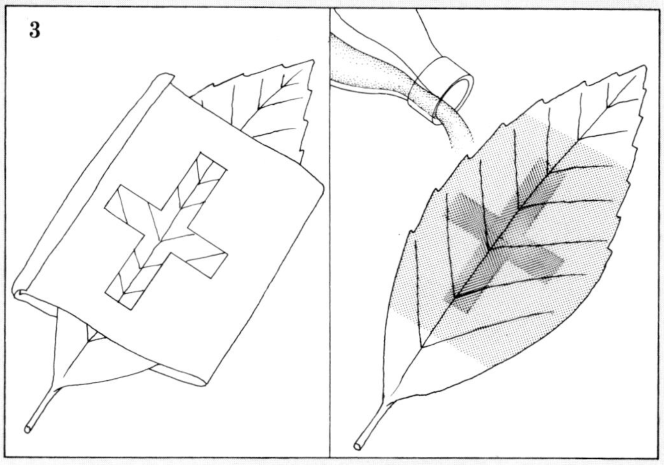

Looking at the garden, that sounds rather like stating the obvious. Everyone knows that a couple of weeks of hot weather, particularly with some rain as well, can turn a well-ordered garden into something approaching a jungle. However, the fact that temperature affects the rate of photosynthesis means that you can get the best possible results from your plants by keeping the temperature in which they live as near the optimum as possible. In the greenhouse that means using a heater in winter perhaps – but it also means remembering that greenhouses often get too hot in the summer and should be shaded with blinds. Some people apply a thin coat of whitewash over the whole greenhouse but, although this is much cheaper than installing blinds, it is not as flexible a system. Blinds can be pulled up and down to follow the vagaries of the summer weather, but whitewash is left on for the whole season.

From sugar to starch

Plants form starch by linking together several hundred, or even over a thousand, sugar molecules together into a long spiral. As each sugar molecule links to the next, a molecule of water is lost, which is why starch is less bulky than sugar and easier to store. The giant starch molecules are sometimes a single spiral and sometimes branched.

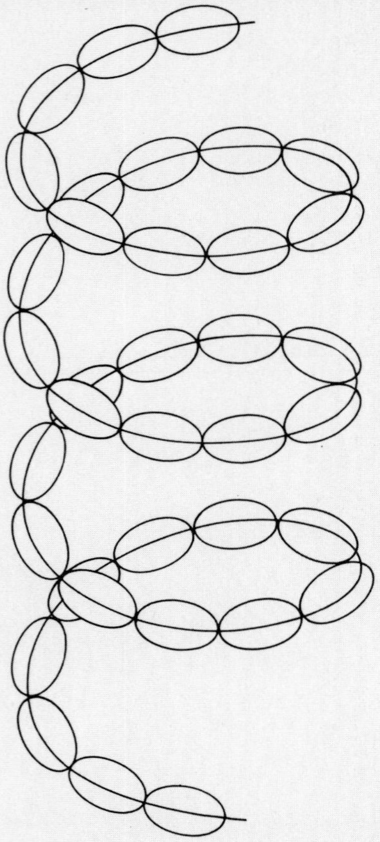

Outside in the garden it is harder to have much influence on the temperature, but cloches and cold frames can raise it enough to extend the growing season a few weeks into the spring and autumn.

The supply of carbon dioxide from the air is not generally any kind of problem for the gardener. In tightly closed winter greenhouses the level sometimes drops a bit as the plants use it up, but even this is unlikely to be a worry for the domestic gardener. Commercial growers, with giant glasshouses and tight production schedules to meet, sometimes give their plants a boost by pumping in some of the gas. If you construct a makeshift 'greenhouse' over a pot of cuttings by supporting a polythene bag on a frame of sticks, some people recommend blowing into the bag first to increase the amount of carbon dioxide available to the fragile young plants. There does not seem to be any real evidence to support this, but it cannot do any harm and may even help, especially as you will also be blowing water vapour into the bag, which will give the 'greenhouse' a nice humid atmosphere, cutting down transpiration and lessening the chance that the cuttings will wilt.

The natural growth cycles of many plants give them a period in flower and also a period in which they bear only leaves. This green, leafy stage may be rather boring for the gardener, who would prefer a splash of colour, but it is vital to the plant. Once the daffodils have finished flowering it is a temptation to cut away the floppy leaves that remain behind them. But these leaves are photosynthesising and pushing all the food that they make down into their 'larder', underground in the bulb. If you cut the leaves away before they turn yellow and die, you will prevent the plant storing up the food that will power the growth of the lovely yellow flowers next spring. Even tying the leaves into neat little bundles lessens the area of green that is exposed to the light, though in a small garden this may be necessary to make space for other plants to grow up beside the daffodils.

The effects of varying amounts of light on plants are most easily seen in the house, where many of them get light only from one side. Plants that are grown on window sills almost always grow towards the light, providing a beautiful display of leaves and flowers for anybody who happens to be on the outside looking in (see Chapter 4, page 59). If you turn the plant a little each day, it will, in fact, be zigzagging from side to side to keep up with the light source, and, inevitably, this must slow its growth. However, it is about the only way you will get full value from your plant.

If a house plant is too far from a window it will become very long, thin and pale in its attempts to get nearer to the light. This distorted growth is called 'etiolation'. An etiolated plant has very small, yellowy leaves, and the sections of stem between the leaves, the internodes, are greatly extended. If you

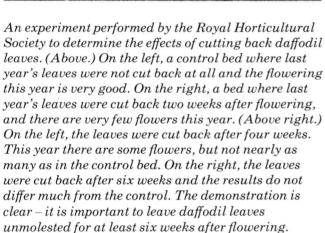

An experiment performed by the Royal Horticultural Society to determine the effects of cutting back daffodil leaves. (Above.) On the left, a control bed where last year's leaves were not cut back at all and the flowering this year is very good. On the right, a bed where last year's leaves were cut back two weeks after flowering, and there are very few flowers this year. (Above right.) On the left, the leaves were cut back after four weeks. This year there are some flowers, but not nearly as many as in the control bed. On the right, the leaves were cut back after six weeks and the results do not differ much from the control. The demonstration is clear – it is important to leave daffodil leaves unmolested for at least six weeks after flowering.

have a plant like this, the first thing to do is to move it. Having left it for a week or so to recover, you then have to decide whether you can live with its new straggly shape (because the growth is irreversible), or whether you will cut it back or take cuttings and start again. Even if low-light damage has not got as far as severe etiolation it is, from the point of view of the plant, a waste of feeding and growing time. Any time that the plant spends with leaves that are not brightly and completely green, whether they are pale from light shortage, chlorotic from a nutrient deficiency or discolored by pests and disease, is time that the plant is not spending feeding and developing to its greatest potential.

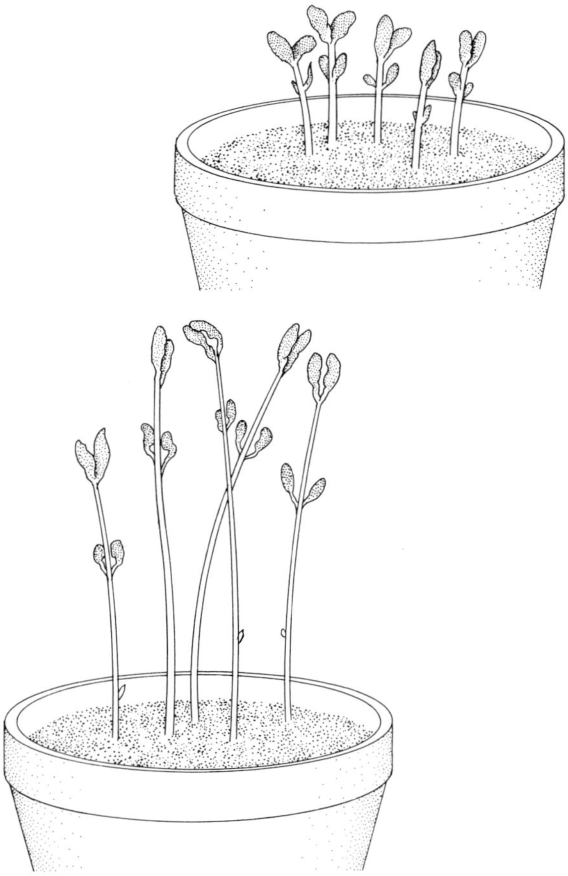

Healthy seedlings grown in normal light and long, thin or etiolated seedlings grown in darkness.

It would be very satisfactory, and a great help to the indoor gardener, to be able to make some sweeping generalisations about which sorts of plants need what intensity of light. In fact, although there are some features which are usually common to plants needing a particular environment (like shade lovers often having dark leaves), the house plants we keep come from such a range of natural homes that it would be absurd to expect the same conditions to suit them all. As usual, their needs reflect the surroundings in which they evolved. Desert cactus thrive on sunny window sills, but many of the foliage plants come from shady, humid jungles and cannot live in a strong direct light. The best approach is to ask for information in the shop where you bought the plant or to consult a specialist book.

NON-GREEN PLANTS

Some plants are not green, or not entirely green. Variegated leaves can photosynthesise only in the green part of each leaf, so they are less efficient. Other plants have green chloroplasts right through their leaves, but the colour is masked by another pigment. A good example of this is the purple tradescantia. In the wild, a pigment like this acts like a sun tan and protects the plant from too much sunshine, but in the house the striking purple colour fades unless the plant gets plenty of light. Plants that are quite without chlorophyll cannot make any of their food and must get it all from another source. Some are parasitic on other plants, and several of these can be a nuisance in the garden. Dodder and broomrape have pad-like absorptive organs that penetrate deep into the tissues of the host plant to obtain food. Their leaves, which are not needed because the plant has no ability to photosynthesise, are very small, like tiny scales. (See colour photos on page 112.)

Insect-eating plants 'feed' in rather a dramatic way, trapping and digesting any small insects that land on them, but these rather gruesome meals are not taken as a substitute for photosynthesis. Insect-eating plants are green and produce their own sugar perfectly well, but they grow in swampy soils which contain very little nitrogen. The animal bodies that they digest contain protein which includes the element nitrogen, and it is this that the plant needs. The insects are devoured to avoid a nutrient deficiency rather than to replace photosynthesis.

It is strange to think just how much we higher mammals depend on the activities of green plants. If they did not exist, nor would we, for without the oxygen they exude, air-breathing animals like ourselves could never have evolved. We live in a very delicate balance with the plants of our planet. Satellite photographs show what a vast area of the earth is green and growing, and the atmosphere we breathe depends on this. The more we hack into the jungles and woods of the world and destroy the trees, the greater the chance that we will damage our atmosphere, our world, our chance of life, in a way that cannot be repaired.

CHAPTER TEN

GARDEN ENEMIES

A formidable number of pests and diseases lurk in the garden. They can attack both flowers and vegetables, damaging the plants and threatening crop yields for both the gardener and the horticulturist. There are birds, like the pigeon and the bullfinch, mammals, like rabbits and mice, as well as an enormous number of smaller pests – slugs, snails, nematode worms, millipedes, mites and insects. In addition, there are diseases, caused by fungi, bacteria and viruses. Pretty well all of these problems can be controlled by applying (and sometimes repeatedly applying) a chemical, and you can find out just which one is best for the job by asking at any good garden centre. The research departments of the big chemical companies have produced almost as many pesticides as there are pests, and there is absolutely no doubt that these work. There are, however, disadvantages in using chemicals too freely.

The first is that chemicals are expensive. On the garden scale it may not cost much to protect a few rows of vegetables, but, on a commercial scale, huge sums can be spent on pesticides, knocking the price up to the consumer and cutting profits to the farmer.

Furthermore, the organisms at which the chemicals are directed can become resistant to them. A strain of the pest evolves which is unaffected by the poison poured upon it and it becomes necessary to develop yet another pesticide, further increasing the strength and complexity of the chemicals that we throw at our environment.

Very few chemicals are specific enough; they almost all affect every animal with which they come into contact, so when you attack an enemy in the garden, you are likely to jeopardise the lives of some friends. Fruit crops in particular suffer badly when bees, which are vital to fruit pollination, are harmed by too liberal use of pesticides. In every garden there is an unseen animal kingdom which lives, like all natural communities, in a state of balance. Killing almost anything will upset this balance. Animals that are unnoticed and generally unrecognised (but that benefit the garden by preying on its pests) may be disrupted or destroyed.

Chemical pesticides can also contaminate food plants. Many of them carry a warning that the chemical should not be applied within some number of days of harvesting, and these instructions should, of course, be followed with great care. Even when it proves impossible to trace the specific damage done by a particular poison, it nevertheless remains true that all pesticides increase the general pollution of our environment. The damage spreads through the food web, so that predatory birds die as a result of eating smaller animals that have fed on poisoned insects. This spreading pollution cannot simply be blamed on the chemical companies that make the pesticides. By and large, they spend a great deal of money on research to minimise these toxic effects, but any poison that is spread around the garden or the countryside must have some undesirable side effects. Chemical pesticides are undoubtedly efficient and valuable, but their use is increasingly regarded as a last resort.

What, though, are the alternatives? The gardener finds it hard to live with pests that damage his crops, and the commercial grower finds it impossible, so some control is vital. In recent years, a lot of research has been directed towards 'biological' controls. These involve controlling pests by manipulating, in some way, their life cycles or by using their own natural enemies – rather like using a thief to catch a thief.

BIOLOGICAL PEST CONTROL

On a commercial scale, where crop losses may be huge, attempts to control the size of a harmful population have recently included the release of large numbers of sterile males, which are prepared in the laboratory and set free in the vicinity of the crops. They mate with the normal 'wild' females, which are then unable to produce viable eggs. The size of the next generation is greatly reduced, and so is the damage done to the crop – but only for a while. Animal populations are able to withstand natural catastrophe because they constantly over produce offspring. Most of these die, either from starvation or because they have insufficient living space, but, when a neighbouring population is wiped out, the excess young animals simply migrate. In their new home, with ample food and space, life goes on much as before. This simple ecological principle will apply whether a pest is attacked by a chemical or a biological method. The gardener may win an occasional battle, but the pest will always win the war.

There are, however, some situations where these environmental influences do not apply. The greenhouse can be almost completely isolated, so it functions as a closed system. This not only allows the gardener much greater control over the plants growing inside, but it also allows him much greater control over their pests and diseases. When a particular problem has been dealt with, pest numbers will generally remain low for some time, because closed doors prevent migration from another area. For this reason it is in the greenhouse that biological controls have proved most effective and most useful.

There are, in fact, not as many different pests in the greenhouse as there are in the garden, because most of the plants grown in the greenhouse are not native to this country, which means that they are generally less susceptible to attacks from British insects. Because most glasshouse plants originate in warmer climates, the pests from their homelands do not occur here, and if they arrive by accident they do not often survive in our colder weather. On the other hand, when pests do attack glasshouse plants, they can be a very serious problem because, like the plants they prey upon, they find the warm, humid atmosphere of the greenhouse very much to their liking, and their numbers increase astronomically.

PREDATOR AND PREY

The greenhouse red spider mite attacks most of the plants that are grown under glass. It breeds quickly and is difficult to control with chemicals. Tomatoes, *Chrysanthemum*, orchids, melons, grapes, carnations and pot plants all suffer from its attentions. It feeds on chloroplasts taken from the foliage, which can cause a severe check in the plant's growth. There is, however, another mite, a fast-moving predatory little animal from South America, that can eat as many as five adult or twenty young spider mites in a day. Its name is *Phytoseiulus* and, since its introduction in the 1950s it has proved a most effective way of combating red spider mite in the greenhouse. Red spider mites can survive the cold of winter, hiding in corners in the greenhouse, while their Chilean predators perish, so each spring the number of red spider mites increases sharply. For control by *Phytoseiulus* mites to be fully effective, they need to be introduced every season.

The glasshouse whitefly is another greenhouse pest that causes a lot of damage, particularly to tomatoes. Whitefly feed by sucking sap from the leaves, which can cause a check in growth, but it causes even greater damage by depositing a sticky substance called 'honey dew' all over the plant. This encourages the growth of a dark fungal mould that dirties the fruit. When honey dew is deposited on the leaves it prevents them photosynthesising properly, and, in very severe cases, sometimes kills the plant. Commercially it is a menace because it lowers yields, and growers must bear the considerable expense of washing affected fruit.

PARASITE AND HOST

The biological control of whitefly is effected by using *Encarsia*, a wasp which is just over half a millimetre long and black and yellow in colour. Like *Phytoseiulus*, *Encarsia* comes from South America, but, unlike *Phytoseiulus*, it does not eat its prey. *Encarsia* controls whitefly by parasitising it. It lays its eggs in the immature stages of the whitefly, which are immobile and called 'scales'.

The eggs hatch into larvae which remain inside the scale, eating the tissue of the whitefly, for five weeks, when the adult *Encarsia* emerges through a hole and the life cycle of the wasp begins again. *Encarsia* lives for several weeks and each one will lay eggs in up to one hundred whitefly scales. The scales are normally whitish in colour but turn black when eggs are laid inside them, so, by comparing the number of healthy white scales with the number of parasitised dark ones, the progress of the control can be observed.

The populations of predator and pest will remain in balance. If there is a sudden influx of whitefly, then the number of *Encarsia* will rise correspondingly. This means that biological controls can be very cheap, because the predator is only introduced once each year, while spraying may have to be repeated if the pest population rises again later in the season.

Interestingly, it was the discovery of *Encarsia* at the Royal Horticultural Society Gardens in 1914 that stimulated the first successful biological control experiments. The wasp was bred and distributed for use by amateur gardeners and professionals alike until after the Second World War, when it was made redundant by the development of new and effective insecticides, like DDT. Now that strains of whitefly have evolved which are resistant to DDT and other pesticides, *Encarsia* finds itself in favour once again. One of the major advantages of biological controls is that it is extremely unlikely that a pest, like whitefly, could develop resistance to a controlling predator or parasite in the way that it can to a pesticide, because these natural relationships (between host and parasite or prey and predator) evolve over millions of years.

These two biological controls – *Phytoseiulus* for red spider mite and *Encarsia* for whitefly – are probably the two most commonly used in this country at the moment. They are of most use to commercial growers whose glasshouses are measured in acres rather than square feet, but they are also available through the post for amateurs.

Another, more recently developed control system is for mealy bugs; this is particularly useful because they are hard to get at and kill chemically. They live in rather inaccessible nooks and crannies around the plant, and cover themselves with a coat of white, waxy fibres which protects them from all but the most powerful pesticide sprays. Both the mealy bugs and their young (called nymphs) are eaten by a kind of ladybird, *Cryptolaemus montrouzeri*, which has recently been introduced to this country. The nymphs are particularly voracious, eating almost thirty mealy bugs every day.
(See colour photos on page 120.)

The use of biological controls is not without its own problems and difficulties. For example, most

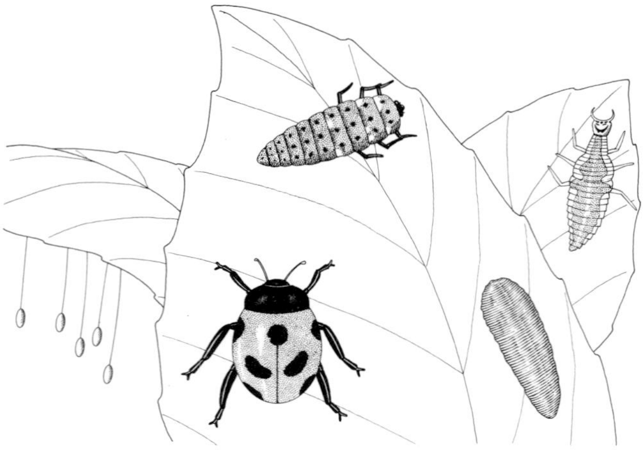

The natural agents of biological pest control in the garden. (Centre.) A ladybird and (above.) its larva. (Left.) The eggs of the lacewing, hanging below a leaf, and (top right) the larva. (Below right.) A hoverfly larva.

parasites and predators need a high light intensity if they are to do well, so their effective season is really only from April until September. They also need warmth, and are most useful when the daytime temperature does not go below 21 °C (70 °F). When conditions are cooler than that, *Encarsia*, for example, breeds more slowly than the whitefly it parasitises and will not form an effective control.

A further problem with biological controls is that you cannot introduce a predator until the pest population is large enough to feed it. It is impossible to use a biological control as a precaution against a build up of pests because, without its prey, the predator will starve. So the pest population must be established before the control agents are introduced. But, on the other hand, it takes some time for the predator population to build up and become effective, so it is important to bring them in before the pests become too numerous and beyond their control. The practical way out of this quandary is actually to infect the glasshouse with the pest, and then, soon afterwards, to introduce the predator or parasite. This establishes a balance between the two, with enough pests to maintain the population of predators and enough predators to minimise damage to the plants.

All these beneficial predators and parasites are killed by most of the insecticides that are available. When a biological control is in operation it thus becomes very difficult to treat any other pests in the greenhouse. Caterpillars, however, can be attacked by a second biological method which is extremely specific and does no harm to any other animal, bird or insect. The caterpillars of moths and butterflies are susceptible to *Bacillus thuringiensis*, a bacterium which produces resting spores containing a toxic protein crystal. The spores can be sprayed on to plants, and are taken in by the caterpillars as they feed on the foliage. Once inside the gut, the spores become active, and release the toxic crystal which poisons the caterpillar. A suspension of spores for spraying is more expensive than conventional insecticides but it can be used without disturbing the balance of life in the greenhouse.

Biological control was not invented by scientists. It happens every day and in every garden, within the natural animal community that lives there, and some of it can easily be exploited by the gardener for the benefit of his own crops. Hedgehogs and birds take slugs and snails, and the thrush that comes into the garden to visit the bird table may find a snail for an extra snack. Sparrows and blue tits will strip the aphids from rose-buds, particularly if they are encouraged by hanging strips of fat above the bushes. Other natural enemies of aphids are ladybirds and their larvae and the larvae of the lacewing and hoverfly.

In the spring it is easy to collect all the ladybirds you see and re-house them on the roses and currant bushes, plants that are badly threatened by aphids. Later in the summer they can be transferred to beans and cabbages. Experience indicates that friends and neighbours find this hilarious – and, indeed, moving ladybirds about the garden probably does look funny – but providing you begin early in the year, before the aphid population gets too large, you get the last laugh. Ladybirds and their larvae are a great help in keeping this particular pest under control, without resorting to an insecticide.

The larvae of hoverflies also eat aphids. The adults feed on nectar and can be attracted to the garden, where they may also lay eggs, by planting the flowers that they particularly enjoy. They like buckwheat, rose of Sharon and one of the bindweed family, the annual *Convolvulus tricolor*. This has brightly coloured flowers, similar in shape to those of the common bindweed, but it does not have the strong white bindweed rhizomes and can be planted without the fear that it will take over the whole garden (see page 119). Larvae of the hoverflies that feed on it will consume a huge number of aphids.

The gardener has one major advantage over the commercial grower when trying to control pests without pesticides, and that is the size of the problem. The area maintained by most horticulturists is so large that chemical pesticides often seem the only practical answer, but the gardener, with many fewer plants, can try other approaches. Most gardens are small enough to allow the gardener a good look at every plant at regular intervals, so many pest invasions can be spotted and dealt with before they become established.

This must be the simplest and most basic kind of pest control there is, but picking pests off plants before they do too much damage really is effective in all but the largest gardens, and even aphids can be kept down in this way, providing you start early enough, around June, before their numbers get too enormous. A nocturnal prowl with a torch will usually yield a good collection of slugs and cutworms that have emerged from hiding for their nightly feast. The slugs that you can catch at night probably spent the day sheltered by weeds and garden rubbish along the edge of a path, so tidiness and general garden hygiene can also help in the battle against pests and diseases.

Cutworms are the fat green-brown larvae of the turnip moth. The juveniles thrive on weed seedlings, and as they mature they move into the vegetable plot, where, in the course of a night, they can eat enough of the stem of a young plant to break it right off. In a garden without weeds, cutworms probably will not appear at all, but if they do become a problem, in a less than perfect plot, the best solution is to dig gently in the soil around the base of the affected plants, find the cutworms that will be hiding there and squash them.

Where to buy Biological control agents.

A number of suppliers will sell biological controls to gardeners as well as to commercial growers. When writing to any of these companies, you should include the size of your greenhouse and the main plants grown in it as well as the degree of infestation that you are experiencing.

Perifleur Limited
Hangleton Lane
Ferring
Sussex BN12 6PP
(*Encarsia, Phytoseiulus, Cryptolaemus, Bacillus thuringiensis*)

Natural Pest Control (Amateur)
Watermead
Yapton Road
Barnham
Bognor Regis
Sussex PO22 0BQ
(*Encarsia, Phytoseiulus, Cryptolaemus*)

Applied Horticulture Limited
Billingshurst
Sussex RH14 9EH
(*Encarsia, Phytoseiulus*, but only in large quantities, *Bacillus thuringiensis*)

Kent County Nurseries Limited
Challock
Near Ashford
Kent TN25 4DG
(*Encarsia*)

GARDEN HYGIENE

Both insects and disease-carrying spores can overwinter in garden debris, so an untidy corner near a vegetable patch can harbour all kinds of trouble. The heavy stalks that remain after cutting cabbages, sprouts and other Brassicas are the prime offenders. They provide a safe and comfortable winter home for a wide variety of pests and diseases, including grey mould, whitefly, clubroot and aphids. It is safest to burn this kind of rubbish because, although some spores will be killed by the heat generated in a compost heap, many are tough enough to survive. Clubroot spores, in particular, can easily live in the heat of the compost and remain viable for up to twenty years, so any infected material should be burnt.

A Brassica showing the symptoms of clubroot.

If you do have a garden that is infected with clubroot, you can stop it spreading and increasing by burning all infected plants. It is also possible to raise disease-free plants by growing each one in a six-inch pot of sterilised soil and planting out the whole root ball. This benefits the garden plant in two ways. Firstly, clubroot only attacks new roots so, whatever happens, each plant has a whole potfull of healthy and functioning roots. Secondly, the number of roots that will grow out from a strong root ball is very large, so there is a good chance that some of these will avoid infection, and the plants will survive. A small quantity of soil can be sterilised by heating it to 150 °C (300 °F or gas regulo 1) for a period of one hour. The same method can be used to reduce the damage done to Brassicas by the maggots of the cabbage root fly.

Crop rotation is a useful technique in the control of some pests. If you plant the same vegetables in the same piece of ground year after year, then pests that attack that particular species will increase in number because there is always a host plant on which they can feed. Most pests and parasites are very specific, and can live or feed on only one kind of plant, so by changing around and using each bed for a different crop each year, a number of parasites can be kept down to an acceptable level.

Potato root eelworm, properly called the potato cyst nematode, can be controlled in this way. Nematodes, or eelworms, are microscopic, thread-like worms that live in the soil and on plants. There are very many different species, feeding on a wide range of garden plants. *Chrysanthemum*, *Iris*, *Clematis*, daffodils, tulips, carrots, celery, lettuce and onions all suffer from the attacks of one species or another, and these minute creatures are very hard to treat chemically. The best way to keep the infection under control is to destroy any affected plants (but not by putting them on the compost heap), and avoid planting the crop affected in the same bed for at least three years.

Nematode cysts on the roots of a potato plant

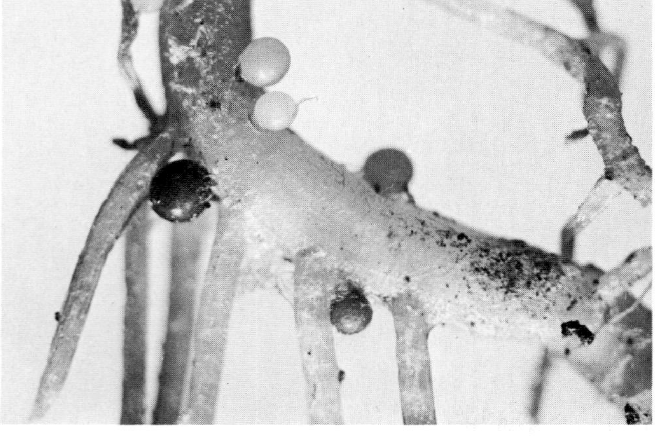

Potato cyst nematodes

These tiny worms attack the roots of potato plants. They stop the roots growing properly and prevent them reaching out through the soil for water and nutrients. This retards the plants' growth, causing them to wilt easily and produce a smaller yield of potatoes. Generally the plants are damaged rather than killed, but the loss of roots makes them particularly vulnerable in dry weather and, in badly infested plots, some plants may die when there are drought conditions.

The eggs of the nematodes lie in the soil. When in some way they detect the presence of potato roots growing nearby, they hatch, and the microscopic larvae wriggle through the soil to invade the roots, where they feed and grow. After a few weeks the male nematodes move out into the soil but the females stay in the roots and continue feeding. Their bodies lie outside the root and swell into round cysts, each of which is about the size of a pinhead and contains eggs. When the cysts begin to grow, they are white, but when they are ripe and full of eggs they turn brown. These brown cysts are very easily dislodged from the roots into the soil where they wait for next year's potato crop, when many of the eggs will hatch and the cycle will start again. If the cysts do not detect potatoes growing, very few eggs hatch and any larvae that do emerge soon die, because there is no suitable host plant in the area.

If the appearance of your potato plants leads you to suspect an attack by these eelworms, you can check for their presence quite easily any time after June. You should gently lift one plant, wash its roots and examine them with a magnifying glass. It is important to lift the plant carefully because the cysts easily fall off into the soil. If the plant is infested, you will be able to see the cysts on the roots. They are about one millimetre across and vary in colour between white and brown. If you find the cysts, it is important to destroy all the roots when the crop (which will be small) is harvested. This lessens the number of eggs in the soil and the strength of future attacks.

It is also possible to check the ground for the presence of nematodes, before planting a potato crop, by preparing a soil sample and searching through it for cysts. This is not absolutely reliable because distinguishing the cysts of different nematode species is difficult. The potato nematodes, however, are the most common. If, therefore, you find any cysts in the vegetable garden, it is best to assume that potatoes could be attacked.

To prepare the sample, take about ten spoonfuls of soil from all over the area you want to examine, soon after the garden has been dug. Mix them thoroughly together, dry them (in the air or a cool oven) and sieve them to remove any pebbles or large pieces of plant debris. Weigh out about 100 grams (roughly four ounces) of this dry soil, crumble it to a powder, then sprinkle it into a jar or jug which is half full of water and stir for one minute (1). It is really very like treating a soil sample to separate particles of different sizes. (Chapter 6, page 94.) The inorganic, mineral part of the soil sinks to the bottom and the organic part, which includes any nematode cysts, floats on the top.

There are two ways of separating this organic fraction for examination. The first is to add water gently to the jar, until the surface, with its floating debris, is right at the top, where it can be examined with a magnifying glass. The second method is to line a funnel with a piece of kitchen paper (2) and filter the soil sample through that. When the heavier, inorganic part of the soil has settled in the funnel, make a small hole through the paper in the bottom, so that the water can run out. The powdered soil sample, surrounded by a tide mark of organic matter, will remain. Spread the paper out (3) and look at this surface debris through a magnifying glass. Potato nematode cysts in the soil are the size of pinheads, shiny brown in colour and more or less spherical, with a knob or head on one side. Cysts that are lemon-shaped or have two knobs are from other nematode species.

If you find more than ten potato nematode cysts in your 100 gram soil sample, you can assume that a potato crop would be damaged. The plants can be helped by manuring the soil well, which may lessen the number of nematodes and will certainly strengthen the plants so that they are better able to cope with the attack, but the best solution is to grow other crops in that soil, and plant potatoes somewhere else. After four years most cysts will have died but, if you do not have enough garden to practise that kind of rotation, there are some varieties of potato, like Maris Piper and Pentland Javelin, that are resistant to nematodes. In their first year, these are invaded and damaged by nematodes if the cysts are present, but they will prevent the production of new cysts and so cut down future damage.

The problem is that there are two species of nematode that attack potatoes, but the resistant varieties are actually only resistant to one of them. If you know your garden contains potato nematodes, you can identify them by growing one of the resistant varieties, lifting a plant in June and examining its roots. If you find cysts, then the nematode species in your soil is the one that can attack resistant varieties and some kind of rotation is the only answer. If there are no cysts, then the yield this year may still be low, but the plants are resistant and the worms will not be able to breed, so future crops should be safe. A good deal of the research going on into the treatment of potato cyst-nematodes involves attempts to breed better and more resistant varieties.

Another very interesting area of investigation is the way in which hatching is stimulated. The majority of cysts only hatch when there are potato roots nearby – quite rightly, because if the nematodes emerge when the host plant is not available, they very soon die. If we could mimic the action of the potato plant and synthesise the secretion of their roots that says to the the cysts, 'safe to hatch, food nearby', then we could confuse the eelworms into hatching under another crop, that cannot act as host, and the nematodes would soon starve.

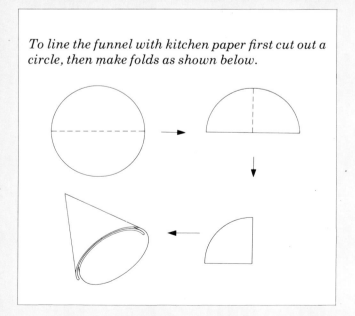

To line the funnel with kitchen paper first cut out a circle, then make folds as shown below.

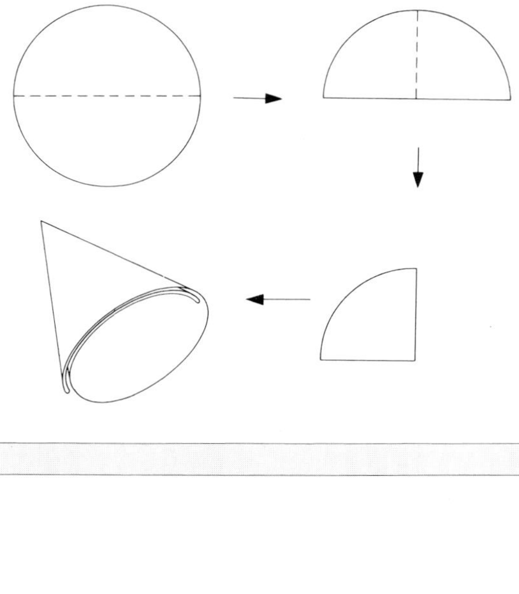

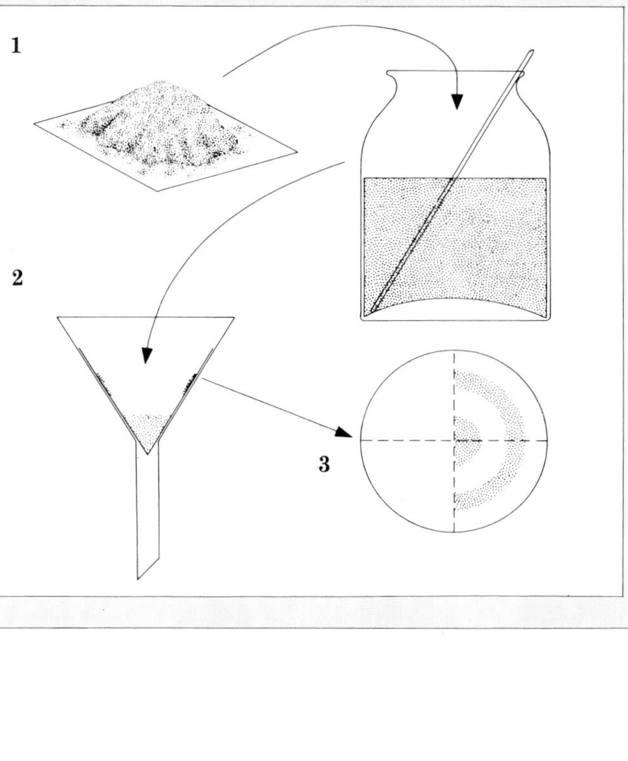

With potatoes, it is best to practise a three-year rotation even when crops show no sign of infection, because rotation will prevent a large number of cysts building up in the soil. Tomatoes are members of the same family as potatoes, the Solanaceae, and they too can act as host for the potato cyst nematode, although they are not damaged by the pest themselves. Tomatoes should not be grown after potatoes in a crop rotation because they will maintain nematode numbers.

Crop rotation is harder for the gardener than it is for the commercial horticulturist, who has more space in which to move about. Walking around the garden, weeding and digging all tend to spread spores from one area to another, so an infection is very hard to contain. Flying insects will find their host plants wherever they are in the garden and long-living spores, like those of clubroot, remain viable for far longer than any rotation cycle lasts.

Some diseases spread more quickly between plants growing closely together. When the leaves of neighbouring plants touch, or nearly touch, the foliage forms an 'umbrella' that traps a layer of still, moist air, and this favours the spread and growth of many infections, both above ground and under the soil. Ventilation between plants slows the progress of most diseases, but for many gardeners this has to be balanced against the need to make the most of limited space by growing as much as possible. One precaution worth taking is that of inspecting plants very regularly – perhaps twice a week during the growing season – and pulling out any that show signs of disease, before the infection spreads right through the garden.

Another profitable approach to pest control in the garden can be summarised by the philosophy 'Know thine enemy'. The more that you know about the life and behaviour of the pests in your garden, the easier it is to retaliate. For example, the cabbage root fly feeds on the nectar of a common hedgerow plant, cow parsley. The flies become a danger to a row of cabbages at just the time the cow parsley begins to flower, so, by keeping an eye on the hedgerows around your home, you can judge the time to begin protecting your garden from this pest.

Because carrot flies use scent to find the carrots in which they lay their eggs, some people plant a row of something smelly, like onions or garlic, in the hope that this will confuse the flies enough to make them miss the carrots. Unfortunately, the flies are not fooled; carefully controlled and observed experiments show that this method only marginally reduces the damage done by the pest. However, it is true that carrot flies are drawn by scent. Because the broken stems of carrot plants exude an especially strong and attractive smell, disposing of thinnings well away from the row in which they grew will lessen the chance of attack.

Protection from the cabbage root fly

These flies lay their eggs around the roots of Brassicas. When the eggs hatch, the larvae tunnel into the roots and stems, feeding on them and often killing the plants. For more than a hundred years, plants have been protected by laying a flexible disc on the soil around each stem. Traditionally, the discs have been made from tarred roofing felt, but scientists at the National Vegetable Research Station have also tried a whole range of more modern materials. The most successful, they discovered, was rubber-backed carpet underlay, coated with grease. This rather unpleasant-sounding combination stops the flies getting at the roots to lay their eggs and also shelters a number of other insects that feed on maggots of the fly, and will eat any that evade the barrier. The discs should be roughly twelve centimetres across; larvae from eggs laid outside that circle will not be able to reach the stems or the roots. The holes in the discs must fit closely around the plant stem, which can grow without hinderance, because of the flexible nature of the underlay. Established plants can generally withstand attack from maggots without suffering too much damage, so it is only seedlings that really need protecting.

The larvae of the cabbage root fly attacking the stem of a cauliflower.

(Above.) A brassica with a protective disc.
(Below.) The clear difference between protected and unprotected plants shows the method's success.

COMPANION PLANTS

Planting vegetables in alternate rows rather than in beds (called intercropping), has, like the related practice of using companion plants, attracted a good deal of attention in recent years. Companion plants are generally non-crop plants that are grown alongside crop plants, for their inhibitory effect on pests and diseases. Some gardeners claim that they completely remove any need for pesticides, and others find them useless. Unfortunately, most of the carefully conducted, critical experiments to check their effects seem to confirm that they have a very limited use. One exception is the use of the Tagetes family, the French and African marigolds, which greatly reduce the numbers of nematodes in the soil. Sixteen varieties of Tagetes have been found effective, but they require a growing period of three or four months to work well, so the plants need starting early, under glass. The most effective of all is *Tagetes minuta*, so named because it has tiny flowers. The plants however have nothing 'minute' about them and can reach eight or ten feet in height.

Many experiments performed using companion plants have shown conflicting results. For example, some researchers have found that planting clover between Brussels sprouts greatly reduced damage by cabbage aphids and root flies. Others found that it made little or no difference. Clearly there is an

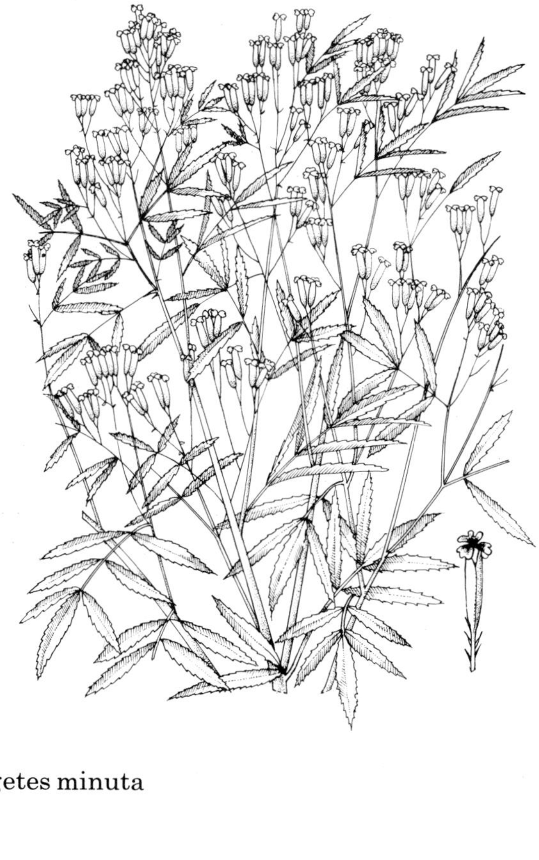

Tagetes minuta

urgent need for more detailed research in this area but, meanwhile, there are a number of theories why ground cover plants (not necessarily clover) between Brassicas might cut down attacks by pests.

One idea is that the companion plants in some way change the outline of the crop plant (as it appears to the approaching aphid) and the pests simply do not land. Another theory is that cabbage root flies will only lay eggs on open ground, so any plant growing around the crop prevents damage. A further reason why companion plants might help in the pest battle is that a monoculture (like a whole field or bed of cabbages) attracts a very restricted fauna, most of which are pests and only there because cabbage is their favourite food or the best place to lay their eggs. Different plants will draw different insects, perhaps including some predators, and will introduce a biological control. In particular, ground cover around Brassicas attracts large populations of nocturnal beetles, which eat cabbage root fly eggs and also climb up the stems of the cabbages to devour the aphids.

Some pests attack crops only when both insect and plant are at a particular stage in their develop-

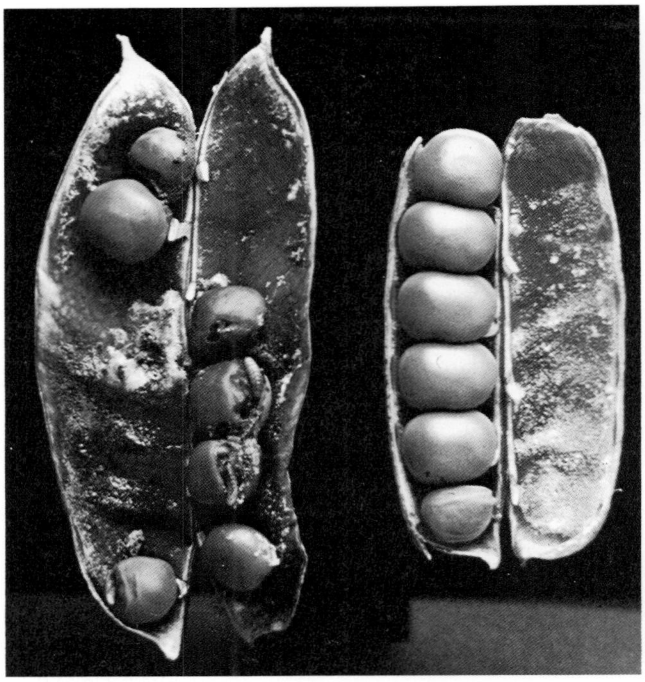

Damage done by the pea moth

The story of the aphid

The blackfly that mutilate the broad beans are aphids. Many species of these tiny insects invade the garden each year. They feed by pushing their long, piercing mouth parts into the cells of the phloem tissue and sucking sap. Aphids sometimes infest a plant in huge numbers and they can consume so much sap that the host is severely damaged; older plants become stunted and distorted, and younger ones may die. Even more injury may be inflicted by viruses that the aphids inject into the plant as they feed. The debris created by a large colony of insects is also unpleasant, with dead aphids, cast skins and honey dew which fosters fungi that dirty the plant.

The life cycles of the different aphid species are varied and complex. Some, like the cabbage aphid, can exist on plants all the year round but many others lay eggs in autumn on a different, woody, host plant. The blackfly that lands on the broad beans in June, for example, spend the winter as eggs on the common spindle tree. When the eggs hatch in spring, the insects multiply rapidly and then a winged form flies off to find the summer host plant and food. Curiously, these winged aphids can sometimes be deterred by laying a strip of shiny foil alongside the plants. As the invading insects come in to land, they expect to see a plant and the soil. What they actually see is the sky, reflected in the foil, and this so confuses them that they fly off and seek for food elsewhere!

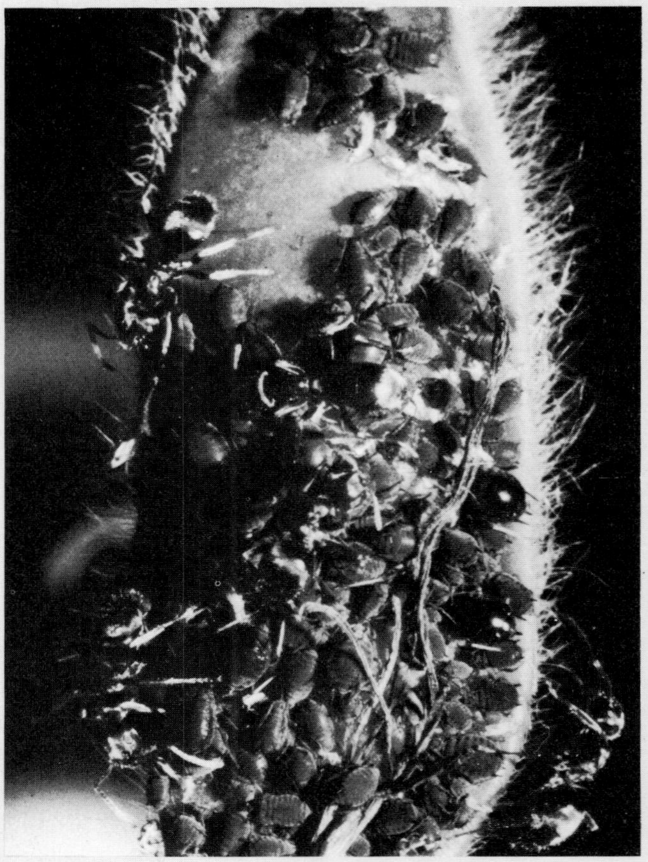

A massive invasion of blackfly feeding on the pod of a broom bush.

ment. The pea moth lays its microscopic eggs on the leaves of flowering pea plants in late June and early July, and, when the eggs hatch, the larvae burrow into the young pods. If the peas are sown very early or very late, the plants will not be in flower when the pea moth needs to lay its eggs and the crop will escape attack.

A similar approach can be used to protect broad beans from blackfly, vast numbers of which infest the crop in June. The aphids show a distinct preference for the succulent growing tip, but, if the plants were grown from beans sown the previous autumn, rather than in the spring, they will be big enough to have this tip, and the aphids on it, pinched right out. This treatment also improves the crop by destroying the apical dominance of the growing tip (see Chapter 4, page 65) thus stimulating the growth of bean clusters lower down the stem.

One of the most fundamental forms of biological control is resistance – the natural, inherited resistance that some plants have to certain pests and diseases. The major goal of many plant breeders is the production of plants that are resistant to some of the gardener's greatest enemies, including aphids. The problem is often that the resistant varieties of a plant lack other desirable qualities – like colour, size or flavour – and the aim of the plant breeder is to combine all these characteristics in one perfect, healthy plant (see Chapter 2, page 32).

PHEROMONES

One area of research, that may provide a way to deal with aphids, is the synthesis and use of pheromones. A pheromone is a substance that is released by many species of animal and affects the behaviour of other members of the same species. It is part of a kind of chemical communication system by which animals exchange vital information – the presence of a mate perhaps, or, in the case of aphids, the approach of an enemy. When this 'alarm pheromone' is used, all the aphids in the area leave, immediately. Sometimes they just drop from the plant to the ground. The pheromone will not get rid of the aphid permanently but its use in conjunction with a pesticide may prove an effective remedy in the future.

The combination of chemical and biological methods of fighting pests can sometimes combine the best of both and the problems of neither. For example, a sex pheromone that is exuded by the female pea moth attracts the male. If a similar synthetic sex attractant is used to lace a sticky trap and the trap is placed in a field of peas, it catches the male insects. It cannot catch enough male insects to prevent breeding and egg laying, because there will still be female moths exuding real pheromone to

A pheromone trap for the male pea moth.

attract more males from the country around. But it can be used as an indicator of population.

The farmer sets two traps in each field of peas and inspects them every two days. When more than ten moths are found in one trap on two successive occasions, it is assumed that there are plenty of male moths about, that they are mating, and that the females are laying eggs. Between ten and twenty-one days (depending on temperature) elapse between laying and hatching, when the tiny caterpillars are crawling around on the leaves and are vulnerable to pesticides. The pea moth trap tells the farmer when the eggs are being laid and a simple calculation using the daily temperature, enables him to work out the best time to spray.

The result is that the crop is treated at the very best time and will not need spraying again. The pea moth trap takes the guess work out of using pesticides.Both farmer and consumer benefit from the money saved and the environment is protected from unnecessary pollution.

Another combined attack, using both a chemical and a biological method, is used against silver leaf, a disease of fruit trees (particularly pear and plum). Silver leaf is caused by a fungus called *Chondrostereum purpureum* which has airborne spores that can easily infect a tree through a fresh wound, like a pruning cut. Once inside, the spores germinate and grow threads that spread into the trunk, where they produce substances that are carried in the sap to the leaves and fruit. This causes the characteristic silvery colour that gives the disease its name (see page 119). There is no cure for silver leaf, once a tree has been infected, so it is important to prevent infection. A common fungus, *Trichoderma viride*, is highly antagonistic to *Chondrostereum* and this battle between the two fungi can be used to protect trees against silver leaf infection. The problem is that the protection given by the *Trichoderma* is not immediate; it takes a little while for the protective fungus to get established and, by that time, it may well be too late.

The solution is to use a combined method; a chemical for instant results and a biological control for long term protection. *Trichoderma* is fortunately tolerant of some fungicides that kill *Chondrostereum*, so it is possible to apply fungus and fungicide together – the fungicide to destroy *Chondrostereum* immediately and the fungus, *Trichoderma*, to carry on protecting the tree long after the effects of the chemical have worn off. Researchers at the Long Ashton Research Station have developed special pruning shears which carry a small tank of this fungus and fungicide mixture. The action of closing these shears covers the face of the cut with the mixture and protects the wound from infection.

It is unrealistic, at the moment, to condemn completely the use of all chemical pesticides. Without them, we have no hope of growing enough to feed the world. But as more and more people recognise the hazards of pollution and look into the future with fear, biological methods of pest control must surely become more important. The treatment of silver leaf and the trapping of the pea moth are interesting and rather exciting examples that combine the best of both worlds. Perhaps that is where the future of pest control lies – in using a few carefully chosen chemicals for their undoubted speed and power, alongside the much less harmful, long-term action of biological controls.

GLOSSARY

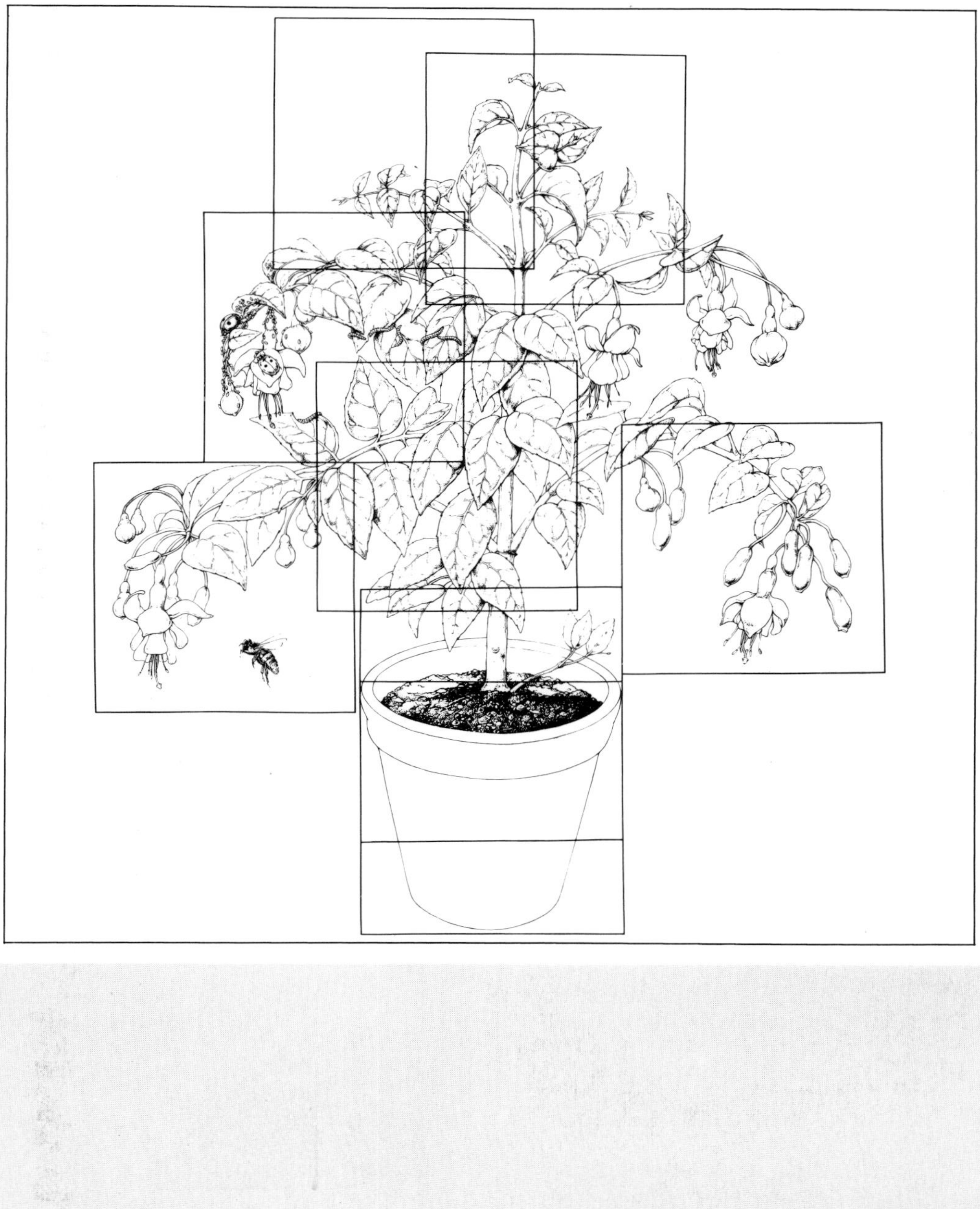

A diagram to name the parts of a flowering plant.

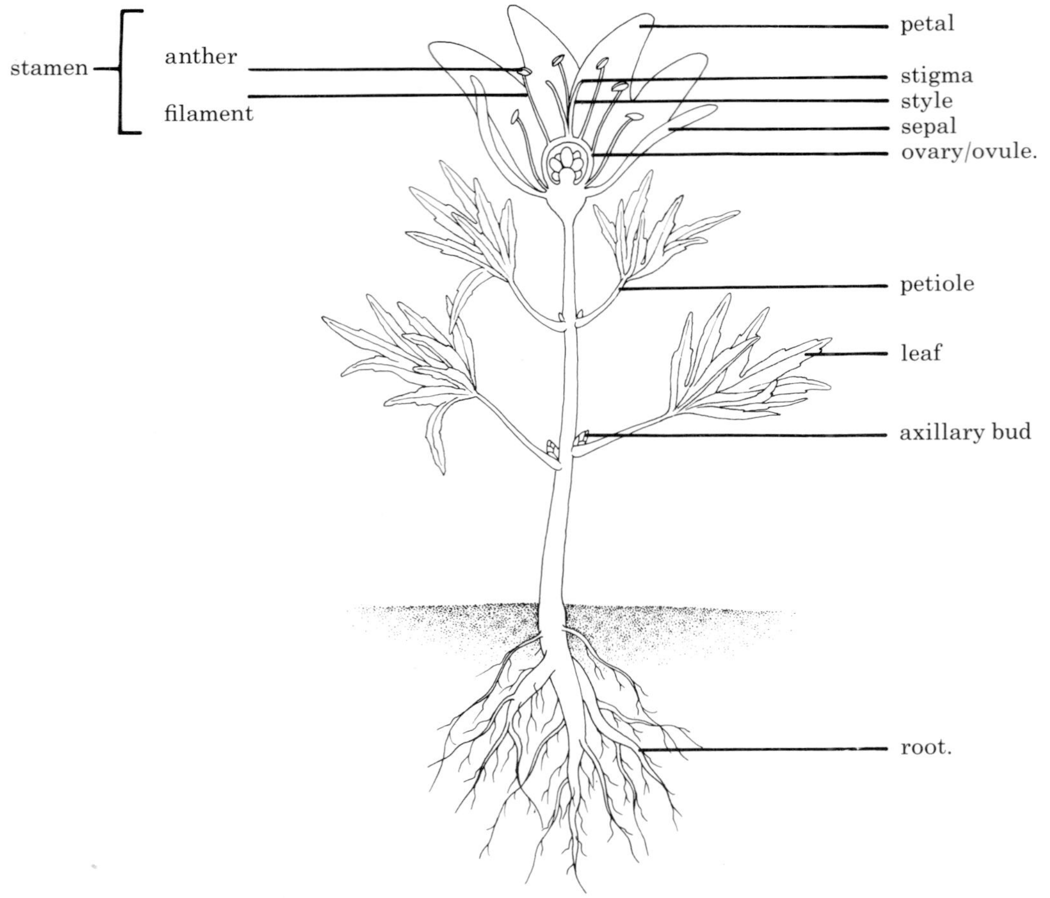

Cross-references to other entries in the glossary are in **bold** type. Numbers in brackets refer to pages in the main text where there is more detailed information. The index contains a complete list of page references.

Abscisin An inhibitory **growth substance** or hormone, found in senescent leaves, **dormant** buds and some fruits.
It is involved in the abscission or drop of young fruit, in leaf fall and in the autumn 'shut down' that protects plants from frost damage during the winter.

Adventitious A plant organ growing in an unusual position; so an adventitious root is one growing from a **node** on the stem and an adventitious **bud** is one growing (for example) from a root cutting.

Annual A plant that completes its life cycle – from **germination** to **seed** production – in one season and then dies. Many common flowers are annuals, as are some vegetables. Some plants (like *Gazania* and *Pelargonium*) are grown as annuals in this country but are perennials in their warmer country of origin. (See also **biennial, ephemeral** and **perennial**.)

Gazania

Anther The upper part of the stamen. **Pollen**, which contains the male sex cells, is produced in the anthers.

Apex The tip of a root, stem or leaf.

Apical bud The **bud** at the tip of each stem. See also **auxins**.

Apical meristem A single **cell**, or a group of cells, lying at the **apex** of the root, stem or leaf, which continually divide, both to maintain themselves and to provide new cells by which the plant grows.

Auxins A group of **growth substances** or hormones that are produced in the growing tips of stems, leaves and roots. They regulate plant growth, in particular by increasing the rate of elongation of **cells**, and are involved in the bending of a plant in response to light (**phototropism**, page 60) and gravity (**geotropism** page 62). Auxins also cause the dominance of one part of a plant – in general the **apical bud** – over another, and it is the manipulation of this dominance that is the basis of pruning (65). Auxin has been synthesised and is used in the garden as a selective weedkiller for lawns (66), but has far wider applications in horticulture and farming (66–69). Auxins are one of the three major groups of growth substances. The others are **cytokinins** and **gibberellins**.

Bacteria A group of microscopic organisms. The activities of bacteria are various and often very important. In the soil, they are involved in the decay of plant and animal matter that releases and makes available compounds containing nitrogen (122). Other bacteria are agents of plant diseases.

Bark A collective term for several different tissues, all of which grow outside the vascular **cambium** of a secondarily thickened stem or root (110). Also generally used to describe the protective cork on the outside of such a stem or trunk.

Bastard trenching A system of digging, in which the soil is circulated around the plot.

Biennial A plant which takes two seasons to complete its life cycle, from seed **germination** to **seed** production. During the first year the plant builds up a food store and in the second year it uses this stored energy to grow and produce seeds. There are a number of biennial flowers and vegetables in the garden and several root vegetables are actually the storage organs formed by biennial plants at the end of their first season. Some biennial vegetables (like lettuce and cabbage) tend to flower in their first season, and this is called 'bolting'. (See also **annual, ephemeral** and **perennial**.)

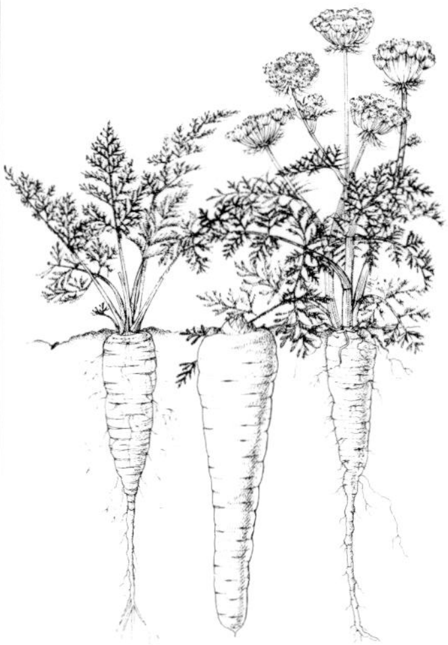

Biological pest control A system of control which uses some aspect of the behaviour or life cycle of the pest, or which introduces one of its natural predators or parasites (Chapter 10).

Bract A small, undeveloped leaf, that lies at the base of the flower stem. In some plants the bracts are enlarged and modified, for example, the poinsettia (22) and lords-and-ladies (28).

Break A term used in pruning to mean the growth of lateral (or side) shoots as a result of cutting back (or **stopping**) the main shoot.

Bud A compact, undeveloped shoot, made up of a short stem with tiny, overlapping leaves.

Budding A type of **grafting** in which a single **bud** is implanted on to a **stock**. Budding is usually performed on roses, It is more economic than other forms of grafting, because each parent plant will provide more buds, for budding, than complete shoots for conventional grafting. Two of the more usual methods of budding are the T-bud and the chip-bud (89).

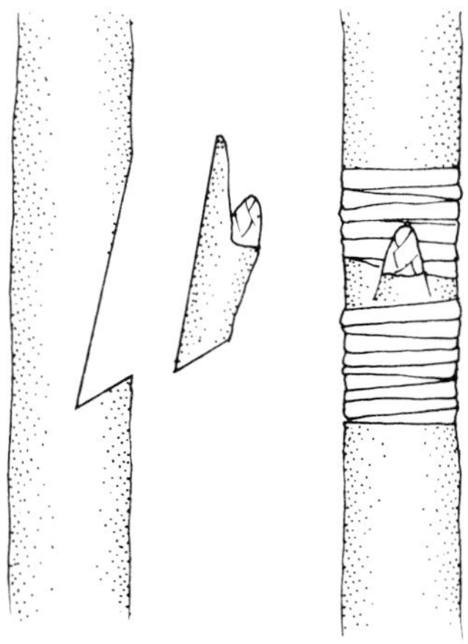

Chip budding

Calcicole A plant that grows well on soil that is alkaline, or has a high **pH**. In contrast with a calcifuge – a plant that will only thrive on soil with a low pH.

Callus 1 A tissue made up of undifferentiated cells that usually develops when a plant has been wounded. Callus formation is an important stage in **grafting** (83–87).
2 The mass of undifferentiated cells that grows during tissue culture (82). (See **differentiation**.)

Cambium A group of cells that retain the power to divide and make new cells throughout the life of the plant. The vascular cambium and the cork cambium are important in increasing the diameter of a woody stem or trunk (110).

Casparian strip An impermeable strip that runs around the radial and horizontal walls of the cells in the endodermis (in the root). This means that every root contains a cylinder of cells that have water-proof cell walls, and the only way that water and nutrients can get inside that cylinder is through the living cell contents of the endodermis. This, in some way, monitors and controls the uptake of nutrients (126–128).

Cell A unit of living matter, surrounded by a cell wall which is made from cellulose. All plants are built up from cells and, as the plant grows, these become differentiated or specialised to perform all the many functions necessary for the plant's life – for example, water transport, protection and **photosynthesis**.

Cellulose The material from which the cell walls of plants are made. Cellulose consists of long, complex chain molecules and is fibrous in nature, which is why plant material, like cotton and linen, is so valuable in the textile industry.

Chlorophyll The pigment that gives green plants their colour. Using chlorophyll, which is found in chloroplasts, green plants trap the energy of the sun, using carbon dioxide and water to make carbohydrates by the process called photosynthesis.

Chloroplasts The body that contains chlorophyll and is the site of photosynthesis. In higher plants, chloroplasts are generally disc shaped.

Chlorosis (Adjective chlorotic.) A yellowing of green leaves due to a lack of chlorophyll. Caused by a number of nutrient deficiencies and a lack of light. Chlorotic plants cannot photosynthesise properly, so they show poor development and growth.

Chromosome Thread-shaped bodies that occur in pairs in the nucleus of every cell, but are usually only visible when the cell is dividing. They contain the genes and, therefore, determine the activity of the cell and the appearance of the individual.

Class See **classification**.

Classification The placing of plants in groups, according to some or all of their similarities and differences. The flowering plants make up one class of the plant kingdom and this is further divided into two subclasses, the **monocots** and **dicots**. Each of these subclasses contains a number of orders, each order is made up of families, each family of genera and each genus of species. Cultivated plants also often have several varieties within each species.It is possible to give complete 'credentials' for every single plant – including its species, genus, family, order and so on – but the usual convention is to use only the name of the genus and species. So the common daisy on the lawn is properly called *Bellis perennis*, where *Bellis* is the name of the genus and *perennis* is the species.

Compost 1 The dark **humus** material that is produced

when vegetable waste is rotted by **bacteria**, usually in a compost heap.

2 The mixtures of peat or soil and sand that are sold and especially prepared for growing seeds, cuttings or a particular kind of plant.

Cotyledon

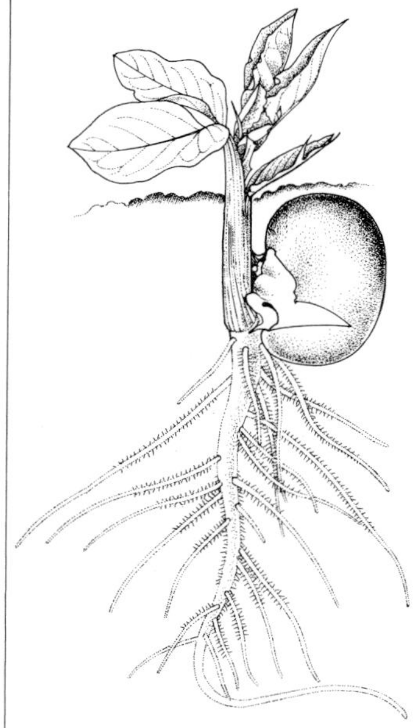

A modified leaf that makes up part of a **seed**. Also called a seed leaf. In some seeds, the cotyledons contain a food store and in others they absorb food from a store in the **endosperm** (42). During **germination**, the cotyledons of some seeds come out of the seed coat and above the ground, where they turn green and begin to **photosynthesise**. They are, however, strikingly unlike the true foliage leaves which follow. In other species, the cotyledons remain below ground. Seeds contain either one or two cotyledons and this difference is used to divide the flowering plants into two groups, called sub-classes. (See **monocot, dicot** and **classification**.)

Cross-pollination

When **pollen** from a flower is deposited on the receptive stigma of a flower growing on another plant of the same species, then cross-pollination has occurred. When the male and female sex cells fuse, cross-fertilisation has taken place. Cross-pollination and fertilisation are vital in the development of variation and in evolution. (See **self-pollination**.)

Cuticle

A non-cellular layer that covers the plant and protects it from damage. It is also water-proof and prevents loss of moisture during hot weather. The cuticle is punctured by the **stomata**.

Cytokinins

One of the three major groups of hormones or **growth substances**. Cytokinins stimulate growth by the division of **cells**. (See also **auxins** and **gibberellins**.)

Cytoplasm

A granular material that contains the living contents of the plant **cell**.

Deciduous

Plants that shed their leaves in autumn as a protection against winter frosts. (Compare **evergreen**.)

Deficiency disease

Symptoms that are seen in a plant that is growing in soil (or some other medium) that does not contain enough of a particular nutrient. Plants that are short of nutrients are generally slow-growing and unhealthy, but they also show specific symptoms, depending on which nutrients are lacking from their 'diet' (117, 52). Some nutrient deficiencies are easily confused with **virus** diseases.

Dicot

Member of the larger of the two **sub-classes** of the flowering plants, the dicotyledoneae, and distinguished from members of the other sub-class (the monocots) by having seeds with two cotyledons rather than one. There are dicots of every size and shape, including forest trees (like oak, ash and beech), food plants (like potatoes, beans and cabbages) and many, many garden flowers. (See **cotyledon, monocot** and **classification**.)

Differentiation

A change in the structure and/or function of **cells** during the development of a plant. Some cells do not change as part of the plant's normal development, and these are said to remain undifferentiated.

Diffusion

The movement of soluble material from a region where it is concentrated to a region where it is less concentrated, usually without any energy being expended.

Dormancy

A state of low activity, analogous to a coma in a human being. The plant is definitely alive, but it ticks over very slowly. Almost all plants experience some time during their life cycle when growth is temporarily suspended, but it is most commonly seen in **seeds** and **buds**. A 'resting' plant is said to be dormant only when the period of arrested growth is caused by internal factors, rather than by something in the environment – the striking feature of dormant seeds or buds is that they will not resume growth, even when external conditions are ideal, until dormancy has been 'broken' (47–50).

Ecology The study of the inter-relationships between living organisms (both plants and animals) and their environment.

Endodermis A layer of closely fitting **cells** that surrounds the vascular tissue in the root. Its most characteristic feature is the **Casparian strip** (126–128).

Endosperm The nutritive tissue, present in most **seeds**, that surrounds and feeds the embryo plant.

Enzyme A naturally occurring chemical substance that promotes or speeds up a metabolic reaction but is not itself used up in that reaction. Many of the nutrient **trace elements** are used in various enzyme systems around the plant, which is why they are so vital to its health and growth.

Ephemeral A plant with a short life cycle (from **germination** to **seed** production), that grows whenever conditions are suitable and usually has several generations in one season. Many of the desert plants are ephemerals, as are a number of garden weeds, including groundsel. (See also **annual, biennial** and **perennial**.)

Groundsel

Epidermis The outermost layer of cells of a plant. On the parts of the plant that are above the ground, the single layer of epidermal cells is covered by the water-proof **cuticle**.

Evergreen Plants that keep their foliage throughout the year, unlike deciduous plants. Evergreens have leaves that are adapted to cut down water loss and resist frost damage during winter (112).

Family See **classification**

Family tree A fruit tree on to which several compatible **varieties** or **species** have been grafted. The result is a tree that bears both cooking and eating apples, or even plums, peaches and apricots.

Florigen Florigen is a hypothetical **growth substance**. It has not been isolated or identified, but circumstantial evidence leads botanists to assume that it exists. The changing length of day and night, which stimulate the plant's photoperiodic responses, are 'perceived' in the leaves, but it is the tip of the stem, where the flowers form, that is affected. Although no hormone has been isolated, something must be carrying information from the leaves to the shoot, and that 'something' is given the name florigen. (See **photoperiodism**.)

Foliar food A solution of nutrients that is sprayed or watered on to the leaves of the plant, rather than being added to the soil, where it would be absorbed by the roots in the usual way. Foliar feeding is particularly useful when the acidity of the soil has made one of its nutrients insoluble, for example, calcium in an acid soil and iron in an alkaline one.

Food chain The 'chain' of organisms that exists in all natural communities, and through which energy is transferred in the form of food. Each link in the chain eats the organism below it and is, in turn, devoured by the one above. At the bottom of every food chain is some part of a green plant, because green plants are the only living things that are able to make their own food (by **photosynthesis**). All the food chains in a community interlink and make up a food web.

Fruit
A group of tissues that surround the **seed**. The tissues may be well developed (like the apple) or sparse and dry (like the acorn). The fruit is often modified to assist in the dispersal of seed away from the parent plant.

Fungi
A major division of the plant kingdom, including mushrooms, yeasts, moulds and rusts.
Fungi do not contain **chlorophyll** and cannot **photosynthesise**. They live as **parasites, saprophytes** or in **symbiosis**.

Gamete
A sex cell, produced by a form of cell division called **meiosis**. The female gametes are egg cells and the male gametes are **pollen** grains.

Gene
The units of heredity. Genes are found on the **chromosomes** and express themselves in the appearance and behaviour of the individual.

Genus
See **classification**.

Geotropism
The growth movements of plants that are stimulated by gravity (62). Shoots are said to be negatively geotropic (because they grow upwards) whereas roots (which grow downwards) are positively geotropic. If a growing plant is laid horizontally, the shoot will bend upwards and the root will grow downwards. (See **phototropism**.)

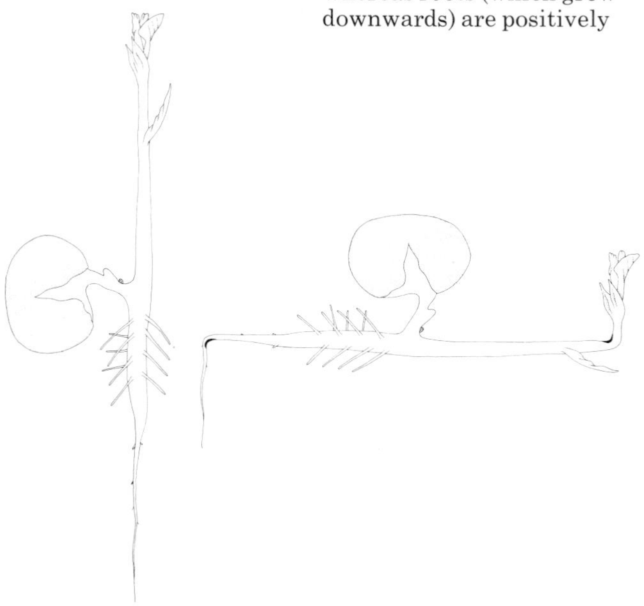

Germination
The development of a seedling plant from a **seed**. A viable (live) seed that is not **dormant**, will germinate, providing it receives enough water, adequate oxygen and a suitable temperature.

Gibberellins
A group of **growth substances** or hormones found in some fruit, seeds, seedlings and growing plants. Involved in many plant responses and growth patterns, including **dormancy** and flowering. Particularly important in the stem elongation of **biennials** (like carrots and cabbages) during their second year. There are three main groups of plant growth substances. The others are the **auxins** and **cytokinins**.

Grafting
A technique for joining together parts of two plants so that they will grow as one. Grafting is used to combine the best qualities of both the **stock** and the **scion**. It is used on a wide variety of plants, including fruit trees. (See **family trees**.) There are dozens of different ways of grafting, but three of the most common are cleft, apical wedge (86) and whip and tongue grafts (85). **Budding**, which is used to propagate roses, is a special form of grafting.

Graft union
The point on a grafted plant at which tissue from the **scion** and **stock** meet. This is generally the weakest part of the combined plant.

Green manure
A crop that is grown on an otherwise fallow plot of land, in order to enrich the soil. Green manure crops can be dug straight into the ground or rotted on the compost heap. The plants used are sometimes **Legumes**, which are particularly valuable because nitrogen fixing bacteria live in the nodules on their roots. (See **nitrogen-fixation**.)

Growth substance A chemical that plays the same role in the plant that hormones play in animals. Growth substances circulate through the plant and changes in their concentration communicate changing circumstances. Their action regulates all aspects of the growth and development of the plant. There are three main groups of growth substances: **auxins, gibberellins** and **cytokinins**. (See also **abscisin** and **florigen**.) Growth substances are sometimes called plant hormones, but this is not strictly correct (59).

Guard cells The two crescent shaped cells that surround each **stoma**. Changes in the turgidity of these cells alter their shape, which opens or closes the pore (108), and controls the rate at which gases and water vapour enter or leave the plant.

Half-hardy A plant that will flower and set **seed** in a normal summer season only if it is germinated under artificial conditions early in the year. In the British Isles, the natural life cycle would not normally be completed.

Hardy A plant that will withstand the seasonal changes of temperature and rainfall experienced in the British Isles.

Heel cutting A cutting that includes a 'heel' of bark and stem tissue, obtained by tearing a shoot from the main stem of the plant (78). The heel is trimmed before planting, and this is often the region from which roots grow. *Daphne, Forsythia* and many other shrubs are propagated using heel cuttings.

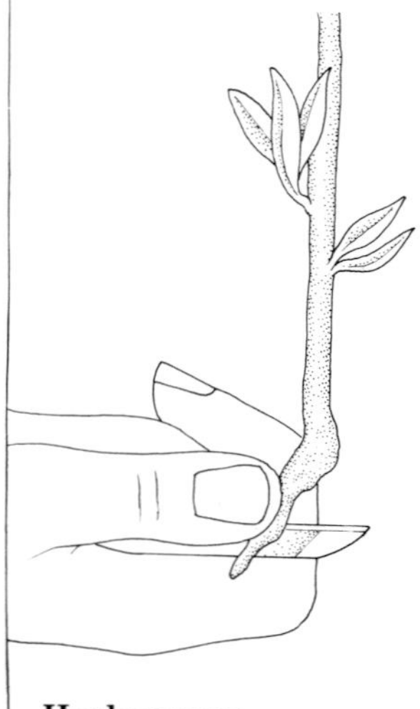

Herbaceous A plant that is soft and green, rather than hard and woody.

Honey guides The patterns of lines or dots on the petals of a flower that 'guide' a foraging insect towards the **nectar** store at the base of the petals.

(Left.) A foxglove.

Hormone See **growth substance**

Hormone powder A mixture of **growth substances** (particularly **auxins**) that promotes rooting in cuttings.

Host See **parasite**.

Humus The **organic** part of the soil. It is a blackish-brown material which is formed by the decomposition of organic waste and holds water in the soil. **Bacteria** and **fungi** are saprophytes feeding on humus, so it continually needs replacing.

Hybrid A plant resulting from a cross between two parents that are genetically different. Often restricted to the offspring of two different varieties within a species or two different species within a genus. (See **classification**)

Hybrid vigour Increased vigour and growth that is found in some hybrids and is attributed to the fact that the plant is descended from two different species or varieties.

Inorganic Not part of any living thing and not a chemical with a structure based on carbon. The inorganic part of the soil includes mineral particles of different types and sizes (92–94) but not the **humus**.

Insect eating plants Plants that engulf and digest insects and use the protein they contain to supplement the nitrogen that they get from the poor and boggy

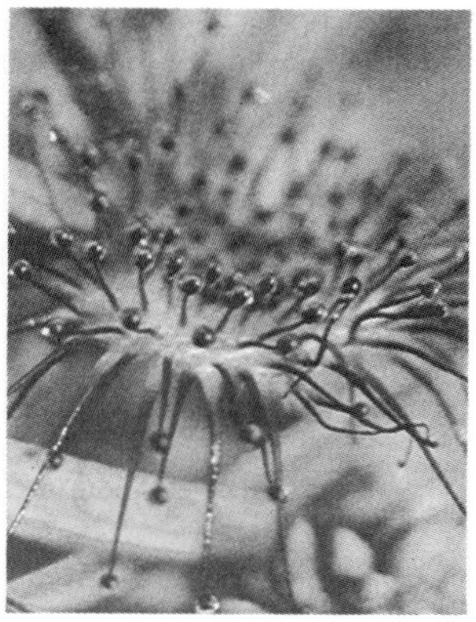

A sundew leaf

soils in which they grow. Several species are now sold as house plants, including the Venus fly trap, which snaps shut on its prey (114) and the sundew, which has sticky leaves that trap landing insects and then curl over to digest them There are a number of insect eating plants growing naturally in the British Isles, including two species of butterwort (*Pinguicula*), three species of sundew (*Drosera*) and the greater bladderwort (*Utricularia vulgaris*).

Internode The length of stem between the **nodes** or leaf joints.

Larva A juvenile stage that some animals (including insects) pass through before undergoing metamorphosis, or changing into an adult. Garden pests are often larvae rather than adults – leather jackets are crane fly larvae, cutworms and caterpillars are the larvae of various moths and butterflies, and it is the maggots or larvae of the carrot and cabbage root flies that actually damage the vegetables (148).

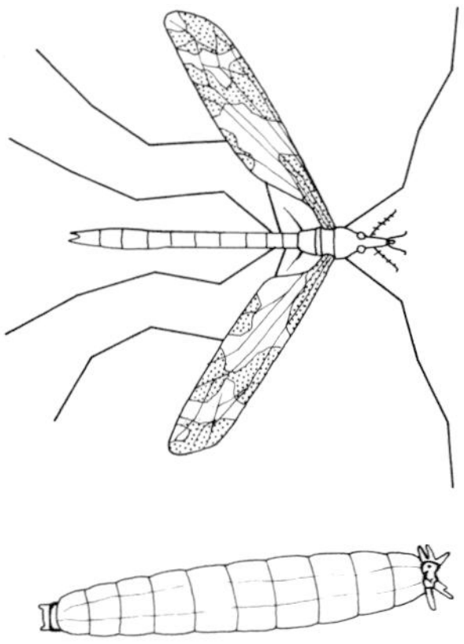

(Left.) The crane-fly and its larva, the harmful leather-jacket.

Leaching The washing of plant nutrients downwards, out of the soil, during normal drainage.

Legume Member of the plant family Leguminoseae. This includes peas and beans as well as many flowering plants, like vetch, clover and gorse. Apart from their value as vegetables or flowers, they are often important to the gardener because most of them carry nitrogen-fixing bacteria in nodules on their roots and some can be used as **green manure**. All members of the family carry **seeds** in dry pods that disperse the seed by splitting into two, sometimes with an audible 'pop'.

(Left.) A popping gorse pod.

Lignin A complex chemical compound that is deposited in the walls of some cells (particularly in the **xylem**) and makes them very strong and rigid.

Meiosis A process of **cell** division which results in four 'daughter' cells, each of which contains half the usual number of **chromosomes** and is a sex cell or **gamete**. When fertilisation takes place, two gametes fuse, restoring the full number of chromosomes. (See **mitosis**.)

Meristem A tissue that undergoes division to produce new **cells** which are then capable of **differentiation**.

Mitosis A process of **cell** division that makes new cells for growth and for the repair of tissue. During division, the number of **chromosomes** in the original nucleus is doubled, so that each of the two 'daughter' cells has a full complement. (Compare **meiosis**.)

Monocot A member of one of the two **sub-classes** of flowering plants, the monocotyledoneae, fortunately abbreviated to 'monocots'. Distinguished from **dicots** (the other sub-class) by having one **cotyledon** in each seed rather than two. There are, however, other differences between the two groups. **Vascular bundles** in the stems of monocots are scattered, rather than being symmetrically arranged as they are in dicots. The leaves of monocots have parallel veins; not the vein network that characterises dicot leaves. The grasses and grain plants that are so vital in growing food around the world are monocots and, in the garden, there are also some flowers, like lilies and the flamboyant red hot poker. (See **cotyledon** and **classification**.)

Mutation A spontaneous change in the **chromosome** or **gene** structure that leads to a change in the appearance and/or behaviour of the plant. Some mutations are of benefit to the gardener or horticulturist and are maintained by **vegetative propagation**.

Mycorrhiza
An association of a **fungus** with the roots of a higher plant. Said to form a pathway, along which water and nutrients pass into the root (128).

Nectar
A sugary fluid that is secreted by a gland called the nectary at the base of many insect pollinated flowers. Various insects feed on nectar and are attracted by its presence. As they climb down the flower in search of the fluid, they may pick up pollen on their bodies or deposit pollen from another flower on the stigma, thus effecting pollination. (See **cross-pollination** and **self-pollination**.)

Niche
An ecological term, used to describe the place of an organism in its surroundings, including its habitat, the way it affects and is affected by other organisms, and its influence on the environment.

Nitrogen-fixation
The process by which certain organisms absorb atmospheric nitrogen and use it to synthesise nitrogen compounds. In the garden, the most important organisms which can fix nitrogen are the **bacteria** that live in the roots of plants, particularly the pea and bean family (118, 120).

Node
The leaf 'joints' or the places on the stem where the leaves arise. The length of stem between the nodes is called an internode.

Nucleus
A body contained within the **cytoplasm** of the **cell** which controls its activities and contains the **chromosomes**.

Order
See **classification**.

Organic
A chemical whose molecular structure is based on carbon or a substance that originates from a living organism. The organic part of the soil comes from dead and decaying plants and animals.

Osmosis
The diffusion of a solvent (usually water) through a **semi-permeable membrane**. The **diffusion** is from pure solvent into a solution or from a dilute solution into a more concentrated one.

Ovule
The structure that contains the egg cell, a food store and a protective coat which, after fertilisation develop into a **seed**.

Parasite
An organism that lives in or on and feeds from another organism, called the host. Parasites usually harm their host in some way but do not often kill it, since this would deprive them of a home.

Perennial
A plant that continues its growth from year to year. There are many **herbaceous** perennials in the flower garden (including hollyhocks, red hot pokers and Michaelmas daisies) and some in the vegetable garden (rhubarb and horseradish). The aerial parts of these die back each autumn and then grow again, from scratch, every spring. Woody perennials have permanent hard stems above ground, that gives them a starting point for new growth each year, and this enables shrubs and trees to attain a large size. (See also **annual, biennial** and **ephemeral**.)

pH
A measure of acidity and alkalinity on a scale from 0 to 14 (18). Below 7 is acid, 7 is neutral and above 7 is alkaline.

Pheromone
A chemical substance which is secreted and released by an animal and which alters the behaviour of other members of the same species. Many insects secrete pheromones as part of the process of finding a mate, and this has been exploited as a form of **biological pest control** (151).

Phloem
The tissue that transports soluble carbohydrates and other metabolites up and down the body of the plant.

Photoperiodism The responses of a plant to the relative duration of day and night (21). (See **phytochrome**.)

Phototropism A growth movement in response to light (60). The response may be positive (towards the light) or negative (away from it). (See **geotropism**.)

Photosynthesis The synthesis of a carbohydrate food (sugar) from water and carbon dioxide in the presence of light and **chlorophyll**. Photosynthesis is performed by all green plants. It is the source of their food and, indirectly, the source of food for all other organisms. (See **food chain**.)

Phytochrome A blue pigment, found in plants, that detects daylight (21). Many plant activities, including flowering, germination and fruit ripening are regulated by the relative length of day and night and by the reactions of phytochrome.

Pollen The powder produced by the anthers. Each pollen grain contains a male **gamete**.

Pollen tube A tubular growth that develops from the **pollen** grain after it has become attached to the stigma. It carries the male **gamete** towards the **ovules**.

Pollination See **cross-pollination** and **self-pollination**.

Rhizome An underground stem. There are **buds** on rhizomes, just as there are on ordinary stems above ground, and the growth of these buds can be used as a means of **vegetative propagation** (for example mint). In some species (for example *Iris*) the rhizome is swollen and is also used to store food. (*Iris* propagation page 73) Some weeds (for example couch and bindweed) spread at great speed because they have fast growing rhizomes and are extremely difficult to eradicate because a new plant will grow from even a tiny fragment of rhizome left in the soil.

Root hair A single celled outgrowth from the **epidermis** of the root, used in the absorption of water and nutrients.

Root nodules Small swellings on the roots of leguminous and other plants which contain the **bacteria** that perform **nitrogen-fixation** (118, 120).

Root pressure A pressure which is developed by the roots of some plants and which, if the shoot is cut off, causes fluid to exude from the stump. The origin of this pressure is not really understood.

Rootstock See **stock**.

Rotation The system of swapping vegetable crops around, so that a particular crop only grows in a particular plot of ground every three or four years. One reason for rotation is the control of diseases and **parasites** that lie in the soil and only emerge when the host plant is present (like the potato cyst nematode, page 146, 147). Rotation also enables you to follow peas and beans (which have **root nodules** and increase the available nitrogen in the soil) with a plant that needs a lot of nitrogen, like one of the cabbage family.

Saprophyte An organism that feeds on dead or decaying plant or animal tissue. Saprophytic **fungi** and **bacteria** are of huge importance in breaking down dead matter so that it can be re-cycled.

Scion Twig or **bud** from one plant that is grafted on to another. (See **grafting**.)

Seed The product of a fertilised **ovule**. The seed is surrounded by a protective seed coat and supplied with enough stored food to fuel its **germination** and early growth.

Secondary thickening The thickening of a stem or root by the activity of the vascular and cork cambium (110).

Self-pollination The transfer of **pollen** from the **anther** of one flower to

	the receptive stigma of the same flower or to the stigma of another flower on the same plant. When the sex cells fuse, self-fertilisation takes place. (Compare **cross-pollination**.)
Semi-permeable membrane	A membrane that contains very tiny pores. Small molecules, like those of water, can pass through the holes but larger molecules cannot. A semi-permeable membrane surrounds the **cytoplasm** of plant **cells**.
Species	See **classification**.
Spore	A very small reproductive body produced by **fungi**, algae and **bacteria**.
Stock	Part of a plant, usually consisting of the roots and a portion of the stem, on to which a shoot or **bud** (called the scion) is grafted. Also called the rootstock or understock. (See **grafting**.)
Stoma (Plural Stomata)	A pore in the **epidermis** of the plant, through which gases and water vapour enter or leave the plant. Stomata are found in large numbers on the underside of leaves. (See **guard cells**.)
Stopping	Pinching out an **apical bud** to encourage bushiness. (See **auxins**.)
Sub-class	See **classification**.
Sucker	A shoot that grows from the **stock** of a grafted plant. Suckers are sometimes a particular problem with roses and, if neglected, can even swamp the real variety. They should be removed by cutting back to the stock, scraping away the soil around the plant if necessary.
Symbiosis	The living together of two different species, usually to their mutual benefit. Also called mutualism.
Trace elements	Nutrient elements that are needed by the plant in very small quantities (116).
Transpiration	The evaporation of water through the **stomata**.
Tuber	A thickened, fleshy, food-storing underground root or stem, with surface **buds**.
Turgid	A **cell** that is full of water, so that the cell wall is rigid, is said to be turgid. Changes in turgidity determine the wilting of plants, especially **herbaceous** plants (107), the opening and closing of the **guard cells** that surround the **stomata** (108) and the movements of 'sensitive' plants, like *Mimosa* (114).
Vacuole	One of the spaces in the **cytoplasm**, the contents of which include cell sap, air and water. It is bounded by a **semi-permeable membrane**.
Variety	See **classification**.
Vascular bundle	The transport tissue of the plant – the **xylem** and the **phloem** are separated by the vascular **cambium**.
Vegetative propagation	The asexual reproduction of a plant, usually effected by removing some part of the plant body and treating it so that it develops into a complete plant.
Virus	A **parasite** that only exists as a living being when it is inside another living cell. They are extremely small and only visible under an electron microscope. Since its mode of action is to take-over and control the activity of each cell that it invades, a virus is a major agent of disease.
Xylem	The tissue that conducts water and dissolved mineral salts up the plant. It is made up of dead cells, the walls of which are strengthened and re-inforced with lignin. Xylem acts as a support in woody plants and makes up the bulk of huge tree trunks.

INDEX

Page numbers in italic type refer to illustrations

Many people, particularly the staff of various agricultural and horticultural research stations, helped Ron Bloomfield and Bryn Brooks in the production of the series *Plants in Action*, and much of the information that they supplied is also included in this book. We would like to give special thanks to Dr George Forster of the National Vegetable Research Station; Graham Bremner and Eddie Hawton of the Department of Biology at Portsmouth Polytechnic; Bettina Wilkes who prepared the index and Sally Grover who designed the book.

The illustrations are by:

RACHEL BIRKET of the GARDEN STUDIO cover; AZIZ KHAN pages 20, 42, 134/5; JOANNA LANGHORNE pages 13, 14, 15, 17, 25 (right), 28, 32, 43, 44, 54, 55, 56, 64, 72, 74, 80 (bottom), 114, 123, 136, 149, 155 (top), 157, 158, 161 (bottom); MAGGIE RAYNOR pages 9, 23, 41, 57, 71, 91, 105, 115, 129, 141, 153, 165; JOHN WOODCOCK pages 16, 18, 22, 25 (left), 46, 59, 60, 61, 73, 76, 77, 78, 79, 80 (top), 81, 85, 86, 89, 92, 97, 103, 104, 110, 125, 126, 127, 130, 137, 139, 144, 147, 154, 155 (bottom), 159, 160, 161 (top).

Acknowledgment is due to the following for permission to reproduce illustrations:

HEATHER ANGEL daffodil section page 24, evening primroses page 28, lords-and-ladies section page 29, bees on *Fuchsia*, fleabane and crocus page 34, hyacinth bulb page 53, *Calvaria* page 56, light response page 58, bindweed page 64, honeysuckle & beech page 64, bryony tendrils page 65, centipede page 95, earthworm on surface page 99, soil profile page 101, broomrape and dodder page 102, *Gazania* page 154; BARNABY'S PICTURE LIBRARY oaks and dandelion seed page 54, crop spraying page 66, leaf colouring (top) page 102, blackfly page 150; BBC HULTON PICTURE LIBRARY Tradescant, potato page 10, *Clarkia*, Darwin, Lewis & Clark, Banks, Tournefort, *Rhododendron, Rudbeckia, Pelargonium* page 11, Mendel page 30, Dodo page 56; JUDY BROOKS hogweed page 12, pea plant page 37, *Fuchsia* breeding page 57, seedless apples page 68, hedge page 69, leaf cutting page 76, carnations, tomatoes, grafted cherry, *Monstera* page 101, leaf colouring (lower) page 102, houseplant without soil page 126, foxglove page 160, sundew page 161, hollyhock page 162; BRUCE COLEMAN LTD Bee on vetch (Jane Burton) page 33, chrysomelid in buttercup (Jane Burton), desert flowers (Kahl) and owl's clover (Calhoun) page 34, shaggy cap (Hans Reinhard) page 102, rose of Sharon (Fogden) and *Convolvulus tricolor* (Price) page 119; GENE COX nucleus page 24, dicot and monocot stems page 83, section through vein page 109, lime section page 111, root section page 127, stomata on underside of leaf page 132; HENRY DOUBLEDAY RESEARCH ASSOCIATION Deep bedding page 100; EAST MALLING RESEARCH STATION apples on M27 stock page 84, graft section page 87; GEEST HORTICULTURAL GROUP *Yucca* page 77; GLASSHOUSE CROPS RESEARCH INSTITUTE parasites/pests (4 photos) page 120, tomato cultivation pages 124 & 125; DR. ALAN HIBBERT Shepherd's purse embryos page 47; ICI Irrigating potatoes page 113; LONDON SCIENTIFIC FILMS heather leaf section page 109, chloroplast page 133; LONG ASHTON RESEARCH STATION silver leaf symptoms page 119; THE MANSELL COLLECTION Raleigh page 10, crab apple page 11; NATIONAL VEGETABLE RESEARCH STATION Mildew on lettuce page 35, wild and Avoncrisp lettuces page 36, deficiencies in vegetables (5) page 52, clubroot symptoms page 145, cabbage root fly page 148, Brassicas (both) page 149; NORTH EAST LONDON POLYTECHNIC tissue culture page 82; PORTSMOUTH POLYTECHNIC Pollens pages 26 and 27, scarification pages 48 and 49, bean germination and growth pages 62 and 63, iris root page 73, root initials page 75, plant cell and xylem tissue page 106, lignin page 107, stoma (both) page 108, cellulose wall page 109, *Rhizobium* nodules page 118, soil particles page 120, nodules (both) page 121, Scots pine root page 128, vein network and ending page 131, stoma and air space page 132; ROTHAMSTEAD RESEARCH STATION topsoil micrographs (4) page 93, soil animals page 94/95, drilling experiments (both) page 98, earthworm taking straw page 99, cysts on potato page 146, pea moth damage page 150, pheromone trap page 151; ROYAL HORTICULTURAL SOCIETY daffodil leaf experiments (both) page 139; ROYAL NATIONAL ROSE SOCIETY Pot o' Gold page 88; JOHN TOPHAM PICTURE LIBRARY maize (Markham) page 25, lords-and-ladies page 28, old man's beard page 65; MICHAEL WARREN Martock bean page 38, French bean page 39; S. H. WITTWER, MICHIGAN STATE UNIVERSITY gibberellin treatment page 67.